MW01235333

Yahweh versus Yahweh

Yahweh versus Yahweh

The Enigma of Jewish History

Jay Y. Gonen

THE UNIVERSITY OF WISCONSIN PRESS

The University of Wisconsin Press
1930 Monroe Street
Madison, Wisconsin 53711

www.wisc.edu/wisconsinpress/

3 Henrietta Street
London WC2E 8LU, England

1   3   5   4   2

Printed in the United States of America

Library of Congress Cataloging-in-Publication Data
Gonen, Jay Y., 1934–
Yahweh versus Yahweh : the enigma of Jewish history / Jay Y. Gonen.
p.   cm.
Includes bibliographical references and index.
ISBN 0-299-20330-1 (hardcover: alk. paper)
1. God (Judaism)   2. Messiah—Judaism.
3. Jews—History.   4. Psychohistory.   I. Title.
BM610.G656   2005
296.3—dc22   2004012857

In memory of my dear parents,

PINHAS and MALKA

Contents

Preface

The Jewish sacred lore, a rich body of biblical and postbiblical literature, teaches a variety of lessons. In recent times this historical literature was combined with more contemporary political and journalistic writings to reinforce a set of related basic assumptions concerning Jewish life. These assumptions, actually a set of interconnected group fantasies, delineate what it feels like to belong to the Jewish group and what are the unshakable rules by which Jewish history supposedly works. These shared fantasies shape Jewish attitudes toward God, the Land of Zion, other Jews, the goyim, the past, the future, and, not to be forgotten, the End of Days. This work looks at the appearance and reappearance of some of the most prominent shared themes that conditioned Jewish expectations from history.

It is important to clarify two major issues in order to facilitate readers' understanding of this psychohistorical study. The first issue has to do with the field of psychohistory itself. Psychohistory is the application of psychology to history with the aim of uncovering the underlying motivations. It tries to understand why the actors on the historical scene behave as they do, sometimes in repetitive patterns. The field of psychohistory can be roughly divided into psychobiography, which focuses on the individual, and into group psychohistory, which deals with the collectivity at large. The two can easily shed into each other, since individuals need to be understood in the context of their group.

A cardinal thesis of this work is that individuals are born into a group that shapes them just as it was able to shape their parents before them. The group culture is a major factor in the psychological formation of individuals. Even though a good deal of this formative work is carried on by the parents, the primary determinants of the shaping of identity reside nevertheless in the group heritage and culture, be it the old sacred lore or newly sanctified myths. Parental conduct and child-rearing modes still count, but not as much as the historically overriding cultural factor of group belongingness. This is why, regardless of child-rearing modes, Jews from Yemen, Poland, and other diverse countries used to share in common the deeply traumatizing conviction that "it is for our sins that we have been exiled from our land."

The domain where group processes occur is the public arena of ideas. The deceptively simple Israeli slogan "We shall not die without *yesha*" can serve as a good example of the hidden complexity of this process. Yesha means "help" or "rescue," but it is also an acronym for Yehuda (Judea), Shomron (Samaria), and Azah (Gaza). Because Israelis and other Jews have the traumatic collective memory that during the Holocaust most Jews died without yesha, this particular word is emotionally charged. With this slogan, therefore, some Israelis assert, with the force of myth, that giving up the occupied territories of the West Bank and Gaza would be a throwback to a Holocaustal fate. This is how images are tossed around in competition for winning over the group mind. The group mind is, so to speak, the percolation of an idea or a combination of notions and images to the point of mobilizing group action. When this happens we sometimes talk of the Zeitgeist, or spirit of the time.

What determines when an idea's time has come in the group's consciousness is not unlike what can be observed in clinical practice with individuals. When an unconscious idea becomes conscious depends on different factors. The forcefulness of the impulses that the ideas represent is one such factor. Concurrent reinforcements from associated ideas or events that historically happen to take place is another factor. The strength or weakness of behavior controls is also very important in both individuals and groups. Finally, the occurrence of a new or a repetitious trauma can compel action or else impose paralysis.

But unlike the case with individuals, this dynamic interplay within the group domain plays itself out as a shared activity of the collectivity at large. In intricate maneuvers, followers and leaders negotiate and manipulate what is to be prioritized in the Zeitgeist. In these negotiations some of the messages are quite overt, but many others are delivered through symbolism, associations, and reading between the lines. Consequently, it is possible for the participants to dance their way toward group consensus and collective action without full awareness of it.

All this raises the methodological issue of how adequate any sampling of the historical cultural repository of a group with its Zeitgeist changes can be. When is a sample comprehensive enough to meet the requirements of even the more rigorous methodologists that it does indeed represent its population fairly adequately? In a field that includes a good deal of reading between the lines, there may not be a satisfactory answer to this question.

I suggest, though, that the validity of the results of each work could be judged by at least two criteria. The first is whether the central themes under discussion are readily recognizable as being prototypical and dominant in a group's life across generations. The second is whether there is an adequate explanation of just what determined the timing of each theme for it to break into the Zeitgeist. To be fully comprehensive, group psychohistory should provide an analysis of the dominant, prototypical themes in a group's life across generations. In the present work, the examples of how such factors come to coalesce provide only highlights of what would otherwise be a very lengthy description that exceeds the scope of this work.

The second major issue that needs to be clarified for readers of this book concerns the Jewish deity, Yahweh. This is the accepted spelling in scholarly publications. It was actually written as YHWH in the ancient Hebrew writing system, which included only consonants, and was in all likelihood pronounced YaHaVeH. This name consists of the verb "to be," which is conjugated in the causative *hiphil* verbal stem. It therefore means either "he makes (something) be" or "he will make (something) be." The related biblical phrase "he makes armies be" has been traditionally translated into English as "the Lord of Hosts."

Yahweh's name was actually pronounced only until the time of the First Temple in Jewish history. Afterward it became the ineffable name that is never to be pronounced. So strong was the prohibition and the fear of even inadvertent violation of this taboo that when vowels were finally added to the Hebrew writing system in the early Middle Ages, YHWH was provided with modified vowels, which were borrowed from the Hebrew term for "My Lords." (It was customary in the Hebrew Bible to address the Lord in the plural form as a special show of reverence and respect.) The result was YeHoVaH, better known to English readers as Jehovah.

The image of Yahweh lies at the core of the Jewish perception of identity and history. A collective invention of the ancient Israelites, Yahweh was endowed with a conflicted personality and given the copyright to the enigmatic rules of how Jewish history was supposed to unfold. Unfortunately, these rules of history turned out to embody a fateful duality of either angry or loving acts by the mixed-up Lord and creator. The result was a breached world that included a Jewish-Gentile divide and a history that fluctuates between catastrophic destructions for Jews and ultimate messianic redemptions. As we shall have more than one occasion to see, these interactions were fraught with intricate dialectics because of the conflict that was woven into the personality of the deity from the very start. Yahweh was a mixed-up ruler whose behavior was capable of abrupt switches. Why he was the way he was and why he selected the Jews to be his chosen people is an enigma that was generated in the collective mind of the ancient Israelites. Its impact on Israelis and other Jews has lasted throughout the generations and continues in the present.

Readers will sometimes encounter Yahweh presented here as an actual bona fide historical player. This literary device was introduced in order to portray more vividly the imagery and conceptualizations of the true believers as they likely saw them. However, from time to time, references to him in this book clearly identify him as the fantasy creation of the ancient Hebrews. Armed with these clarifications, readers can now embark upon what might prove to be an interesting excursion.

Yahweh versus Yahweh

CHAPTER I

The Enigmatic God

The Bible designated the Jews as a chosen people. There are numerous references to this notion, but the basic idea is fairly clear: "For you are a holy people to Yahweh your God and Yahweh chose you to be a precious people for him out of all the peoples that are on the face of the earth" (Deuteronomy 14:2). Being chosen is a mark of distinction and is therefore a privilege indeed, or so it seems. It turned, however, into a mixed blessing. This can be gleaned even from Jewish humor, when the Jews complain about the Lord. ("Can't he find someone else to choose for a change?") Apparently from the very start, being chosen was a mixed blessing because the God who did the choosing was himself mixed up.

He identified himself in Exodus 20:2 as "I am Yahweh your God who brought you out of the land of Egypt from a house of bondage." After issuing a warning against worshiping other deities, he went on to describe himself: "I Yahweh your God am a jealous God who visits the sins of the fathers upon the children to the third and fourth generation of those who hate me, but who shows benevolence to thousands of those who love me and keep my commandments" (Exodus 20:5–6). The jealous God, in Hebrew el kana, carries the meanings of God of anger, God of zeal, and God of vengeance. But, as we shall soon see, God is also el ra'hum ve'hanun, one who shows benevolence, or hesed in Hebrew. That word refers to grace, mercy, charity, benevolence, and love.

The philosophical question arises: Why punish the innocent descendants of sinners? This remained a difficulty for Judaism that the great Jewish philosopher Moses Maimonides tried to resolve, but not very successfully (1969, 126–27). He wrote that God is called "jealous" and "avenging" because this is what we call human beings when they engage in such actions. But, unlike humans, God does not feel anger, wrath, or other emotions. All he does is act. As for punishing the offspring of sinners to the fourth generation, this is a preventive measure in the special case of idolatry that is designed to root out this corruption. This rationalistic discussion by Maimonides was not likely to quell the deep anxieties of ordinary Jews. In them a psychological sense of uneasiness was aroused by this self-introduction by Yahweh. What if he ever forgets who are those who honestly love him (the children of Israel) or gets a bit mixed up about who are the ones who truly hate him (polytheistic Gentiles) or are the enemies of Jews (monotheistic Gentiles)?

The fateful duality that is imbedded in God receives expression in other biblical passages. In Exodus 34:6–7 Yahweh descended in a cloud in front of Moses: "Yahweh passed before him and Yahweh proclaimed: Yahweh is a merciful and compassionate God, slow to anger and abundant in benevolence and faithfulness, keeping benevolence for thousands, forgiving transgression, crime and sin, but who by no means clears the guilty, who visits the sins of the fathers upon the children and the children's children, to the third and the fourth generation." Somewhat later in the chapter God sounds a warning to the Israelites not to emulate the worship of other nations: "For you shall not bow to another god for Yahweh his name is jealous, he is a jealous God" (Exodus 34:14). Clearly, what we witness here is the juxtaposition of Yahweh the jealous God—el kana—with Yahweh the merciful and compassionate God—el ra'hum ve'hanun. A similar juxtaposition recurs in Deuteronomy, where the Israelites are reminded, on the one hand, that "Yahweh your God, a consuming fire he is, a jealous God" (4:24) but, on the other hand, that "a merciful God is Yahweh your God, he will not let go of you and will not destroy you and will not forget the covenant with your fathers which he swore to them" (4:31).

Thus a dread of fateful duality runs throughout Jewish history in various incarnations and reincarnations. It saturates the Jewish heritage. Its origin, however, is the split image of Yahweh as a merciful and compassionate God who is nevertheless also a zealous and vengeful God. This is the starting point from which other biblical, then talmudic, and later Jewish mystical, philosophical, and ethical elaborations ensued. It has become a shared fantasy that conditioned the Jews' collective responses and their expectations of history. The problem lies with the unpredictability of Yahweh. It is hard to stay secure in the knowledge of God's boundless love when he is also known to suddenly convert to a ferocity that signals cosmic anger. At that point he is ready, able, and willing to inflict punishment on future generations of innocent souls. In the official doctrine the punishment can never be truly unexpected. Throughout the generations the sinners know that they have sinned and can therefore expect punishment. But this is not how things work out psychologically. Even if most of the sins could come under the rubric of normal human fallibility, some of the dreaded punishments seem abnormally harsh. It is difficult to trust a loving God who intermittently flies off the handle. It is a juxtaposition of contradictory emotions that are too extreme and that therefore seem too unstable. At any given moment God may be given to a mood shift. At no time, therefore, can the well-being of the people be considered as truly safe or stable.

Consequently, throughout the generations, Jews felt a basic sense of insecurity. They never felt safe. Only too frequently they felt compelled to turn their gaze to heaven, wondering how God is doing right then. Is he smiling or is he frowning? Is Yahweh el kana for now, God forbid, or is he at least for the time being el ra'hum ve'hanun, thanks be the Name. The constant dread and insecurity led to obsessive monitoring of everything that was happening in this world. Fear was the driving force behind the recurrent and obsessive enquiry concerning each and all events whether they were good for the Jews. This chronic and compulsive viewing of the world through Jewish glasses has even acquired the name of "the elephant and the Jewish problem," the title of an imaginary doctoral dissertation on elephants as produced by a Jew in a Jewish joke (Gonen 1975, 33–34). Yet as Jews were scanning the earth, they were also gazing at heaven. And when they were explicitly asking whether something down here was good for the Jews, they were also implicitly asking whether he up there was good for the Jews. It was as if everything on heaven and earth required constant monitoring.

We shall now look at the question of why God needed to exercise a choice regarding which group of people he favored in the first place. The answer to this question may cast additional light on God's enigmatic character. Returning to Deuteronomy 14:2, we once again read the following: "For you are a holy people to Yahweh your God and Yahweh chose you to be a precious people for him out of all the peoples that are on the face of the earth." Aided by psychoanalytic insights, we just might be able to unlock the secret of this conversion of the Israel-ites by an act of choice from a normal people into a very special entity. There are two key terms here that need to be explored. The first is "holy people." Holy, or kadosh, means sanctified, dedicated, devoted, and even sacrificed. The term connotes also the meanings of taboo and of exclusive possession. The holy people are therefore dedicated to be the exclusive possession of God. The second term is "precious people," or people of sgulah. This Hebrew term means a precious object, a dear possession, or a choice treasure. Adding the two terms together we get the combined notions of a very precious object that is the exclusive pos-session of Yahweh. When does it first happen in human development that an exclusive possession becomes a very precious object? It happens in the case of a "transitional object."

This term was coined by the British psychoanalyst D. W. Winnicott (1986) to describe behavior patterns displayed by babies in their "use of the first not-me possession." He was referring to the development of an attachment to a teddy bear, a doll, a blanket, a mere piece of a blanket such as the edges or fringes, a soft toy, or even a hard toy. This develop-ment occurs anywhere between four and twelve months of age. The in-fant attaches himself to the transitional object for its soothing effects, carries it around, and clings to it when going to sleep. In short, it serves as what is widely known as a security blanket, which is sometimes nick-named by adults "the blankie." The infant himself would call it "da" or something similar.

Transitional objects are so named because they provide an inter-mediate area of experience to serve as an in-between phase during the transition from fantasy to reality. The infant is not yet ready to accept the reality that Mother's breast in particular or warm body contact in general is not available all the time. In the past, he responded to this deprivation by imagining Mother's breast and treating it as a real one. Now, however, he is able to forgo the fantasy because he can derive the necessary calming and soothing effects from a replacement object. That particular object is his first possession of something outside the realms of his own body that is specially and exclusively his. Winnicott empha-sized that a very important quality of a transitional object is that the in-fant assumes rights over it while the adults play along with his action. In the course of years, as the child outgrows the transition phase, the tran-sitional object is relegated to limbo; this occurs as the intermediate ter-ritory between inner psychic reality and the external world spreads out and is elaborated into the areas of play, creativity, arts, and religion.

It is possible to view the transitional object as a portable mother substitute that, unlike the real mother, is always available. But unless it is in the exclusive possession of the infant it could not be always available. Thus the infant must assume total control over it. And unless it is very special and uniquely precious, it could not deliver the magic of the security and comfort that come with Mother's presence. At this point it behooves us to compare the infant's behavior to that of mighty Yahweh.

Yahweh's assumption of exclusive rights over the children of Israel by making them a "holy people" and his conferring upon them the status of a people of sgulah, or precious object, is very reminiscent of the development of an attachment by an infant to a transitional object. Of course, God did not crawl on his belly like an infant and hug the fuzzy teddy-bearish people of Israel to his chest. The fact remains, however, that in the Jewish sacred lore an image has been conjured of a God who clung to one people as his exclusive and most precious possession. And such an act of the development of a special attachment to a very precious possession shares important features with a psychoanalytic model of infant attachment. The question arises, therefore, What might all this mean? From a purely religious point of view, it may mean no more than heresy. From a philosophical outlook, it might seem illogical. But from a psychological vantage point, it makes a lot of sense. It suggests that God is a projection of human beings and that the Israelites created Yahweh in their own image. From the recesses of their unconscious thoughts and dim feelings they drew out an image of vulnerability and of a tenacious infantile reaching out for the security and soothing impact of a transitional object, that is, of a first outside-the-body or not-me possession that is most precious and also exclusively one's own. It was a vulnerable God who needed to attach himself to the Jewish people as his transitional object. And it was a vulnerable people who invented this bargain to begin with and then bought into it. Everyone needed his or her specific "da" or blankie.

The consciousness of being a chosen people is deeply ingrained in Jewish identity and can easily color historical perspectives. It is not something that is merely buried in biblical pages and subject to ritualistic recitations. Rather, it is an ongoing conviction that at any moment can affect the perception of current events such as the chain of events that took place in mid-2001. On 18 May 2001 a Palestinian suicide bomber blew himself up in a crowded mall in the city of Netanya, killing five people. Israel retaliated with bombing runs by F-16 fighter jets and attack helicopters against select Palestinian Authority targets inside

Arab towns on the West Bank and the Gaza Strip. It was a foolish Israeli response born out of anger and frustration. It was therefore no surprise that Israel immediately received international condemnations for deploying American F-16 airplanes against the Palestinian cities. Many exasperated Israelis were especially irked by the fact that even the Russians, the so-called butchers of Chechnya, were among those willing to give Israelis lessons about what constitutes a measured response.

On 21 May one incensed Israeli man called the There Is Somebody to Talk With show of the Israeli armed forces radio. His statement included the following: "Russia condemns us because we are a chosen people. The whole world hates the Jews because they are a chosen people. We are a chosen people, and it is impossible to run away from it." As a clue concerning how Israel should carry on now, the caller advised the talk show host to read Psalms chapters 83, 120, and 130. When I looked them up, I found the main thrust of each chapter to be that God will destroy the goyim, that we are for peace and they are for war, and finally that God will redeem Israel. This "analysis" of the current situation and future course of action supposedly stems from the reality of being a chosen people. Many Israelis, both secular and religious, are not as fanatical as that particular caller. But the conviction of being chosen for a select fate runs deep. It results in the notorious Israeli mood of "the whole world is against us" that is rooted in the biblical Jewish-Gentile split and that is known to grip even secular Israelis every so often. This particular radio listener call was a glaring example of how the identification with the chosen people conviction serves as a key ingredient of a historical sieve with which to filter current events. Current events come and go, but some features of the historical sieve, such as the Jewish-Gentile divide, tend to resist change and to remain timeless. This happens with many secular and not just religious Jews.

People seek protection when they live in a precarious world. The ancient Israelites were no exception, and it is ironic that in effect the protection they so badly needed was in some cases from their own protector. Yahweh was a creature of moods and had a historical track record of cosmic rage. In sweeping anger he was able to exercise genocidal sweeping judgments. And that was the way it was when he decided to do away with humankind by means of a flood. "And Yahweh saw that the wickedness of man on earth is great and that every urge [Hebrew, yetzer] of his heart's thoughts is evil throughout the day, and he regretted that he made man on earth and his heart became sorrowful. And Yahweh said, 'I shall wipe out man whom I have created from the face of the earth, from man to beast, to crawling creatures, and to the birds of the sky for I regret having made them.' But Noah found favor in the eyes of Yahweh" (Genesis 6:5–8). Apparently, Yahweh was in one of his el kana moods, during which his anger swelled into a flood and spilled over from humans to all life on earth. The urge of his heart's thoughts was evil, much as Yahweh projected such urges upon mankind. Flooding everything was the way to vent ferocious anger rather than a measured attempt to make the punishment fit the crime. And the "crime" we are talking about was the possession of an urge, that is, being human. Luckily, however, just in the nick of time the el ra'hum ve'hanun mood of compassion rose up to mitigate the sentence. Yahweh recalled that he liked Noah, and this feeling prompted him to activate the escape clause from the flood by means of an ark. The continuation of some life on earth was assured.

Yetzer is habitually translated as inclination. But this mild word fails to convey the full force of impulse that typifies yetzer. I therefore prefer the word "urge." An urge signifies a drive that is wired into the psycho-biological make-up of human beings. The concept is actually derived from the Hebrew verb "to make," "to shape," or "to form" that was used to describe the creation of man. Yetzer is therefore elemental to human nature, and as such it became a much-discussed topic in Judaism. Talmudic tales involving yetzer are legion. Much later, in the second half of the eleventh century, Rabbi Bahya Ben Joseph ibn Paquda, who lived in Muslim Spain, returned to the subject. In chapter 5 of gate, or part, 5 of his famous work The Duties of the Heart, he provided an eloquent exhortation to his fellow Jews that includes as good a description of the urge as has been written:

> Son of man, you should know that your greatest enemy in the world is your urge [yetzer], which is blended into the powers of your soul and is mixed in your temperament and participates with you in the conduct of your bodily and spiritual senses. It rules in the secrets of your soul and in which it is implanted within you. It is your counselor in all visible as well as hidden acts that you wish to make. It is the one who stalks your steps in order to tempt you. While you are in a state of sleep regarding him he is alert regarding you, so you ignore him, but he does not ignore you. For you he puts on the garments of friendship, and for you he wears the jewel of love. (Ibn Paquda 1856, 257, my translation)

With "friends" like that, who needs enemies? The friend, however, resides within man and is an essential part of him. Nevertheless, God was miffed at man for being a creature of yetzer. But God was unable to create man differently because he created man in his own image! Poor Yahweh, he had the yetzer too. Eventually, talmudic literature split the urge into the good urge and the bad urge. In later Jewish mystical movements this split was applied, at least implicitly, to the deity itself.

After first regretting the creation of man, God regretted the results of his regret—the unleashing of a flood. He therefore drew up a covenant, between himself and all flesh, of no more flooding and set up the rainbow in the cloud as a sign of the covenant. He was contractually bound not to rescind his latest decision. Things were by no means safe for the human race from then on, but at least punishments inflicted by the zealous God could no longer amount to a total destruction.

But subtotal destruction was still in the cards, making life decidedly uncomfortable. Should any particular human group on earth wish to further limit its liability to destruction, it would have to secure for itself a separate covenant. When this subsequently happened, as Abraham succeeded in appealing to the merciful side of God, a new covenant was established for Abraham and his Jewish descendants. In turn this covenant too was soon modified in a crucial way, so that by the end of this process the sign of the covenant was a surgical removal of the foreskin from the penis. It was significant on more than one level.

The famous covenant that came to be known as brit bein habtarim, or the covenant among the cuts, is described in chapter 15 of the book of Genesis. Abraham cut in half a heifer, a she-goat, and a ram and also presented an uncut turtledove and a young pigeon. In those days covenants were "cut"; therefore, the cutting of animals symbolized the conclusion of a covenant. The covenant among the cuts would prove a very decisive factor in the fate of the Jews because it gave them a divine and eternal title deed to their promised land: "On that day Yahweh cut a covenant with Abraham, saying, to your seed I give this land, from the river of Egypt to the great river, the river Euphrates" (Genesis 15:18). This was God's most tangible promise to his children—real estate. If Abraham had recognized a good deal, he could have said to Yahweh, "Now you're talking." But promised lands do not come free of charge. The deal came with a price that was enumerated two chapters later in Genesis.

Yahweh appeared again to the aging Abraham, who was now ninety-nine years old. He reiterated the notion of the covenant and promised once again to give the land of Canaan to Abraham and his descendants for an everlasting possession. But Yahweh insisted on a more updated cutting of the covenant. To quote Yahweh: "This is the covenant that you shall keep, between me and you and your seed after you throughout the generations. Thou shall circumcise every male. Thou shall circumcise the flesh of your foreskin that it would become the sign of the covenant between me and you . . . and my covenant in your flesh would become an eternal covenant. But anyone with a foreskin, a male who does not circumcise the flesh of his foreskin, that soul will be cut off from its people for he has violated my covenant." It seems that chapter 17 provided the never-to-be-ignored fine print that was attached to the insurance form of chapter 15. And what a fine print it was. As usual, the devil, or, should one say, el kana, was hidden in the details.

The revisions in the updated covenant went way beyond mere formalities. A fatal switch had taken place. The switch was from the cutting of covenants by cutting animals to the cutting of covenants by cutting humans. And the choice of the specific organ was no coincidence, as will soon become clear. The covenant among the pieces has become in effect the covenant among the foreskins, and it was referred to by Yahweh as "my covenant in your flesh." God's order was an offer one could not refuse. Abraham, the ninety-nine-year-old patriarch, and his entire household underwent the painful cuts on the threat of death. It was no idle threat. Yahweh could turn murderous if disobeyed. As we learn from Exodus 4:24–26, the enraged Yahweh accosted Moses and was about to kill him for failing to circumcise his son. Luckily for Moses, his wife, Zipporah, rushed to circumcise her son, threw the foreskin at Moses' feet, and called him "my groom-of-blood," thus re-affirming that a Jewish betrothal necessitates the bloodshed of circumcision of all male offspring. Yahweh then let go of Moses. It all goes to show that you just do not mess with Yahweh.

Thus, long before American ranchers ever branded their cattle to signal ownership, which is a fairly painful procedure, Yahweh branded his herd in an affirmation of his possession. And the pain, especially for adult converts, was excruciating. By yielding to this procedure Jews demonstrated their unconditional submission to the heavenly father. But circumcision defined not only the proper attitude toward heaven but also the proper conduct vis-à-vis the other peoples of this earth. Through circumcision Jews have marked their flesh to distinguish themselves from all other nations or goyim. Gentile nations and Gentile persons were thus rigorously set apart from Jews.

The Jewish-Gentile split has become henceforth a basic emotional perception that occupies its safe place in the psychological grid that conditions the Jewish view of history. Jews were not to mingle with or marry into Gentiles. To this day it is considered a tragedy in many Jewish families if the son marries a Gentile woman, or shiksa, that is, someone to be avoided and abhorred. The goyim became the hereditary enemies of Israel. The covenant in the flesh that put a mark of distinction on the Jews accentuated the psychological "us versus them" separation of Jews from Gentiles. The Jewish-Gentile split was internalized and fixed in the collective psyche of Jews. It remained a mark of Jewish distinction in spite of the fact that circumcision was performed by some non-Jewish groups as well. And once there was an insurmountable Jewish-Gentile split down on earth, it became logical to entreat and even badger the mixed-up Yahweh in heaven to be a compassionate el ra'hum ve'hanun for the Jews but save his el kana disposition for the Gentiles. It was one of the psychological consequences of becoming the people of the brit, or covenant. The term became synonymous with circumcision.

Of all the limbs in the human body, why choose the penis? One obvious reason is that women lack it. Consequently, covenants can be cut only between God and men but not between God and women, who do not count for much. Women were considered to have feeble minds, which is the reason why Eve was successfully tempted by the snake. The snake, by the way, was Adam's penis. In the Garden of Eden story, the snake served as both an allegory and a symbol. As an allegory it represented the yetzer by means of a fictitious figure, a talking snake, who uses the gift of speech to urge on behalf of the urge. These allegorical elements were later picked up and elaborated in the Talmud. As a symbol the snake represented the penis, the primal organ of yetzer, by virtue of it too being in reality a slippery elongated object with the capacity to spit or "ejaculate." This equation may seem far-fetched to some persons, but in Jewish kabbalistic writings the theme does appear of a demonic mythical snake crawling into the Shekhinah, who is the motherly presence that hovers over Israel, and biting her womb. If he bites once, blood flows out. If he bites twice, water flows out. All of these phantasms were related to speculations concerning the origin and birth of pure souls (one bite) versus contaminated souls (two bites). But after all is said and done the basic fact still remains that for a snake to "ejaculate" it needs to bite. The symbolic meaning of the snake is therefore no mystery.

At any rate, Yahweh insisted on curbing the powers of both the symbol and the allegory, that is, the temptations of the penis as well as the more general inclination to follow the urge in various ways. For this reason the circumcision edict was later extended from the primal organ of sex to the presumed organ of feelings and thoughts in the ancient world, namely, the heart. Yahweh commanded: "And thou shall circumcise the foreskin of your heart and no longer stiffen the back of your neck" (Deuteronomy 10:16). Like the urges of the penis, the urges of the heart too must be tempered by the removal of its "foreskin." In addition, a warning concerning being stiff-necked is thrown in for good measure. Stiffening of a man's neck muscles may take place during copulation as well as whenever he digs his heels into the ground in a stubborn posture of refusal. Thus the chain of associations takes us all the way from one stiff organ to another. The implied suggestion is that stubbornness, a mental stiffness of sorts, is at the service of the urge. There was therefore no "if" or "and" or "but" in Yahweh's direct order, as can be learned from Jeremiah 4:4: "Circumcise yourselves to Yahweh and remove the foreskins of your heart, men of Judah and inhabitants of Jerusalem, lest my wrath go forth like fire and burn with none to quench it, because of the evilness of your deeds." As was said before, you just do not mess with Yahweh.

Circumcision is a symbolic wound. Not everything is always symbolic. Sometimes a cigar is only a cigar and a banana is only a banana. But when it comes to religious rituals, circumcision is never just a circumcision. It is always symbolic of something more. That something more may be castration or even complete immolation of the penis, which could easily result in uncontrolled bleeding and death. That something more may also be decapitation, during which by analogy the body loses its head the way the penis has its foreskin cut off. The symbolic meanings of circumcision are clearly fear-evoking. The Jewish rules of the game of life are such that members of Yahweh's flock live under the threat of death. To avert the danger they yield to a ritualistic token sacrifice of a highly symbolic body part, hoping that it will serve as a substitute for the real thing—the full sacrifice of life. The ritual of circumcision thus serves as an acknowledgment of total submission to an angry God who must be appeased.

According to the Jewish holy writ, Abraham's token sacrifice in the form of circumcision was not quite enough. The full appeasement of God required further demonstration that, in addition to the foreskin of the penis, the foreskin of the heart has also been removed. This could be shown through a readiness to sacrifice something very precious to oneself at God's command. This was the case with the "binding of Isaac" when "God tested Abraham" (Genesis 22). At God's command, Abraham would have sacrificed his son if it were not for the last-minute intervention of the merciful God. But the merciful God was an insecure God who first needed to run a test in order to find out whether circumcision really works. Did Abraham's earlier submission to circumcision really indicate an attitude of total submission to God? Was it sufficiently clear to everyone that disobedience could spell death? By demonstrating total submission to the heavenly father, Abraham won a reprieve for his earthly son. Actually, Abraham played more than one role. He played the role of the obedient son in relation to God his father, just as Isaac was fully obedient to his father, Abraham. And Abraham also played the role of the angry father turned merciful toward Isaac, just as God was finally merciful toward Abraham himself. Everyone in heaven as well as on earth fully understood the rules of the game. It was a full confirmation that the lessons of circumcision were learned well by all.

The theme of dual circumcision of sorts has been reiterated in Judaism throughout the generations. This theme represented a major diagnosis of man's imperfections and offered a partial remedy for the impulsivity of the human condition. It all goes back to the mythological snake that made its appearance in the book of Genesis both as a symbol and as an allegory. This biblical snake always lurks within man and poses a never-ending danger. As a symbol the wiggly snake represented the penis and sexual urges. In order to curb the power of these impulses Judaism issued the injunction to physically remove the foreskin of the penis. As an allegory the talking snake stood for the heart's desire to follow evil. In order to counteract and weaken this constant urge to sin, Judaism issued the added injunction to spiritually remove the foreskin of the heart. Thus the well-known dual injunction concerning two circumcisions was designed to counteract the sexuality of the symbolic snake and the immorality of the allegorical snake.

The covenant among the cuts and, even more so, the covenant among the foreskins were imbued with symbolic cutting. The cutting of pieces implies a division and sharing, that is, a deal in which each party receives its cut. The cutting also takes animals' lives away, an act that serves as a reminder that treaty violations could be punishable by death. This was especially true in the case of failure to circumcise, in which case "that soul will be cut off from its people for he has violated my covenant." Males were put on notice here. Any breaking of covenants is to be followed by justice with a cutting edge.

It was man rather than woman who was the greatest cause for concern to Yahweh. Man has the necessary wherewithal, whether a penis or a brain, for being a major player on the world scene. A woman remains a passive receptacle who as such could still tempt man. But she is not a first-class human, as man is. The antifemale bias ran deep within

Judaism throughout the ages, hence the talmudic saying "Women their mind is light." This is why the twelfth-century philosopher Moses Maimonides believed that, just as form should rule matter, so should man rule woman (1969, 430–31). This is necessary because it is in the nature of deceitful matter to behave like a married harlot who runs around on her husband. Yahweh, whose own frolicking with his consort, Asherah, was censored out by the early editors of the holy Jewish writ, was more concerned with suppressing men than suppressing women. Since women were only second-rate beings and were already so thoroughly dominated, there was little danger of their mounting a successful challenge. But men, Goddamn men with their percolating testosterone known in antiquity as yetzer, they were another matter. Yahweh was as afraid of them as they were of him. They may have circumcised the foreskins of their penises, but did they also circumcise the foreskins of their hearts? Only God can see what is within men's hearts. And what he saw was scary. Men were not sufficiently tamed. They could rebel and mount challenges about everything, even including forbidden sexual prerogatives such as consorting with the fertility goddess Asherah. The business of their penises was therefore also Yahweh's business.

All this goes to show that dread and fright were not the exclusive lot of God's flock but also of God himself. Omnipotent as he was thought to be, he nevertheless remained a fantasy projection of humans. Yahweh was a very frustrated heavenly potentate. The good old times when he used to engage in prolific frolicking with his favorite consort, Asherah, were gone. Long before there ever was a rigid Jewish rabbinate that follows the harsher law interpretations of the house of Shammai, unnamed ancient Jewish sages had already stepped in and reined Yahweh in through rigid strictures. Consequently, he has become an almighty male God ruling in loneliness. Through an act of censorship his sexual delights were deleted from the holy writ. His wings were clipped because the intellectual elite of his ever-obedient subjects disapproved. The only trace left of the bygone but joyful days of a fertility cult were the two winged cherubim who stayed first in the desert Tabernacle and later in the First Temple (Dobrowski 1995). They, at least, were still able to copulate once a year (Ein Gil 1995). But all-powerful Yahweh, the miserable victim of censorship by despotic men, could no longer get himself some action. In the seventh century B.C. he had a period of reprieve that lasted for about fifty years when Manasseh, king of Judah, reinstated the statue of Asherah within the Temple (2 Kings 21:7), but it was later removed from the Temple and burned by King Josiah (2 Kings

23:6). In spite of this short period of reprieve, Yahweh was in effect sentenced to social isolation and sexual deprivation.

Yahweh's grim fate was nevertheless not shared by his subjects. They continued to preoccupy themselves with their fertility goddess. "Asherah was a problem for the Israelites even before Manasseh installed her image in the Temple" (Hestrin 1991). Already in the ninth century B.C. Asa, king of Judah, had burned the idol of Asherah that his own mother had made, and as punishment he removed her as queen mother (1 Kings 15:13). But dealing with the image of Asherah was prevalent. Because they were stiff-necked in spite of Yahweh's warning not to be, the Sons of Israel had the tendency to disobey. And this is where the old repression that was imposed by the Jewish sages broke down. It so happened that the Sons of Israel just adored Asherah and paid her numerous love visits. Through his prophets the fascinated Yahweh harshly condemned these practices the way an enchanted antipornography crusader condemns smut. So numerous were the acts of disobedience that the prophets of old needed to wage an almost incessant war against the Israelite love affair with Asherah. So it was, through his prophets, that the incensed "new" Yahweh who no longer had Asherah desperately tried to get the Israelites not to behave like the "old" Yahweh. Put differently, Yahweh was trying to suppress in others that which was repressed within him.

The situation was fraught with an ambivalence that became even clearer after a new battleground was formed between the father in heaven and the sons on earth. The battle was waged over a new symbolic feminine figure whom the ancient Jewish sages granted to God as a legitimate replacement for the forbidden Asherah. She was the motherland of Zion—the land that was promised to the Sons of Israel in the covenant. She was now transformed into God's bride as well as into the mother of the Sons of Israel. The dual role of Zion was not devoid of its own dialectics, which becomes clearer when compared with the roles of Asherah. According to the prevailing ancient Jewish party line, Yahweh never really had Asherah, but the sinning Israelites did, even though Asherah was forbidden to them. By contrast, as wife and mother Zion was now permitted to both father and sons with the stipulation that she be shared in different fashions. But neither father nor sons adhered to these distinctions. Psychological forces were in play that caused a fusion of the images of father, mother, and sons that in turn caused a blurring of role distinctions.

Yahweh was the first victim of monotheism. From the very start the monotheistic coup served the purpose of masculine domination. In consequence, the Judaic monotheistic requirement of a one and only one deity deprived Yahweh of his beloved Asherah. In no way could this requirement of monotheism have resulted in a female goddess, eternal Asherah, losing her beloved Yahweh; to imagine that kind of a monotheistic world is akin to imagining a universe made of antimatter. The antifeminine masculine bias was already deeply rooted among the male founders of Jewish monotheism who shaped Yahweh to their own liking, ergo, in their own image. And this is also why when Yahweh, who was the fantasy product of the Israelites, lost his beloved Asherah by the edict of the ancient lawgivers, he regressed galore. His initial response to this deprivation of the feminine touch was to revert back to the security and comfort of a transitional object. He therefore conferred upon the Israelites the status of a holy and a precious possession, and, as a result, they became his chosen transitional object. For a while the transitional object provided occasional comfort in the absence of maternal comfort. But in the course of growth and development, children, including the regressed Yahweh, outgrow the phase of deriving succor from a da or a blankie. But Yahweh remained a deprived God, and that made him an angry God. A permanent condition of feminine deprivation could not have been sustained. Both father and sons needed badly the missing feminine comfort.

In a certain psychological sense the reactions of all the participants in the universal drama of deprivation point to the underlying need of children to have two parents and of adults to have mates. After all, why should people who feel like vulnerable children have only a "father in heaven" but not also a "mother in heaven"? Why could not the creators be a loving pair? Philosophically, it goes against the monotheistic grain, but psychologically, it is actually pleasing. Adults need mates and children need parents. But when by a monotheistic decree one mate was removed from the scene, both God and children were deprived of elemental security and joy. The deprived God turned angry and insecure and regressed to the level of seeking a transitional object for recompense. He was now programmed to carry out parenting as if he were a deprived and angry child himself. Dreading his frightful anger and childish temper tantrums, the founding fathers of Judaism nevertheless chose him as their best-bet protection from catastrophes that could be unleashed by him. But Yahweh was destined to fail in this protective task because he could not override the fateful duality that was built into his character and written into his program. Thus, from the very start, insecurity and explosiveness were introduced into the guiding rules of Jewish psychohistory.

The deprivation of feminine comfort resulted in a state of psychological instability. The situation was ripe for a return of the repressed, and future conflict was also brewing. While God yearned for a wife who would also be a mother, the Sons of Israel longed for a mother who would also be a wife. In response to these psychological needs, Zion evolved into God's bride on earth. Zion, by the way, short for Land of Zion, referred to the Land of Israel, which was so named after Mount Zion in Jerusalem. Zion was therefore the motherland of the Sons of Israel. As such she was also their mother and the target of Oedipal attraction. The attraction and temptation by the sons to the mother could only be exacerbated when, as the Bible reports, Zion began knowingly and willfully acting like a prostitute. The sight of a hot-to-trot whoring mother reinforced the generational conflict between the father in heaven and the sons on earth. From the very start sexual urges were interwoven into the story to erupt into a lasting conflict that in time engulfed even Zionism in the modern era. There had just been too much of a suppression in Judaism of males and even more so a repression of the primary role of femininity for things to remain quiescent. Unfortunately, this repression resulted in a traditional relegation of women to a degrading subordinate role based on denigration of their mind. But already in olden times the oppressive repression produced rebellious countermoves. Lo and behold, Zion—beloved bride and mother—started to behave like an overactive fertility goddess, that is, like Asherah.

Zion turned her back on Yahweh, her husband, and turned to prostitution with a relish. The Jewish prophets were of course enraged by Zion's scandalous behavior. The prophet Ezekiel was especially incensed. Speaking of Jerusalem personified as a woman who received from God the term of endearment oholivah (my tent is in her), he roared: "Yet she multiplied her harlotries, remembering the days of her youth, wherein she had played the harlot in the Land of Egypt. And she doted upon their male prostitutes, whose flesh is like the flesh of asses, and whose flowage is like the flow of horses" (Ezekiel 23:19–20). Those Egyptian men must have been out of this world. These envious fantasies concerning the phallic prowess of the better-equipped goyim were clearly related to circumcision. In the twelfth century Maimonides reiterated, in his The Guide of the Perplexed, that circumcision reduces the strength of the sexual drive and sexual performance (1969, 609). As an old talmudic saying goes, any woman who has sexual intercourse with an uncircumcised man finds it difficult to break away from him. Therefore, because of the covenant in the flesh, Jewish men are at a disadvantage.

To this day Israeli advocates of the abolition of circumcision make their views known from time to time. In the ensuing arguments medical reasons pro and con are usually cited, and the probable social consequences for the minority of uncircumcised Israeli babies are also mentioned. The real underlying issue, however, is whether to be freed from the archaic Jewish-Gentile split by means of complete secularization.

The prostitution of Zion or Jerusalem included complex psychological issues and had wide-ranging historical implications (Gonen 1975, 11-19). The psychological issues involved first and foremost a failure to develop a mature and wholesome love that unifies affection with sensuality (sexuality). Freud (1957a) discussed such failure. It could result from the sons' fear of a harsh father that leads to the repression of sensuality in relation to the mother. Inevitably, this banishment of sensuality separates it from the more tender kind of affection. In terms of Jewish psychohistory, it is not difficult to assert that Yahweh, during his el kana periods, was a harsh father to his children. But we can also hypothesize that he too had his own anonymous harsh fathers, the ancient Israelite lawgivers who deprived him of female companionship. This harsh act affected his personality development. The censorship of feminine comfort engendered in Yahweh the repression mostly of sensuality rather than tenderness. Once again the likely result was a failure to integrate affection with sensuality.

Frequently, the failure to integrate the two currents of feeling leads to the splitting of the object of love into either a mother or a prostitute (Freud 1957b). A mother may receive tenderness, and a prostitute may get sensuality, but never the twain shall meet. If this becomes a permanent pattern, the treatments of mothers, on the one hand, and of prostitutes, on the other hand, go their separate ways. Sexual desire for a mother remains repressed, while affectionate or tender feelings toward prostitutes or cheap women stay suppressed. Yahweh did not embark on this clear-cut course of splitting the object of love into two distinct figures. With his kind of mixed personality, being the vengeful yet merciful type, he fell into another pattern in which the love object is not fully split but retains mixed images.

According to Freud (1957b), neurotic forms of love can sometimes culminate in rescue fantasies during which men try to rescue morally degraded fallen women. Psychologically speaking, to rescue is to save a life. Saving a life is like giving a life. It can therefore be equivalent to the sexual act of fathering a child, which is also the giving of life. The fantasy implication here is that if a man rescues a woman's life, it is as if he gave her life and as if he had sexual union with her and therein made her his own woman. Thus the rescued woman belongs to the man who did the rescue. All these themes came into play in the biblical narrative because of the fused images that are imbedded in Zion. Zion is Jerusalem, the Land of Israel, the motherland, and the mother of the Israelites because she is God's bride. She also, and this is very important, stands for a collective image or representation of the Sons of Israel. As a result, whenever the treachery of forsaking Yahweh is brought up in the Bible, one can say that the Sons of Israel sinned, that the land sinned, or that Zion sinned. The long-term historical consequence of this psychological mixture of motives and images was the age-old drive to rescue Zion. It buttressed the return to Zion after the Babylonian exile, and it gave rise to modern Zionism, which was the rescue operation of Zion by the Sons of Israel. For a better understanding of the biblical references to Zion's harlotries and her subsequent rescue, it is necessary to bear in mind this fusion of images that saturated the psychological entanglement of father, bride, and sons.

Yahweh's problematic rescue of Jerusalem appears in Ezekiel 16. At her birth in the land of the Canaanites, the infant Jerusalem was neglected by her Amorite father and by her Hittite mother. (What can one expect from goyim?) Her umbilical cord was not cut, and she was not washed in water or rubbed with salt or swaddled. As Yahweh passed by and saw her weltering in her own blood, he said to her, "In your blood live." Thus Yahweh saved the infant Jerusalem or gave her life, and, as befits rescue fantasies, she was going to be his, and he was going to give her life once again. He passed by her on a later occasion and duly observed the growth of breasts and the appearance of pubic hair. He covered her nakedness, wedded her, and took care that she enjoyed luxurious clothes and delicious food. But Yahweh was ill rewarded for his magnanimity, of which he boasted without timidity. Jerusalem capitalized on her beauty and engaged in incessant whoring. The clothes and food that Yahweh gave her she shared with her lovers, and, as an added affront, she used some of the jewels to form male idols, with which she played the harlot. As if all this was not enough, she slaughtered and sacrificed for others to devour the sons and daughters whom she bore to Yahweh. It was as if yetzer became her undisputed king, as she loved to spread her legs for every passerby, especially the Egyptians, who were large of flesh—another reminder that the uncircumcised Egyptians must have really been something else.

We have seen that the children were also victimized in this tale of treachery. God, mother, and children were embroiled in a triangular situation. Psychologically speaking, the situation could be both tempting and threatening to the sons. They could have felt, after all, that if Mother is free for all, then the family should come first. But they were also aware that Yahweh was a zealous father. Nobody was safe from the injured potentate once Mother started whoring around.

Yahweh's rage reached a boiling point. His long tirade of condemnations and punishments culminated in the naked Jerusalem being stoned as well as cut to pieces with swords. But somehow she still remained alive after he vented his anger. He was therefore able to proceed with a highly ambivalent forgiveness after reminding her first that, unlike her, he did keep covenants. He delivered his forgiveness by emphasizing that his very act of forgiveness would exacerbate her shame to the point that she would no longer dare open her mouth. It was a sudden shift of moods. How could he so quickly forgive her after such furious indictments? Of course, an almighty God can do anything he wants, but it seems that a bit of human psychology lent him a helping hand. Yahweh behaved like a neurotic lover who continues to overvalue a woman who has already proven unworthy if not utterly worthless. Such a lover must forgive the vulgar prostitute because he yearns to find loving tenderness in her. In other words, he is still searching for his mother.

Even while Yahweh exhibited a neurotic form of love toward his treacherous bride, the Sons of Israel entertained their own rescue fantasies, which were imbued with Oedipal longings. The proto-Zionist manifesto of love for Zion, return to Zion, and rescue of Zion appears in Isaiah 62:4–5. It foretold the ingathering of the Babylonian exiles back in Zion:

> You shall no more be termed Forsaken,
>> and your land shall no more be termed Desolate,
> for you will be named My Desire Is in Her,
>> and your land Husbanded,
> for Yahweh desired you,
>> and your land shall be husbanded.
> For as a young man husbands a virgin,
>> so shall your sons husband you,
> and as a bridegroom rejoices over a bride,
>> so shall your God rejoice over you.

Yahweh displayed surprising generosity in allowing his sons to husband his wife. It can only be explained as a result of yet another fluctuation in the state of the fusion of images, this time of father and sons, whereby the rivalry between them is masked while the longings of both for a tender, yet sexual, mate and mother are promised fulfillment. It was nevertheless a dangerous situation. At any given moment Yahweh could revert to an el kana mood and punish the sons for husbanding (the Hebrew term stands for intercourse) their mother, Zion.

The promise of a happy repossession of the motherland remained alive in Jewish hearts and fueled the modern return to Zion that was carried out by Zionism. The early Zionist pioneers returned to the motherland of Zion. Their slogan was "making the desolate land bloom." They came to rescue their mother Zion, and they fertilized her. They husbanded her and made her bloom again. In the process they experienced a Zionist rebirth. They kept singing, "We came to the land to build and be rebuilt." In a fusion of images they descended upon their mother as both father and sons. They were therefore able to simultaneously impregnate her and also be born to her. In a psychological translation therefore the song would run "We came to the motherland to beget and be reborn." In short, the returning sons husbanded their mother and fathered themselves in a Zionist rebirth.

The Zionist settlement of Israel was carried out mostly by secular pioneers. Yet for the time being Yahweh seemed more tolerant of these secular pioneers than most rabbinic authorities who actually opposed the Zionist venture. The ensuing conflict between the conservative religious authorities and the younger pioneers was shaping up as another battle between fathers and sons for control over how to relate to the motherland. The rabbinic authorities believed that redemptive work belonged to God alone, and he will miraculously execute it in his own sweet time via his Messiah. They feared that for Jews to engage in such an undertaking on their own was to infringe upon the territory of the heavenly father. It could evoke a terrible punishment. But at first el kana was not stirring up and seemed to allow the Zionist venture to go on, albeit not smoothly. There were difficulties in handling Arab antagonists, with their legitimate national claims to the land, and Turkish or British authorities. But the Zionist policy of gradual buildup through laborious pioneering work was bearing fruit. As more and more land was being husbanded and as more and more Zionist pioneers were being reborn, it also looked more and more as if the latest return to Zion was becoming a success. God must have given his blessing to this multiple return to land, mother, and potency. He was going to abide by the covenant in the flesh in which, in return for circumcision, he granted the Promised Land to his chosen people.

But Yahweh did not stay quiescent. Like the volcano God that he once upon a time might have been, he rumbled every so often and erupted as his belly filled with fire. He visited the earth with a second world war and with a holocaust in which a third of the Jewish people were annihilated. Then he mercifully allowed the State of Israel to be established, but only through a war with the Arabs. And afterward he rekindled Jewish fears of impending holocausts during further Arab-Israeli wars. In short, he never tired of reminding his people of his fateful duality in which at one moment the merciful Lord grants revival but at another moment the vengeful Lord unleashes death and destruction. Jewish resurrection in the Land of Zion was to proceed under the auspices of a mixed-up God who was destined to revert back and forth between being an el kana and being an el ra'hum ve'hanun in endless fluctuations that will not stop until such time as the Messiah arrives. Small mercy it was indeed that during moments of smiling rather than frowning he let the reclamation work of the motherland go on.

Realizing that the Zionist love affair with the motherland was blooming, some of the Jewish religious authorities sought a pragmatic accommodation to Zionism. They did not want to be left behind when the land was being rebuilt, and they also desired to influence its future development. After the State of Israel was established they were very adroit not only at supervising the Jewish character of the newly born state but also at securing even more than their fair share of power and economic largess. Their increasing use of the state and its resources as a cash cow has grown so egregious that by the end of the twentieth century there was increasing clamor to disconnect them from the udders of the state. It thus seems that, even though some religious misgivings over the reestablishment of a Jewish state without the Messiah persisted, it was nevertheless clear that certain benefits need not await his arrival and that it is no sin to enjoy them in the here and now. As my high school teacher in Haifa, the literary critic Baruch Kurzweil, who was a religious man, used to say, "The greatest enemy of religion in the State of Israel are the religious parties."

This deplorable development was clearly foreseen by the Zionist leader Chaim Weizmann, who became the first president of the State of Israel. In his autobiography he sounded the following warning:

> It is the new, secularized type of Rabbi, resembling somewhat a member of a clerical party in Germany, France or Belgium, who is the menace, and who will make a heavy bid for power by parading his religious convictions. It is useless to point out to such people that they transgress a fundamental principle which has been laid down by our sages: "Thou shalt not make the Torah a crown to glory in, or a spade to dig with."

There will be a great struggle. I foresee something which will perhaps be reminiscent of the Kulturkampf in Germany, but we must be firm if we are to survive. (Weizmann 1966, 464)

But in spite of Weizmann's hopes Israelis have not been firm at all, perhaps because they saw their survival threatened by their Arab foes and therefore figured out that they cannot afford a culture war between secular and religious forces in modern Israel. The underlying dynamics of the Israeli political alliances among secularist and religious factions resulted in the implementation of aggressive nationalism and in the granting of religious concessions that caused the postponement of a Kulturkampf (Gonen 1975, 328–33). Skirmishes continue to take place, but so far an all-out war has been avoided.

So far Israelis have not succeeded in casting off Yahweh's shackles, even though Israel offers Jews the most propitious opportunity to forsake religion without running the risk of assimilation. Many Jews who regard themselves as secular still buy into Yahweh's doctrine of a chosen people, a special Jewish fate, and a primordial Jewish-Gentile divide. The special fate imposes permanent tsores, or troubles, on the Jews because it is a rule of history that "it is difficult to be a Jew." Because of the special fate requirements, the perceived need to preserve the Jewish character of the state compromises its democratic character notwithstanding the pretense that there is no inherent contradiction between the two. On radio talk shows, however, one hears more revealing expressions such as "We do not need democracy. We do not need to emulate the goyim. We have our own way." Such blatant expressions let the cat out of the bag. Yahweh continues to rule among religious and nonreligious Jews alike. His special rules concerning Jewish psychohistory may seem like transcendental decrees that are imposed from the outside, but they are self-imposed. Consequently, Yahweh's fateful duality will continue to rule supreme. Till when? When will the end of tsores come? Jewish tradition provided its own answer to this question—when the Messiah arrives.

CHAPTER 2

When Will the Messiah Arrive?

The arrival of the Messiah involves two basic questions. The first is, What will happen when he arrives? The second is, When is his arrival likely to happen? And there is an added issue. Do the answers to these questions lie outside the realm of the fateful duality that has been so characteristic of the moody God?

The prophet Daniel, who was getting impatient with waiting for redemption, once posed the question, "Until when the end of the wonders?" The cryptic answer he received was that "in a time of times and a half, and when the shattering of the hand of the holy people is completed, all these would be completed." The puzzled Daniel asked for more clarification. He was then provided with more numerical clues but was urged to just wait patiently for his fate at the End of Days (Daniel 12:5–13). The "when" question has therefore remained a mystery, but the "what" question did receive a fairly clear answer. Only after the last disaster to befall the holy people has run its full course would redemption come. Premessianic cataclysm is preordained and is therefore inevitable. Putting up with this kind of a futuristic vision of history required an inordinate amount of patience. Frequently, however, patience ran out.

The scholar Raphael Patai (1979) grouped together the Jewish Messiah texts with added comments and perceptive analysis. The following discussion of Jewish messianic legends relies heavily on his excellent work. It was he who raised the difficult psychological question, Why did the Messiah fail to come? Why was his advent always delayed? The traditional answers fell pitifully short of meeting these goals: the generation was unworthy; there were too many sinners in Israel; Satan's machinations; the pious were unable to complete all the necessary prayers; and there were unborn souls still left, so that the celestial Hall of the Souls, the mystical Guf, was not yet emptied. Recognizing that these were lame explanations, Patai proposed that what lay behind them was an unconscious perception that God was not a free agent after all and was therefore incapable of implementing his own wishes. The unconscious perception that he referred to smacked of dualism. This is the Manichaean perception of the division of the divine realm into two domains where the good God and the evil God perpetually battle it out. Well aware that he was treading on a very sensitive issue, Patai suggested that if one substitutes the people of Israel for God, this unconscious notion "becomes psychologically inevitable and theologically inoffensive" (xxix).

But why should unconscious stuff remain theologically inoffensive to begin with? Psychologically speaking, would it not be more logical to assume that it was repressed exactly because theologically it was very offensive? Could it also be that the offensive and repressed notions included the conviction that it was not only a case of God not being able to bring the Messiah but also of God not wanting to salvage his people? For one thing, it was not out of character for the mighty el kana to inflict prolonged punishments. For another thing, since when was Yahweh impotent? It is therefore more likely that the lame explanations for the delays in the arrival of the Messiah enumerated by Patai represented an avoidance by people who felt impotent to challenge an omnipotent God. The rules of Jewish history as laid down by Yahweh could not be challenged. His rules extend from the days of Creation to the End of Days. And the most important edict was a severe warning not to violate any of the rules through rebellion or stiff-neckedness. Yahweh's people must accept his rules and fully submit to them if they know what is good for them.

Treading gingerly over this sensitive issue led to the conviction that one should not even mention that the Messiah is delayed. Moses Maimonides placed this injunction within the twelfth of his thirteen principles of the faith, quoted here in Patai's translation: "The twelfth pertains to the days of the Messiah: it is to believe and to hold true that he will come, and not to say that he is delayed, for even though he tarry, wait for him" (xxxix). Maimonides implied here that to say that the Messiah is delayed is akin to questioning the belief in his coming and even to questioning belief in general. That is why it is forbidden. Of greater psychological interest is his dictum "for even though he tarry, wait for him." It seems too much like a contradictory dual message. Each day one is supposed to wait for him even though he is evidently not coming. It is a somewhat paradoxical form of waiting with the expectation that it will never happen; that is, it will happen when the Messiah arrives.

And there is the gist of it. In common parlance the very phrase "when the Messiah arrives" became equivalent to "never." Adults used the phrase frequently, and, consequently, children learned it early. As a little child in Haifa in the late 1930s I grew accustomed to two standard Hebrew utterances that meant "never." The first was "when the Messiah will come," and the second was the more vulgar "when a beard will grow in your ass." Children are not shy in responding with "never" to other children's requests, and on many occasions I took both expressions as well as dished them out. At any rate, the actual use of the language carried with it its own implicit answer as to when the Messiah will arrive — never, that is, when the Messiah will come. By the way, in the 1970s still another phrase for "never" appeared on the Israeli scene: "when peace comes."

Language games are not merely kid stuff. They are a very serious matter for adults who fight for political causes. This was clearly the case in an article by Israel Harel, a proponent of Jewish settlements in Greater Israel. His article is titled "Better the Golan than Peace" (Harel 1992). The title represented a takeoff on Moshe Dayan's famous statement in Tel Aviv on 17 February 1971 before a group of veterans that a state of no peace with Sharm al-Sheikh was preferable for Israel than a state of peace without Sharm al-Sheikh. Sharm al-Sheikh, at the southern end of the Sinai Peninsula, was captured by Israel during the Six-Day War. In 1977 Dayan repeated the same statement, maintaining that "Israel will have to state, in spite of the discomfort involved, what it prefers — Sharm al-Sheikh without peace or peace without Sharm al-Sheikh" (Dayan 1977, my translation). He went on to emphasize that the decision applies not only to Sharm al-Sheikh but also to the Golan Heights, Gaza, the Rafah Salient, and the West Bank. Just as Dayan then was reluctant to relinquish most of the occupied territories, Harel later did not want to give up the Golan that he considered as *nahalat avot*, or the inheritance of the forefathers. And this is how he stated what he termed "the true Israeli position" at the end of his article: "I believe, with full faith, that this is the way for a true peace. For even though it may tarry, each day I shall wait for it to come" (Harel 1992). This is a clear allusion to the dictum of Maimonides to believe each day with full faith in the coming of the Messiah even though he tarries. The same language that traditionally has served as the expression of a craving for the Messiah to come was cleverly used by a hawkish annexationist to express a craving for peace to come, but only when the Messiah arrives. With this language game of transferring yearnings for the Messiah to yearnings for peace, Harel's religious political credo crystallized, and its implications became self-explanatory and self-understood. The Golan we keep, but even though this act makes peace impossible, we shall wait for peace every day till it comes when the Messiah comes. And since this actually means "never," it decrees that Israel will never have peace and will live by its sword.

With less sophisticated religious fanatics, the cat gets out of the bag in no time at all. A messianic lady called the religious radio station Arutz 7 on 20 June 2001 and flatly stated: "There will be no peace until the Messiah of our justice comes, and there will be peace when there is no longer any Arab in the Land of Israel." What can one say about such militant positions, which doom Israel to everlasting troubles? In the Jewish tradition the harbinger of the Messiah is the prophet Elijah, the Tishbite. This is why unsolvable problems, which may have to wait indefinitely in order to be resolved, are referred to as *tyqu*, a Hebrew acronym for "Tishbite will resolve questions and problems." Yet self-destructive behavior on the part of the modern zealots of Yahweh need not await the arrival of the Messiah to be understood by those who do not wish to be dragged into the abyss.

In Jewish history waiting for the Messiah usually manifested itself in three basic forms. In the first form his future coming was accepted pro forma but actually ruled out. This somewhat dishonest psychological stance was given a blunt literary expression in the story "The Sermon" by the Israeli novelist Hayim Hazaz (1952). In the story Yudkah, a shy and usually silent kibbutz member, surprised everyone at a committee meeting by delivering a prolonged sermon on the meaning of Jewish history. The gist of his message was that Jews do not have a history because they did not make history. What happened instead was that history was done to them by the goyim. Calling the belief in the arrival of the Messiah "the typical Jewish delusion," he characterized it as a legend, an invention that excuses Jews of making any effort on their own behalf and allows them to just sit and wait for the Messiah to do it all. At this point Yudkah uttered the following indictment:

> "How can they believe such a thing! And believe it that much! And believe it for two thousand years! Two thousand years—in what way can people who are by no means naive, who are not at all stupid but, to the contrary, quite sophisticated, people who are quite a bit skeptical, people who are practical, perhaps even too practical, believe in such a thing, in such a thing! And not merely believe but even trust in it and make their whole life depend on it, the entire essence of their life and existence, their national and historical fate! Seriously! Seriously! They do believe in this with full faith—and that is what it is all about that they believe! But nevertheless, nevertheless, in the secret of their heart, you know, deep, deep within some fold, at some hidden point in the heart, a wee bit they do not believe, just a wee bit, at least that he will come now, that he will come this moment, that in their lifetime and their days he will come, and that is the main thing—it is impossible that they do not disbelieve even though they believe with full faith! What? This is also a Jewish characteristic, very, very Jewish: to believe with full faith, with a fervent and crazy faith, with all their heart and soul, yet a bit not to believe, just a little bit, even though this bit is decisive. I cannot explain it well. But this is how it is. I am not mistaken!" (Hazaz 1952, 194–95, my translation)

Through Yudkah's somewhat disjointed language Hazaz questioned the sincerity of the belief in the arrival of the Messiah. In effect he turned Maimonides' twelfth principle of the faith, as recited in the morning prayer, into something like "I believe with full faith in the arrival of the Messiah even though at some hidden point in my heart I just a wee bit, yet decisively, disbelieve." In other words, the twelfth principle of the faith is sometimes recited as mere lip service on the part of those who equate "never" with "when the Messiah comes."

The second form of waiting for the Messiah is a more intense mode and is typified by detecting the footsteps of the Messiah in ongoing events. The Israeli victory during the Six-Day War and the liberation of the Temple Mount rang in some Jewish ears like messianic footsteps. They were taken to mean that the Messiah and redemption are getting nearer to the point that they place additional obligations on the current generation that perforce affect daily lives. Therefore, new steps should be taken each day to help along the acceleration of the process, steps such as increasing Jewish settlement activity in areas heavily populated by Arabs. This messianic assignment was undertaken by the religious and political movement Gush Emunim, or Block of the Faithful. Other steps consisted of fostering more familiarity with traditional Jewish values and a greater appreciation of the Torah among the more secular Jews. Among those who were visibly active in this messianic endeavor, both in the United States and in Israel, and who placed a premium on educating and proselytizing the young army soldiers, was the Habad Hasidic movement.

The third form of waiting for the Messiah's arrival is the one that reaches fever's pitch as a messianic movement convulses its followers. This happened in Israel in the second century A.D. as Jews rushed to join the leaders of a terribly ill advised military revolt against the Romans. Leading the revolt for the Jews was the messianic military leader Bar Kokhba, who was joined by the messianic religious leader Rabbi Akiba ben Joseph. The historical lessons to be learned from that disastrous revolt received a thorough analysis from Y. Harkabi (1982), who regarded it as a catastrophe second in magnitude only to the Nazi Holocaust, in this case, an ancient revolt that was born out of the adherence to a myth that embraces unreality. Another example of a messianic movement on a mass scale took place in the seventeenth century; this time it took place in the Diaspora. It was a classic of feverish behavior. Gripped by a messianic convulsion, the followers dropped everything except for special rituals in preparation for the forthcoming redemption. They gathered together to wait for the great happening in the here and now. This usually occurred under the influence of a charismatic leader, the most notorious among them being the so-called false Messiah, Shabbetai Tzevi. When such instances occur, the messianic fervor reaches such heights that it simply cancels ordinary daily life. Energized by a collective delusion that is enthusiastically shared by all the group members, the followers drop out of normal daily life in anticipation of its replacement by a new messianic reality. The intricate dialectics that characterized the seventeenth-century Shabbatean movement and the paradoxical thinking that propelled it were superbly analyzed by the late Gershom Scholem (1957).

The Messiah idea encapsulates the dualistic internal logic of the way Jewish history is expected to work. Its core essence—the juxtaposition of destruction with reconstruction—is also expanded and projected to the ultimate dimensions of total catastrophe contrasted with a miraculous utopia. The psychohistorical essence of being a Jew is to always fluctuate between *hurban,* or destruction, and *ge'ulah,* or redemption. This is how it has been, how it is, and how it will continue to be whenever history encounters horrible premessianic tribulations followed by a glorious messianic bliss. As noted in the preface, in the Hebrew Bible Yahweh's ineffable name is spelled YeHoWaH by borrowing the vowels of the Hebrew term for "My Lords." The result of using these particular vowels is the meshing together of the verb "to be" in a way that combines all three tenses. In terms of Hebrew grammar the spelling of YeHoWaH can therefore be seen as a combination of "was," "is," and "will be" even though this was not the true original pronunciation of the ineffable name. (One of the traditional ways of referring to God without mentioning him by name was to call him "the Name.") Somewhat similarly, the messianic conception of history stretches across time so that it always was, is, and will be. The Messiah "was" because he preexisted since the days of Creation. He "is" because during each generation it is possible to detect "the footsteps" of the Messiah in the here and now. And he "will be" because he must. He has been promised, he is needed, and there are always either full catastrophes or at least major troubles, or tsores, to indicate that these events might qualify as the premessianic cataclysms that suggest the impending coming of the Messiah.

The myth of the preexistence of the Messiah (Patai 1979, 16-17), who was set up by God at the time of Creation to wait and suffer and long for the day when he is finally allowed to rescue the people of Israel, is an affirmation of the decree that Yahweh's laws of history will prevail from beginning to end. These implicit laws were actually an outcome of Yahweh's basic character. One version of these laws was stated by the prophet Isaiah: "'In gushing rage I momentarily hid my face from you but in eternal benevolence I pitied you,' said Yahweh your redeemer. 'For this is like the days of Noah to me, just as I swore that the waters of Noah will no longer pass over the earth so have I sworn not to rage over you and rebuke you'" (Isaiah 54:8-9). As usual, Yahweh smiles only after having frowned first. The fate of the Jews correlates with his moods. Every so often the omnipotent God is unable to control his anger, raising a fundamental question of justice within Jewish psychohistory. Do historical punishments occur because of Jewish sins, or is it the case that sins do not have anything to do with it, and the punishments are inflicted for no other reason than that Yahweh has once again gotten into one of his raging moods? At no time has this gut-wrenching question been more searing than during the Nazi Holocaust.

The prophet Jeremiah made his own contribution to stating Yahweh's laws of history: "'See, I have set you this day over nations and over kingdoms, to pluck up and to break down, to annihilate and to destroy, to build and to plant'" (Jeremiah 1:10). When I was taught these lines in Bible class during my junior high school days in Israel, the teacher emphasized the importance of the fact that in Jeremiah's statement one passes through four terms of destruction before arriving at only two terms of construction. It was not math that he was teaching. He was giving us a lesson in how Jewish history is supposed to work. Basically, it works in two major ways. You cannot get utopia without getting disaster first. Moreover, the phase of destruction and suffering is at least twice as long as the hoped-for stage of salvation.

Things become even more intriguing with the enlargement of the number of destructions by Jeremiah. "'And it shall come to pass that as I have watched over them to pluck up and break down, to destroy, annihilate and to harm, so I will watch over them to build and to plant,' says Yahweh. 'In those days they shall no longer say, "The fathers have eaten unripe fruit, and the children's teeth will be blunted." But rather each person will die for his own sin; any man who eats unripe fruit, his teeth will be blunted'" (Jeremiah 31:28-29). What we have here is a reiteration of the previous quote but this time including five terms of destruction. Of greater interest, however, is the statement that follows. It contains a modification of el kana's old law that punishes the sins of the fathers down to the fourth generation. When the period of destruction is over and the period of construction is ushered in, each person will die or otherwise suffer for his or her own sin. This amounts to a reform of justice and is tantamount to a future character change in Yahweh. Jeremiah, the prophet of destruction par excellence, promised a tilt in the balance away from el kana and more toward el ra'hum ve'hanun within Yahweh's character. The issue of Yahweh's justice remained alive in Judaism and was given new life in modern Israel. Presumably, the young country has set up new rules of justice, as can be learned from a joke by the noted Israeli humorist Ephraim Kishon about Israel, "a country where the fathers ate sour grapes and the teeth of the children are excellent" (Smith 1973). This assertion was made less than three months before Israel suffered the Yom Kippur, or Day of Atonement, War, during which the children's teeth were blunted galore. One should never underestimate Yahweh's long memory.

But the potential new balance in Yahweh's character that can be deduced from Jeremiah's writings is destined to show itself only after the prolonged period of destruction is over. And there are no guarantees anyway that this balance will hold. Yahweh is known to do things, to regret what he has done, and, subsequently, to even regret his regret. His fundamental rules of history have defined for Jews who they are and what their fate is. They have also conditioned Jewish expectations with regard to themselves and to the Gentiles. Jews are expected to sin, while Gentiles are expected to serve as God's agents of punishment. Such internalized expectations belong to the field of psychohistory. How changeable are these expectations? For Jews who become secular, change is possible, although many internalized expectations remain in force even after the divorce from Yahweh. For Jews who wish to remain within the faith but reform it, change is also possible, provided that they find the strength to revise their marriage contract to Yahweh. For Jews who remain unconditionally wedded to Yahweh, whose faith transcends questioning, or who can only question when questioning represents merely another detour in a convoluted road toward submission, for those Jews change will come only when the Messiah arrives.

In Jewish tradition the figure of the Messiah is not a God but rather a divine human being endowed by God with special powers. He must be a descendant of King David, and he has been designated by God to bring deliverance at the End of Days. Looking at the talmudic legends concerning the suffering Messiah, who as punishment for the sins of Israel has to keep waiting in heaven for his own arrival on earth, Patai very aptly concluded that the Messiah is none other than Israel personified (1979, 42–43). The waiting, suffering, and crying of the Messiah in heaven reflected the anguish, impatience, and despair of the exiled Jews who longed for redemption. His conclusion provides also an inkling of how psychologically boxed in many Jews felt. They were crying while waiting for their savior, who was himself crying while waiting for his own coming. Such a portrayal of the Messiah confirms suffering in the present but hardly affirms salvation in the future.

The messianic era that was projected to the End of Days was destined to unfold in two stages. The first phase was that of *hevlai mashiah,* or pangs of the birth of the Messiah. It referred to horrendous cataclysms that would eventually usher in the second phase of redemption. In his study of the Messiah idea in Jewish history, Julius Greenstone summed up the cataclysms as the breakdown of social order and the prevalence of political explosions (1906, 94). Patai emphasized that the pangs of the messianic times had both earthly and heavenly sources (1979, 95–96). Cosmic cataclysms brought about from above in the form of major natural disasters were to be paralleled by social and religious evils brought by sinful men upon themselves. He also pointed out that the use of the word "pangs" suggests that while waiting for the Messiah the people of Israel were much like a pregnant woman who expects to undergo severe pangs of childbirth before she can enjoy the pleasures of motherhood. Actually, the Hebrew term *hevlai*, which means "pangs of birth" or "throes of birth," attaches itself to various other words to denote the suffering and tribulations that are the price of any major initiation (Gonen 1975, 4–5). A person can experience pangs of birth, of acquiring a new language, of artistic creation, of love, of living, of death, of hell, and, lastly, of redemption. In short, no birth, growth, death, after-death, or rebirth can evolve without the bitter toll of pangs. The final initiation price at the End of Days is no exception to this rule. Hevlai mashiah, or premessianic cataclysms, will precede ge'ulah, or redemption. The final punishments and rewards at the end of time reach the dimensions of disaster and utopia, but the old initiation rule of having to pay the price of pangs still holds. One cannot get utopia without getting disaster first. Before the smiling el ra'hum ve'hanun can ever deliver a messianic bliss, the frowning el kana must first unleash a torrent of pangs to insure that the premessianic price of destruction will be paid in full and in advance. This fateful duality operates in Jewish history from beginning to end. This is how Yahweh governs.

The stormy events that were expected to lead from premessianic cataclysms to a final period of redemption started with the wars of Gog and Magog that were described in Ezekiel 38 and 39 and that served as the basis for later talmudic and medieval myths about the global Armageddon between the armies of Gog and Magog and the forces of the Messiah. Patai reasoned that these myths concerning the divine retribution that God will inflict upon the Gentiles functioned as an emotional safety valve by means of which a suppressed rage reaction could still receive some expression. His hypothesis was right on target. It should be borne in mind, however, that even in the cataclysmic End of Days, vengeance on the goyim came only after the initial phase of a disastrous defeat for the Jewish forces. Thus, even in Jewish compensatory fantasies about the time of the end, Yahweh still imposes a penalty prior to handing over the prize.

In the earlier stories the forces of evil were led by an unnamed king. But the leading role was eventually assigned to Armilus, who was the son of a stone statue of a woman that was impregnated either by worthless people or by Satan himself. This intriguing fantasy raises the specter of dualism once again. In certain respects it serves as an antinomy to an early biblical myth: "The Nephilim [fallen ones] were on earth in those days, and afterward too, as the sons of God came to the daughters of men, and they bore children to them. These were the heroes of old, the men of renown" (Genesis 6:4). It is not clear whether the sexual union between members of God's entourage and earthly women cost the former their heavenly seats, but the progeny were nevertheless heroes. This time, however, the union between Satan, who is God's antagonist or fallen angel, and a daughter of stone of sorts produced the negative hero: the ruthless leader of all the evil hordes. There is a distinct dualistic flavor to these descriptions of fateful battles between the forces of good and the forces of evil that seem independent of God. The hybrid Armilus, the progeny of an evil being and a stone woman, challenged both God and Israel in an attempt to become the new ruler of the world. He mastered enormous forces from among the other nations of the earth, and he struck fear in the hearts of the children of Israel. Most important, his eschatological role, according to Patai, was to slay Messiah ben Joseph (son of Joseph) and to be slain in turn by Messiah ben David (son of David).

At first the Israelite forces were led by Messiah ben Joseph, who won some battles against the armies of Gog and Magog. But eventually the armies of Israel suffered a devastating defeat in which Messiah ben Joseph was slain by Armilus. For forty days his corpse remained unburied in the streets of Jerusalem, but no beast or bird of prey dared to touch it. The choice of forty as the number of days may have been patterned after the forty days of the flood as well as the forty years that the Israelites spent in the Sinai desert under the leadership of Moses prior to arriving in the Promised Land. After forty days, Messiah ben David appeared. He resurrected Messiah ben Joseph and assumed command over the armies of Israel, and the rest is history. Patai provides a poignant summation of this portion of history in the End of Days.

> Under the charismatic leadership of the second Messiah, Messiah ben David, the great wars will continue. God fights the battles of His Messiah and the ultimate victory comes to pass. The final confrontation takes place on two planes: in heaven, where God chastises and subdues the celestial princes of the nations of the world, thereby weakening the earthly armies under their protection; and down on earth, where God intimidates and devastates those armies with fearsome portents. Thus the small nation of Israel, led by Messiah ben David, can overcome its enemies despite their vast superiority in numbers. (1979, 171)

It all amounts to an apocalyptic world war that encompasses both heaven and earth between the united forces of God and his people and the combined forces of the goyim and their celestial promoters. Thus the traditional contrast between good and evil has crystallized around the archaic split between the few people of the covenant and the many uncircumcised others.

The split of the Messiah figure into two was an enigma that preoccupied Patai, who offered two suggestions about it (1979, 165–70). The first was that when the death of the Messiah became an established talmudic tenet, it was felt to be irreconcilable with the hope that someday the Messiah will successfully redeem Israel. By splitting the person of the Messiah in two the second Messiah could still redeem Israel. What is more, the resurrection of Messiah ben Joseph by Messiah ben David serves as a psychological hint of the identity of the two. This explanation seems unsatisfactory, since it only pushes the enigma farther back in time. Why did the death of the Messiah become an established talmudic tenet to begin with? The psychological forces that imposed this belief still remain a mystery.

Patai's second suggestion was that the splitting of the Messiah in two adapted the messianic legends to the old tradition that the Messiah was perfectly prefigured in Moses. Since Moses died before reaching the Promised Land, the Messiah too had to die before reaching the goal of redemption. Nevertheless, the fact that, at least in some of the legends, Messiah ben David brought Messiah ben Joseph back to life suggests the identity of the two Messiahs. Patai's suggestion is an intriguing one. Moses indeed fulfilled the role of a savior. He performed miracles, liberated the Israelites from bondage, gave them the Torah, and led them within sight of the Promised Land, which, after his death, was conquered by his disciple, Joshua. It therefore stands to reason that, to a certain degree, dreams of liberation at the End of Days would be patterned after the legendary liberation of old that is being celebrated each Passover.

But the analogy is not complete. Moses did not die in battle like Messiah ben Joseph. And Joshua, who was not anything like Messiah ben David, did not resurrect Moses. Moses, after all, died for his sin as decreed by Yahweh. And a very peculiar sin it was. It all happened in the Wilderness of Zin, where the disgruntled people of Israel besieged Moses and his brother, Aaron, and harassed them with complaints about being thirsty:

> And Yahweh said to Moses: "Take the rod, and assemble the congregation, you and Aaron your brother, and tell the rock before their eyes to yield its water; so you shall bring water out of the rock for them; so you

shall give drink to the congregation and their cattle." And Moses took the rod from before God, as he commanded him. And Moses and Aaron gathered the assembly together before the rock, and he said to them: "Hear now, you rebels, shall we bring forth water for you out of this rock?" And Moses lifted up his hand and struck the rock with his rod twice; and plenty of water came out, and the congregation drank as well as their cattle. And Yahweh said to Moses and Aaron: "Because you did not believe in me, to sanctify me in the eyes of the Sons of Israel, therefore you will not bring this assembly into the land which I have given them." (Numbers 20:7-12)

What a stickler for detail was the righteously incensed Yahweh in imposing his punishment. In an earlier version of this event (Exodus 17: 1-7) Yahweh instructed Moses to hit the rock with his rod. Moses did exactly as he was told and did not incur punishment. A comparison of the two versions indicates that what really mattered in each case was not whether Moses hit the rock or spoke to it but whether he executed Yahweh's commands with exact precision. This is what Moses failed to do in the Numbers version, and it was for this sin that Yahweh punished him. Yet a forthright acknowledgment of this would have rattled Jewish innards too much. Because of this emotional resistance, the sin of Moses had to remain somewhat of a mystery. Numerous Jewish scholars would grapple in future generations with various creative and even far-out interpretations of the nature of the offense that was committed by Moses. It even reached a point where the nineteenth-century Italian scholar Samuel David Luzzatto recommended the ceasing of new interpretations because they only serve to enlarge the list of the sins of Moses (Becker 2001).

In his book *The Kuzari* Judah Halevi, who may have sensed that it is much easier to figure out the feelings of Moses than of Yahweh, offered a rather genteel comment about the whole sorry episode. Speaking of the Land of Zion, he said, "Moses prayed to see it, and when this was denied to him, he considered it a misfortune. Thereupon it was shown to him from the summit of Pisgah, which was to him an act of grace" (Halevi 1964, 2, 20). Saying that Moses considered it a misfortune is not the same as saying that God's action was unjust. But the underlying ambivalence on the part of Judah Halevi with regard to God's action can be sensed here. Moses may have taken it all in stride, both the "misfortune" and the "act of grace" that came his way from the enigmatic God. It was nevertheless a perfect setup by Yahweh, specifically instructing Moses to take with him the rod that was not needed for the task and that he was not supposed to use anyway. Clearly, Yahweh does not come out of this episode smelling like a rose, and the anonymous biblical editors were well aware of it. They therefore provided Yahweh with an added opportunity to justify his action (Deuteronomy 32:51) by accusing Moses and Aaron of breaking faith or acting in a way that betrays trust. Biblical and postbiblical justifications aside, what we basically see here is that the dual aspects of Yahweh's personality revealed themselves in his treatment of Moses. The harsh el kana prevented him from reaching the Promised Land, but the benevolent el ra'hum ve'hanun allowed him a glimpse of the land before his death. Jewish history is supposed to reflect Yahweh's mixed disposition.

The projection of the unfolding messianic events at the End of Days is no exception. It too reflects the mixed disposition of the deity. This is why the death of the Messiah became established in talmudic times. It was not done primarily in order to conform the figure of the Messiah to that of Moses. It was mostly done in order to conform the messianic saga to Yahweh's rules of Jewish history. He had to be allowed to remain true to his character and to angrily exact the price of disaster before lovingly conferring the prize of utopia, hence two Messiahs.

It was simply not possible to believe in Yahweh without buying into a whole set of expectations of how history is supposed to work. Uppermost among these expectations was the belief in premessianic cataclysm. Israeli author Hayim Hazaz had some choice words to say about all this, and he let these words come out of Yudkah's mouth during his sermon:

> Redemption is their top desire, the whole essence of their hope, yet with it they tied themselves, shackled their hands and feet in chains, and sealed for themselves a verdict that they harshly and pedantically guard and keep so that they will never, ever be redeemed! Well then, and now—and now—pangs of the Messiah—this is a chapter all by itself, a very interesting chapter—why, according to the popular opinion, must there be big troubles before the end? Why?—Why is it not possible without troubles? He is a Messiah and can do anything—why should he not come out of joy, out of goodness and blessedness, out of peace?—and pay attention: not troubles that are particular to the enemies of Israel, to the nations of the world, but deliberately to Israel! And not necessarily troubles, let us say, in order that they would repent etc., but troubles just for the sake of troubles, without any reason or need, troubles as plentiful as a river, decrees and calamities and various torments to the point that the eyes of Israel despair, grieving and sighing, to the point of not being able to withstand it and they will give up on redemption—what is this? A worldview? A wisdom-of-life? Or

is it something that the mouth does not disclose to the heart: fear of redemption?—I wonder! (1952, 195, my translation)

What the mouth did not disclose to the heart, the secret that could easily rattle Judaism's innermost *qishqes* (guts or innards), was the realization that Yahweh's deal is flawed. Who needs redemption if it only comes at the price of such premessianic cataclysms? If Yahweh cannot deviate from his standard historical procedure, how about canceling the whole deal? Bye-bye, utopias; just spare us the disasters. But it is not easy to shake off divine historical expectations.

Frequently, these expectations remain alive and well even among secular Jews who opt to preserve a Jewish tradition. Clinging to the Jewish heritage, these secular Jews are unable to separate language, literature, art, and beauty from the old religious impact that turned them into irrefutable laws of Jewish history. The impact has lingered on even after the outright belief in the ancient deity is presumably defunct. Perhaps they unconsciously continue to believe even as they no longer think so. Why not? The Lord, after all, works in mysterious ways. At any rate, the old expectations concerning how Jewish history works continue to be in operation even as they miss out on true reality. Such expectations are the stuff of psychohistory.

Following victory, Qibbutz Galuyot, or the Ingathering of the Exiles, was to take place. Patai pointed out that the Jews have been praying for this three times daily and underscored the fact that the concept of the ingathering became synonymous with redemption (1979, 181–82). Since redemption is the hallowed goal of messianism, its equation with ingathering takes us right into the point of intersection of messianism and Zionism—the modern Jewish political movement that set up for itself the goal of gathering the exiled Jews back to the Land of Israel in order to rebuild it and regain national independence and collective health. The psychodynamics of the return of the Sons of Israel to the motherland of Zion are discussed in the previous chapter. An addendum to this dialectical saga is now in order in connection with messianism. In order to make the ingathering complete so as to effect a full restoration of Israel to God, not only the tribes of Israel but also the exiled Shekhinah, or Dwelling, that personifies God's presence should return to the ancestral land.

There have been many variations on the theme of the Shekhinah in the Judaic heritage. We will confine ourselves to Patai's two basic assertions. The first is that the Shekhinah is a divine feminine entity who lamented the fate of her exiled children and desecrated temple. In talmudic times she became identified with the "community of Israel." The second is that, in later kabbalistic literature, she came to be regarded as the spouse of God. The talmudic theme is the gentler of the two, consisting of a hovering divine and motherly presence who benefits all people but especially the Sons of Israel, whose plight she shares. By contrast, the kabbalistic myths have a rougher quality to them. The state of the universe fluctuates as the battle between the top demon of the forces of evil, known as Samael or as Sitra Ahra, the Other Side, and between God continues to rage. When the forces of good are ascendant, the Shekhinah is able to rebuff Samael's attempt to copulate with her, and she is even able to use the harsher of the divine powers to take vengeance on the goyim. But the exiled Shekhinah is constantly away from God, her husband. When the evil forces prevail, she may then be impregnated by Samael and thereby conceive impure souls, or else a demonic snake may bite her womb. What is more, during such periods God himself sometimes has a sexual union with Lillith, the demon female figure who then rules over the abandoned Land of Israel.

These descriptions are psychologically significant, but this time the psychodynamic contrast is not intrapersonal but interpersonal. It is no longer an inner conflict between mother and prostitute, as can be deduced from the different behaviors of Zion the motherland. Rather, it is an outer conflict either between the mother figure of Shekhinah and the demonic snake that penetrates her or between the female demon Lillith and God with whom she attempts to copulate. The scales have tilted heavily in the direction of dualism. Instead of conflicted and mixed-up personalities who engage in contradictory behavior, as both Zion and Yahweh were, we get a struggle between Sitra Ahra and the Shekhinah and, even more important, an overall struggle between Sitra Ahra and God. No longer does Yahweh complain about the disloyalty of his whoring wife. Instead, he screws around with Lillith on certain occasions, as disloyal husbands sometimes do. But this seems to take place not because of a neurotic sudden change of heart but because Lillith has the power to get him when the universal demonic forces are on the ascendancy. The Land of Israel is not always under Yahweh's control, and the whole world is partly controlled by the forces of the Other Side. The theological problem as well as the psychological dilemma now shifts from the question, What do you do with an omnipotent but a neurotic God? to the question, How do you help a God whose powers are limited? It is a dualistic picture that suggests that God himself needs allies. Both theologically and psychologically therefore it serves as an inducement to acting on one's own initiative, since waiting for the less-than-omnipotent God to do it all on his own no longer seems valid. This view of the state of the universe reinforced the Jewish predilection to take active steps for the purpose of hastening the messianic end. It strengthened the Jewish tendency at first to follow false Messiahs and later, after the advent of secularization and the rise of modern nationalism, to follow the so-called secular messianism, namely, Zionism.

In the previous chapter we spoke of the duality within Yahweh's personality. Now, however, we talk about dualism as the religious doctrine of two independent deities. It is important to bear this distinction in mind in order to avoid semantic confusion. The injection of a flavor of dualism, albeit never a full-fledged dualism, into Jewish mysticism came as a response to a prolonged exile, continuous persecutions, and delayed redemption. The dualistic themes of an opposition between two Gods implied a growing impatience with God's excuses and a refutation of his traditional habit of somehow explaining away the injustice of punishments that seemed to far outweigh sins. The "authoritative" explanation was delivered long ago by Yahweh with a moralistic and self-virtuous "do not blame me, it is all your fault" style:

> Thus said Yahweh:
> "Where is your mother's bill of divorce,
>   with which I sent her away?
> Or which of my creditors is it
>   to whom I have sold you?
> For it is for your iniquities that you were sold,
>   and for your transgressions that your mother was sent away.
> Why, when I came, was there no man?
>   When I called, no one answered?
> Is my hand so shortened that it cannot redeem?
>   Or have I no power to rescue?
> It is by my rebuke that I dry up the sea,
>   turn rivers into a desert;
> their fish stink for lack of water
>   and die of thirst.
> I clothe the skies with darkness
>   and make sackcloth their covering."
>
> (Isaiah 50:1–3)

Yahweh's excuse of last resort is that he, who is powerful enough to master the forces of nature far beyond man's capabilities, is similarly

wise enough to mete out the kind of justice that far exceeds man's limited understanding. He delivered the same kind of response when Job
complained to him about his injustice: "'The earth is delivered into the
hand of an evildoer; he covers the faces of its judges. If it is not he, who
then is it?'" (Job 9:24). Deeply stung, Yahweh retorted as follows:
"'Where were you when I founded the earth? Tell me if you have known
wisdom!'" (Job 38:4). When I studied this material at high school in
Haifa, my teacher, Baruch Kurzweil, stood up, waving his arms like an
excited God, turned to us pupils as if we were the complaining Job, and,
paraphrasing Yahweh, bellowed: "Where were you when I received my
doctorate in Vienna?" It was his way of signaling that Yahweh's response sounded woefully hollow.

In similar fashion the flavoring of Judaism with dualistic elements
in Jewish mysticism signaled dissatisfaction with the traditional explanations. It was a reaction to a situation during which it was becoming
increasingly difficult to keep the lid on the rage at the Lord that was
evoked by the incessant frustrations. What the dabbling with dualism
implied, without explicitly saying so, was some such reaction as the following: Do not talk to us about creditors or a bill of divorce, and do not
tell us that it is all for our sins and is therefore all our fault. It has never
been all our fault. In a corner of our mind we have always known that it
is sometimes your fault, Doctor el ra'hum ve'hanun and Mister el kana.
But lately we have come to realize that we are not always the victims of
your goddamn neurotic personality with its rapid changes of heart.
Sometimes you yourself cannot help matters because you are not in total
control. Admit it! Do not dance around turning rivers into deserts as if
you are truly omnipotent. You are not. Therefore your hand is too short-
ened to redeem, and you are powerless to rescue. And you do need help
because you are not the sole master. Even if the Sitra Ahra is only the
"other side" within you (duality) rather than side by side with you (dualism), the fact still remains that you are not totally in charge. We will try
to help you. And this also means, God forbid, that we may have to take
it upon our own selves to hasten the end so as to bring about redemption. Just sitting on our behinds and waiting for semi-impotent you to
do it would no longer do. We will do it. So you can stop your bitching
about "Why, when I came, was there no man?" Mr. Complainer.

The description above was but a literary way in a fairly modern
parlance of giving words to the underlying frustration and anger that
fostered the dabbling with dualism. It is important to underscore the
fact that by and large the Jewish mystical movements did not embrace

full-fledged dualism. It has never reached the stage of officially acknowledged two independent Gods, even though Samael was recognized as the rebelling servant. The unity of God and his being the only God remained two of the pillars of Judaism that were emphasized by the leading authorities. Satan was never accorded the de jure status of an independent agent, but de facto he sometimes appeared that way. Thus the perception of Yahweh has tilted somewhat from the image of a conflicted person to the image of a person in conflict with others. This theological shift had an enormous psychological significance in relation to messianism. In the case of a God who is an omnipotent but a conflicted person, any human meddling with his affairs would be an ill-advised transgression. It is therefore prudent to leave the issue of bringing about the Messiah entirely up to him. But in the case of a God who may be less than omnipotent because he is in conflict with another deity, trying to help him bring about the Messiah is commendable. The old sin of *de'hiqat haqets,* or hastening the end, could now be a mitzvah, that is, a commandment.

The psychological origins of messianic tales reside in the tangible oppressions of the present much more so than in the imaginary dreams of a rosy future. Consequently, the period of a struggle for liberation can be expected to carry much more of an emotional punch than the following phase of a steady postmessianic bliss. And this is what happened with the talmudic messianic legends. Victory came, God was the undisputed ruler, all the defeated goyim recognized Yahweh as the only God, and the children of Israel and the Shekhinah returned from exile. Now what? Well, for one thing the Messiah was now reduced to insignificance because the attention shifted to what God would now say and do, as was so poignantly pointed out by Patai (1979, 189–90). And there were still things both big and small left for God to do. There was the resurrection of the dead, as prophesied by Ezekiel's vision of the dry bones: God breathed new life into dry bones and promised to revive the deceased Israelites in their graves and bring them back to the Land of Israel (Ezekiel 37:1–14). Another big matter was the bestowal of a fabulous fertility on all living creatures.

And then there was the smaller matter of throwing a messianic banquet. The food offerings included a choice of fish (the sea dragon Leviathan), meat (Behemoth), and fowl (Ziz Sadai). All this had a bit more to it than the usual joy of eating gefilte fish during a Sabbath meal. Since Yahweh once killed Leviathan by his "hard and great and strong sword" (Isaiah 27:1), there may have been elements here of a victory feast during which one eats the flesh of the slain enemy. The food was offered together with wine that had been preserved in its grapes since the days of Creation. This could mean that the year 3760 B.C. was a very good year for wine, the best vintage ever. Being a good host, God joined the table and even danced for his guests, but he saved his best show for last. He killed the Angel of Death. With this masterpiece performance he presumably rid the world of the curse of dualism as well as duality, that is, outer conflict and inner conflict. No more Satan without. No more yetzer within. Everything could now regress into the merriment of a struggle-free existence.

With the messianic banquet the chain of events reached its end. From then on messianic narratives lapsed into generalities. But even then hard-core Judaic biases remained. Israel was imagined as a community of men only. Women were reduced to the role of childbearing machines. The feminine element in mystical Jewish thinking was confined to the image of the matronly figure who suffers her children's pain. Patai did not pull any punches in criticizing this obvious Judaic male bias. Speaking of Rachel, Israel's *mater dolorosa,* he asserted: "This supernal Female was very much present in the male consciousness — present, in fact, to such an extent that no room was left for thought about the role, tasks, functions, and feelings of mere flesh-and-blood women in the Messianic ambience" (Patai 1979, 249). These were "words like spurs," as the Hebrew idiom goes. Something was indeed overly present in the Jewish male consciousness, and something else was missing as a result. Chances are that the missing element was relegated to the realm of the unconscious.

Clearly, the meat and gravy of messianic tales is to be found in the descriptions of the arduous road of getting there. The stuff of life consists mostly of making efforts, and being in the thick of things means struggling on the long road. On many occasions when life's oppressions and frustrations scraped Jewish guts, the psychological inclination to hit the messianic road in search of an accelerated solution has been reinforced. But the rules of the arduous road, including the final cataclysmic events, were not designed to offer instant remedies. Moreover, the messianic rules were never confined only to the culmination of events at the time of the end. In effect they were also the ongoing rules for the flow of life and history. Every generation can expect major disasters that can be interpreted as progressive steps toward the advent of the Messiah. Each generation can be expected to experience anew the enigmatic mingling of present trouble and future hope. By contrast, blissful descriptions of the wondrous state that would come about after everything else has already happened and the hard journey was completed were not really the stuff of life. These wondrous descriptions were too fluffy to serve as actual rules of history or to indicate what to expect of life. Nevertheless, these descriptions merit our psychological interest.

It is not possible to determine for sure the psychological significance of the descriptions of the end state. One can, however, offer some speculations based on the application of psychoanalytic insights to certain Jewish themes. The killing of the Angel of Death was the clearest indication that henceforward existence would be different from life as we knew it. With the messianic revival of the dead now followed by the cancellation of death itself, existence assumed a different nature. Postbiblical talmudic developments have endowed the Angel of Death or Samael or Satan a semi-independent role. They also equated him at times with the bad urge, or yetzer. All this represented various shades of dualism that crept into the reigning monism. Thus conflict with the "other side" raged not only in heaven between God and Satan but also on earth between the good urge and the evil urge within man's soul. And all this reflected the reality that life is a struggle. But with the final messianic projection of the completion of the arduous journey, struggle has been canceled. The postmessianic era of life without struggle has been ushered in, if one can still call it life. Patai was right in indicating that at that point, with their imagination exhausted, the Messiah texts lapsed into generalities (1979, 247). While it was stated that God would teach the pious a new Torah, not a word was said about how it might be different from the old one. This is a telling example indeed. The concept of a new Torah may sound quite revolutionary, but in the absence of concrete details it dissolves into platitude.

By and large, one gains the impression that these musings about the nature of postmessianic bliss represent the less-than-fertile imagination of tired old men who are not fully in touch with their underlying feelings. The fantasy of dispensing with life's need to exert effort was not exactly a sign of emotional maturity. To old man it may sound nice and pleasant that everything comes their way without exertion. For example, males would no longer need to court females, but instead it would be females who court males. And this is but one example of how all the good things come one's way effortlessly. There is a spoon-feeding quality to it all. No more weeping, sighing, or groaning. Instead of suffering, a hallmark of Jewish history that has been considered to be a Jewish specialty, there is now continuous delight with the readily available food, Torah teaching, women, and what not.

Where does all this leave Yahweh? He now floats in a world with no yetzer, no death, no sin or, for that matter, punishment, and no enemies of Israel. The defeated goyim have already meekly acknowledged the Jewish God as the only true God. Torah study and ritual circumcision may still continue, but the foreskins of people's hearts are gone with the abolition of the notorious urge. In this kind of life without struggle, Yahweh's rules of history no longer apply. Jeremiads, forecasting four or five terms of destruction to be followed by only two terms of construction, are not relevant anymore. Their time has passed. It is somewhat ironic that when Yahweh finally got around to activating his two Messiahs and to establishing the kingdom of God, he became superfluous and lost his raison d'être.

How could the God-baby be thrown out with the bathwater? What could be the psychological explanation for such a surprising turn of events? One possible answer is the reemergence of the repressed feminine side. The constant feeding and uninterrupted satisfaction of all needs that typifies messianic bliss conjures up the image of the nourishing mother. For so long the children of Israel needed it and longed for it all—tender loving care, a feeling of security, continuous feeding, and uninterrupted joy. Finally, the Holy One, Blessed Be He, responds to these yearnings with boundless generosity and provides it all. He may be a male, but he acts in the best tradition of womanly love and care. He might as well be addressed as the Holy One, Blessed Be She.

Another possible answer is rooted in the psychological defense of overcompensation that was born out of overfrustration. Whether consciously or unconsciously, as seen from within the framework of the traditional Jewish religion, Yahweh's yoke was too hard to bear. His laws of history were too oppressing. His reign seemed to sustain hope in theory but to squash it in practice. It was difficult to be a Jew because life under him and his capricious shenanigans was simply too difficult. But the defensive Jewish counterreaction, of dreaming about an everlasting postmessianic bliss, went too far. It went beyond reforming the laws of history so as to make them just. With more just rules, efforts could be rewarded, the children's teeth would not be blunted, the innocent would not be punished, while the guilty would receive only punishments that fit the crimes and not be subject to cataclysms. But from a psychological vantage point the messianic dreams concerning the bliss of the time of the end lapsed into a ludicrous overcompensation. Instead of reforming the rules to insure that life's efforts are justly rewarded, they aspired to do away with struggle altogether. The regressive quality of the wish to carry on an effortless life is apparent. Born of impatience, the messianic dreams abandoned the constraints of reality altogether and found solace in the bosom of fantasy. As a result, instead of reforming the rules of history, they canceled history altogether.

Of course, Yahweh himself was a fantasy made up by the ancient Hebrews. He was primordial, capricious, contradictory, moralistic, and not fully predictable. Because he had troubles in handling his own yetzer, he was too harsh with the Israelites, who experienced similar troubles. To make matters worse, he engaged in too many self-serving justifications of his undue harshness. Now, at the End of Days, he was unofficially supplanted by the talmudic and postbiblical Holy One, Blessed Be He, who cut a more benign figure. He presided over the postmessianic existence of effortless joys that was getting close to limbo. The cancellation of struggle yielded an existence in a continuous bliss that was a bit on the boring side. The excitement of life was gone because it no longer was life as we know it. But there is no need to worry. It would all happen only after the Messiah had arrived.

CHAPTER 3

Fateful Holidays

The fateful duality that runs through Jewish lore was crystallized and given mythic expression in Jewish holidays. By so ritualizing the repeated expression of core beliefs that determine what it feels like to belong to the Jewish group, Jewish identity was even further solidified and given annual reinforcement. And no holiday is as ritualized or as symbolic of the Jewish lot on this earth as Passover.

Passover is the celebration of the miraculous liberation of the Jews from bondage in the ancient Egypt of the pharaohs. The Passover seder spells out all the consecutive steps to be performed during the Passover ritual ceremony. The ritual includes symbolic food items such as saltwater, which stands for the Israelites' tears as they were forced to do hard labor in Egypt, and haroset, a mixture of wine, crushed apples, and crushed almonds that stands for the clay that was used in the building of brick walls. The ceremony consists of a ritualistic recitation of the miraculous transition from slavery to freedom that was brought about by the might of God.

Passover, the legendary deliverance under the leadership of Moses, to a certain degree prefigures the messianic deliverance that is yet to come at the End of Days. This direct connection between the past and the future is underscored by the special custom of allotting a special wine cup for Elijah toward the end of the ceremony. It is the fifth occasion of pouring wine into a cup. This time, however, a large goblet of wine intended for the prophet Elijah is placed on the table. No one drinks from it, and no blessing is recited over it, as was the case with the four previous cups. What is more, the entry door of the house is swung open to allow Elijah to enter should he arrive. Elijah is the harbinger of the Messiah, as prophesied by Malachi: "Behold, I will send to you Elijah the prophet before the great and terrible day of Yahweh comes" (Malachi 3:23). The last poem sung at the ceremony, known as *had gadya* (it refers to the kid that Father bought for two zuz, a silver coin worth about a quarter of a shekel), also indicates a messianic connection. The poem ends with God slaying the Angel of Death. This act never took place during the liberation from Egypt and clearly refers to the upcoming liberation at the End of Days. This allusion plus the injection of Elijah into the Passover ceremony thus reaffirm the continuity of Jewish expectations throughout mythohistorical time.

This is why it is incumbent upon every Jew to consider himself or herself personally as someone who has been liberated from Egypt during his or her own lifetime. It is explicitly stated in the haggadah, Passover tale: "In each and every generation a man must see himself as if he came out of Egypt." When this injunction is paired with the daily prayer "I believe with full faith in the coming of the Messiah, and even though he tarries, with all that, each day I shall wait for him to come," both past and future become fused in a single time. In that kind of time the past as well as the future are expected to shed any aura of remoteness and to assume instead the quality of immediacy. In other words, Yahweh's rules of history are expected to continually prevail throughout all times.

Yahweh being Yahweh, he cannot bend these rules. Regardless of which particular time period it is, deliverance cannot come about unless it is first preceded by bondage. It would be illogical otherwise. If Yahweh is to deliver a deliverance, he must at first afflict an affliction. And if this is what has to be done, then why not do it right—drag it out. So in the story of the Exodus from Egypt Yahweh kept hardening Pharaoh's heart. If in the meanwhile the Israelites only suffer more, what of it? Even greater will be their deliverance. And if in the meantime the ferocity of the plagues inflicted on Egypt escalates to the point of killing the firstborn sons, so what? The greater affliction would only serve as a testimony to Yahweh's might. The fact that this was a problematic stance on God's part did not escape Jewish scholars, who tried to justify it somehow. For instance, in his *Book of Principles* the fifteenth-century Jewish scholar Joseph Albo interpreted God's action as a device to determine whether Pharaoh's repentance was sincere or reflected merely fear of punishment (1893, 329). Only by repeated plagues was it possible to ascertain that Pharaoh no longer attributed the events to natural co-incidences but rather to God's divine providence.

What do we do with a Jewish Lord who imposes his own inner du-ality upon the course of history? Psychology would tell us, of course, that this is a self-imposed constraint by the Sons of Israel on earth rather than a decree from God in the skies above. But given the reality that to genuine believers it all seems to be a transcendental edict rather than an internal compulsion, the question still remains, How do we handle God's personal predilection to dish out a mixture of vengeful-ness and mercifulness? Passover is a prime example of how we do just that. It is so named because God made the destroyer pass over the marked households of the Sons of Israel while he killed all firstborn sons in the Egyptian households. The markings were made by smearing the blood of the slaughtered Paschal Lamb on the doorposts and cross-bar at the entryway of each Jewish house. All this takes us back to an-cient times, when children, especially firstborn sons, were sometimes sacrificed just as the firstborn among animals or the first yield of the fields went for the gods. It also takes us back to the story of the binding of Isaac, when Isaac was saved from sacrifice because the ram served as an adequate substitute. In the Passover tale this revised sacrificial model of animals rather than humans applied to the Jews. But the Egyptians had no such luck, of course. For them, the old insistence on human sac-rifice remained in force. Yahweh, who knows how to stick to the fine print of any contract, took care that his obedient adjutant, the destroyer, would carry on as instructed without showing any signs of indepen-dence. As if aware of the danger of a dualistic or otherwise theologically incorrect interpretation of the destroyer in Exodus (12:23), the writers of the Passover haggadah inserted in it a strongly worded comment that focused on the expression "And I will pass in the land of Egypt" Exodus (12:12). It aimed to nip dualism in the bud, and it ran as follows "And I will pass in the land of Egypt. I, and not an angel. And I will smite every firstborn. I, and not a seraph. And on all of the gods of Egypt I will execute judgment. I, and not a messenger. I am the Lord. I am he, and none other."

God's solo act was very brutal, and it worked. Pharaoh was forced to yield. Although he was uncircumcised and did not remove the foreskin of either his penis or his heart, and although his heart was even further hardened by Yahweh on several occasions, he had to surrender. So there is an answer to the question of how to handle the God who poses an enigmatic mixture of love and vengeance. Lobby with Yahweh to be an el kana with the goyim and save his el ra'hum ve'hanun disposition for the Jews. At this point it behooves us to mention again the Lord's warning: "Circumcise yourselves to Yahweh and remove the foreskins of your heart, men of Judah and inhabitants of Jerusalem, lest my wrath go forth like fire and burn with none to quench it, because of the evilness of your deeds" (Jeremiah 4:4). The clues for a strategy for handling Yahweh are basically all there. Get him to deflect his wrath from those who are circumcised to those who are not. This strategy was institutionalized in the Passover ceremony.

Moshe Davidowitz (1978) viewed the Passover haggadah as an attempt to concretize the collective mythos of the Jewish historical consciousness by setting up a historical model on three different levels. The first was the heroes—the Jews. The second was the oppressor—Pharaoh. The third was the Controller and Master of history—God. It is no surprise that sooner or later inspections of Jewish myths, including the Passover tale, narrow down to the psychohistorical triad of Jews, goyim, and Yahweh. But the rage of exiled and largely helpless Jews toward the oppressing goyim could not be given free reign. In this connection Davidowitz demonstrated how the less-than-coincidental pairing of a certain artistic illustration in the haggadah with a specific portion of the text allowed for a carefully masked attacks on Christianity and its symbols. It is the famous "pour out thy wrath" section:

> Pour out thy wrath upon the goyim
>   that know thee not
> and upon kingdoms
>   that call not on thy name;
> for they have eaten up Jacob
>   and his dwelling place they have laid waste.
>   (Psalms 79:6-7)
>
> Pour out thy fury upon them,
>   and let thy burning anger overtake them.
>   (Psalms 69:25)
>
> Pursue them with anger and destroy them
> from under the heavens of the Lord.
>   (Lamentations 3:66)

Davidowitz examined a fifteenth-century haggadah written by Israel Hasofer Ben Me'ir of Heidelberg in which this very passage appeared together with an illustration of a supposedly Jewish seder scene that was a thinly disguised portrayal of the Last Supper of Jesus. This juxtaposition of the powerful "pour out thy wrath" text with one of the most famous symbols of Christianity provided a clear-cut identification as to who were the contemporary goyim who triggered reactions of Jewish rage. Davidowitz regarded the rage as reaching such explosive dimensions that its release could be dangerous on two counts. The external, and quite hostile, world could retaliate with violence. Yet the alternative of a defensive redirection of the rage inward could lead to the kind of communal implosion that creates a collective depressive state. The seder ritual, which was sometimes augmented by visual illustrations, mitigated some of the impact of the imploded anger by focusing it away from the self but in a visually disguised and therefore safe way.

Nevertheless, the written text as such carries no disguise. Jewish attempts to interpret the word "goyim" in the text as a reference to polytheistic peoples did not fool the Christians. Rage is rage and is not difficult to recognize. And the rage was supposed to last till the End of Days. Davidowitz noted that the "pour out thy wrath" section is read at the seder when the door is opened for the prophet Elijah to enter the home as the harbinger of the messianic age. What we see here is a not-so-subtle reminder to Yahweh that he is obliged to fully unleash his anger at the goyim by the time of the final reckoning. To this day there are plenty of Jews who engage with quite a bit of gusto in this yearly opportunity to urge and cajole the Lord to be sure to fulfill his ultimate destiny of being the avenger.

But other Jews are not comfortable with this expression of outright rage. Sometimes this section is omitted in experimental revisions of the haggadah. Some other times Jews simply skip the recitation of this part of the text. On other occasions they tone down their voices. This was the case with U.S. Senator Joseph Lieberman, the Democratic vice presidential candidate in the 2000 election campaign. Ruth Gil, an Israeli woman who is the wife of Hadassah Lieberman's cousin, reported the following during an interview: "The Lieberman family is keen on conducting the Passover seder according to its regulations. During a Passover seder at the home of Hadassah's parents, who reside in Riverdale, New York, we recited the haggadah just as we do in Israel, according to sitting order, with everyone reciting in fluent Hebrew. I had to recite the section that says 'pour out thy wrath on the goyim,' and Joe asked me to recite it quietly so that the non-Jewish neighbors would not hear or be offended" (Meidan 2000, my translation). Senator Lieberman's gut-level reaction seems to suggest that his heart is in the right place, since he does not let his religious sentiments slide into primitive expressions of rage.

The Passover haggadah is full of heavy stuff that is saturated with emotionally laden themes. In order to lighten this burden, the tale is sometimes handled by Israelis with humor. The seder includes a very jubilant singing of *dayenu* (literally, "it is enough for us"). Ten marvels that God performed for Israel are mentioned separately. After each of them comes the exclamation, "It is enough for us." But in the actual singing the first syllable of *dayenu* is replicated in order to create two words, *dai dayenu*, or, "enough, it is enough for us." This emphatic expression of the "enough" sentiment is sometimes used by Israelis to indicate that they have had it with the whole burdensome ceremony. In other words, enough is enough. I recall having read once a fictional story about an Israeli man who felt dayenu with regard to the elaborate seder ritual. He plotted his escape by scheduling a trip to France with his family during the Passover season. In France the family was robbed and left stranded. Seeking help in what turned out to be a Jewish household, they were of course invited to the seder and ended up singing dai dayenu in France. There is no escape from Jewish fate.

A takeoff on the dayenu poem appeared in a satirical newspaper column in Israel under the title "A Passover Prayer, the New Version." A series of requests were repeatedly addressed to "Our Father in Heaven," asking him to fix the social, economic, political, and security problems of the Israeli state. Yet each bunch of requests concluded with the proclamation *lo dayenu*, or "it is not enough for us." Finally came a request for "a moment of complete quiet . . . a moment in which each person could chose his God, and understand it the way it occurs to him. One moment, our God and the God of our fathers, is not too great a request. And then, in all probability, dayenu [it is enough for us]" (Lapid 1993, my translation). Apparently, it would indeed be enough if one could exercise a choice rather than be already preemptively chosen by Yahweh.

But the whole aim of the Passover ceremony is to reinforce the traditional theological order, thus denying a choice. It is meant to shore up the group identity and to strengthen its exposed and weakened defenses. This point was made by the psychohistorian Howard Stein, who illustrated it by means of the second of "the four sons" of the haggadah (1978, 168–70). These are the wise, the wicked, the simple, and lastly the one who knows not how to ask. Each of the first three sons asks the father a question concerning the meaning of Passover. And here is what the haggadah states about the second son: "The wicked one what says he. What is this service to you? To you and not to him. And since he took himself out of the collective body, he denied an essential principle. You should therefore blunt his teeth and tell him. It is for what the Lord did for me when I went from Egypt. For me and not for him. Had he been there, he would have not been redeemed" (my translation). One can learn from this ritualized exchange what Yahweh truly meant by blunting teeth—death. Stein emphasized that this answer spells out very clearly what a wicked Jew who asks the wrong questions can expect from the Jewish community. He who dares to challenge tradition faces rage, exclusion, and a death wish retroactively displaced to not being redeemed in ancient Egypt. Moreover, "Egypt" is not a single place in time, as poignantly pointed out by Stein. Being redeemed in Egypt could therefore also refer to surviving the Nazi Holocaust of the 1940s or to escaping the schemes of 1970s Egypt, where the image of its leader, Anwar Sadat, merged with the image of the enslaving pharaohs. It all happened, of course, before Sadat became a peacemaker and a martyr to peace, and it was a result of the father's manipulations of imagery. By "father" Stein meant the traditional authorities, who would not hesitate to resort to modern teeth blunting in order to insure theological correctness, that is, psychological submission.

But with the weakening of the religious hold among many Jews and with the secular genie out of the bottle, it was no longer possible to confine the discourse on the Jewish liberation saga to traditionally kosher images. One example of this is the "Palestinian Passover haggadah" that was composed as a tongue-in-cheek political statement by the late Israeli humorist and author Dan ben Amotz. It was written from the point of view of the oppressed Palestinians and repeatedly played on the ironies of role reversal. A few selections follow: "We were slaves to Pharaoh in Israel. . . . In each and every generation an Arab must see himself as if he came out of Israel. . . . If Israel had won the war but did not expropriate our lands—dayenu. . . . Pour out thy wrath upon the goyim who know you not, yah Allah, and upon kingdoms that do not call upon your name and the name of Palestine" (Ben Amotz 1972, 13). In spite of the sardonic humor, this was a serious political and, even more so, ideological challenge to the Israeli authorities. The challenge picked up on the conviction long held by Palestinians that they have become the "Jews of the Arab world." It clearly called for the application of the Jewish sense of justice to people who were suffering a Jewish fate. The Israeli awareness of this role reversal, in which Jews act like goyim toward

Arabs who suffer like Jews, increased during the first Palestinian intifada and sharpened even more during the second, or al-Aqsa, intifada.
More and more Israelis have been asking themselves, These days, who
are the people who are fighting for liberation from bondage, and who
are the ones who are playing the role of the Pharoah? This issue also
was raised by members of the Tikkun Community—a group of liberal
Jews and non-Jewish allies who are committed to a new planetary consciousness. In a full page ad in the *New York Times* on 22 March 2002
they urged support for the Israeli Reserve officers who refused to serve
in the occupied territories, and they urged other American Jews to include in the upcoming Passover seder ceremony "a mini teach-in about
the way that Israel is increasingly perceived as a Pharaoh to a population
that is seeking its own freedom and self-determination" ("No, Mr.
Sharon!" 2002).

Historical ironies aside, it is clear that the Passover celebration has
further cemented several ironclad Jewish expectations from life that are
sometimes referred to here as Yahweh's rules of history. First, it has confirmed, albeit implicitly, that the duality of God's character does indeed
reflect itself on earth through miraculous and radical shifts of fate during which catastrophe has to precede salvation. Second, it has insured
that this fateful duality would be related to and consonant with the
Gentile-Jewish schism. Consequently, Jewish catastrophes were expected to come by way of Gentiles but only as instruments of God, who
is the true initiator of all historical destinies. These convictions came at
a psychological price. There was an enormous anger toward Gentiles,
the suppression of which was emotionally taxing. There was also manifest guilt on the part of Jews regarding themselves but latent rage toward the Lord. It was, after all, for their sins that the just Lord inflicted
severe punishments upon the Jews, hence—the guilt. Yet a nagging and
infuriating suspicion persisted that the magnitude of the punishments
bore no relationship to the alleged sins, hence—the rage.

Finally, the yearly Passover celebration locked all these psychohistorical expectations into a fused time during which everything of the
past or the future happens in an eternal present. As a result, the present
has been experienced concurrently on two separate plans. On the one
hand, the here and now was perceived in a mundane fashion as the flow
of current events. But, on the other hand, it was perceived as both the
here and there in the now and then and always. This was the messianic
outlook—always expecting the recurrence of the eternally dual fate, always detecting the footprints of the Messiah, and sometimes even

hearing his actual footsteps. There is a distinct quality of timelessness to all this. And we know from psychology that the greatest originator of timelessness is trauma. When a trauma cannot be coped with and somehow absorbed in ways that cushion the blow, when a trauma floods one's ego and overwhelms it, it becomes timeless. The experience remains painfully fresh for an entire lifetime. Even when repressed it remains "unforgettable" and tends to manifest itself in repetition compulsions. In short, it becomes timeless.

The ultimate source of the timelessness of Jewish history has not been documented. What the original trauma was that may have given rise to the long chain of Jewish dreadful expectations can be only a subject of speculation. The adoption by the Israelites of Yahweh, the traumatized God who was deprived of his mate, as an originator of their history may have been the start of it all. In that case, it would once again be the old story of the abused turning into an abuser. Yahweh, with his enigmatic character, was only a fantasy projection of the ancient Hebrews. He crowded out and replaced the original mother, but as a new fantasy creation he now reflected the ambivalence of the Israelites toward the suppression of the feminine role that could otherwise be such a source of comfort. Judaism was left with an unbalanced position and an antifeminine stance. Psychohistorian Avner Falk has indicated, with good reason, that such an aggressive antifeminine stance might be traced back to archaic fears of women that originated in the earliest stages of human development (1996, 531). Later religious images of God and the devil or good and evil or heaven and hell represent the splitting of the world in two just as an infant may split its internal images of its mother into an all-good mother and an all-bad mother (Falk 1996, 414). This split is also the source of the later worship of a much-feared goddess of war and a much-adored goddess of love who were sometimes combined into a single female deity (Falk 1996, 50–51).

Bearing in mind that the earliest psychological splitting act by infants applies to the internal image of the mother, it is reasonable to assume that the biblical presentation or badly split image of Yahweh harks back to the primordial psychological split. But the official biblical narration starts with a male God, the creator of everything, who rules over a world in which women are compulsively kept down in a somewhat phobic fashion. Be that as it may, it seems that a long time ago a model of history was set up that presented life as an eternal chain of traumas with intermittent periods of relief. It was a paradigm that was capable of affecting future reality and that has probably already reflected past reality.

It was therefore timeless and almighty in a fashion. This is probably why there is such an obsessive-compulsive quality, one could even say a talmudic quality, to the elaborate Passover ritual. It has most likely served as a defense against existential dread. The compunction and assiduousness with which the Passover ceremony has been set up in the seder betrays the underlying fear that there was no guarantee that the miracle of passing-over would always recur.

As we move on from Passover to the Purim holiday, a stark contrast presents itself. At the beginning of the haggadah it is stated, "We were slaves to Pharaoh in Egypt, and the Lord took us out of there with a strong hand and a lifted arm" (Deuteronomy 6:21). But throughout the entire Purim story, as told in the book of Esther, the Lord is not mentioned even once. Nevertheless, as in other holidays, the deliverance that happened on Purim is considered to be a miracle wrought by God. It was therefore taken for granted that the hand of God was operating behind the scenes. The talmudic sages took care to lift God out of oblivion and reinstate him as the architect of all of Israel's victories. Thus Rabbi Yohanan recommended that the following blessing be recited after the reading of the Purim Scroll: "Blessed art thou the Lord our God, King of the Universe, who fights our fight, and who judges our judgment, and who avenges our vengeance, and who punishes our foes, and who repays all the enemies of our life. Blessed art thou the Lord who punishes on behalf of Israel all their foes." (It is easy to detect in this formulation the predilection of Semitic languages for using together verbs and nouns that are derived from the same root.) It was through such addendums to the holiday ritual that the Jewish sages placed God back at center stage.

But only an earthly potentate has been mentioned in the book of Esther. It is "The King Ahasu'erus" who ruled, from his Persian capital city of Susa, over 127 provinces. The reference to him as "The King Ahasu'erus" is a curious one. Were it not for the fact that he was also mentioned by name, it would have resembled references to the Lord, whose name is ineffable and who is mentioned as "The King." The Lord is also called "The King of the Kings of Kings." But this exalted title was not applied to Ahasu'erus lest it suggest idolatry. The Persian name Ahasu'erus, which is actually pronounced in Hebrew as *ahashverosh*, has been jovially rendered into *ha'hash-berosh*, which means "he who has headaches."

I will now sum up the essential elements of the Purim story as told in the book of Esther, known in Hebrew as the scroll of Esther. Enraged by the refusal of his wife, Vashti, to come to him wearing her crown upon being summoned, the king, "whose wrath burned in him," decided to deprive her of her royal privileges. After "his wrath was abated," he agreed with his advisors' suggestion to compensate himself with a new virginal consort. All the provinces were therefore ordered to send suitable candidates to the royal palace. The Jew Mordecai sent his uncle's daughter Esther, whom he had raised, to the king's court with specific instructions not to disclose her being Jewish. The king found Esther to his liking. Meanwhile, Mordecai incurred the wrath of Haman, the king's most prominent minister, by being the only person who refused to bow before him as ordered by the king. Haman was an Agagite; that is, he belonged to one of the family trees of Amalek—Israel's hereditary enemy. Having been informed of Mordecai's Jewish religion, the furious Haman determined to destroy not only Mordecai but also all the Jews. He therefore cast lots (*purim* in Hebrew) to determine the specific month to be slated for the destruction. What followed belongs to the kind of stuff that always gives Jews the shudders: "And Haman said unto King Ahasu'erus: 'There is a certain people scattered abroad and dispersed among the peoples in all the provinces of thy kingdom; and their laws are diverse from those of every people; neither keep they the king's laws; therefore it profiteth not the king to suffer them. If it please the king, let it be written that they be destroyed'" (Esther 3:8–9). It gives Jews the shudders because it is regarded as a prototype of anti-Semitism. Murderous rage is evoked in reaction to people who are different and who do not abide by the customary rules as all other people do. Why do they insist on being different? Perhaps they feel superior to others and that is why they refuse to conform. And, if this is what they think, then they ought to learn the hard way who is superior to whom.

The decree "to destroy, kill, and annihilate all the Jews, young and old, women and children, in one day" that included also permission to engage in looting was written and sealed with the king's ring. When Mordecai heard of it, he went into mourning and sent word to Esther. Her first impulse was to run for her life. But Mordecai reminded her of her duty to her people. She therefore decided to stay and fast for three days prior to coming unannounced to the king at the risk of her life. When she showed up, the king allowed her to touch his golden scepter, and thus her life was saved. At her request the king also agreed to come with Haman to a wine banquet that Esther was preparing for that day. At the banquet she asked the king and Haman to attend a second banquet the next day. After this first banquet Haman went home and at the instigation of his wife had a fifty-cubit-high gallows tree made specifically for the hanging of Mordecai. In the meantime, having been reminded that Mordecai had once thwarted a plot on the king's life, Ahasu'erus decided to reward Mordecai with a special honor. He therefore asked Haman, "What should be done to the man whom the king delights to honor?" Haman, believing that he was that lucky man, suggested that the man be allowed to wear a royal robe and ride on a royal horse led by one of the king's ministers. To his shock and dismay, Haman was then ordered to personally accord this treatment to Mordecai. At the second wine banquet the next day, Esther divulged to the king her and her family's Jewish origins as well as Haman's plot to exterminate her people. In his anger the king ordered that Haman be hanged upon the same tree on which he had intended to hang Mordecai.

Since it was impossible to rescind the previous order of the king to destroy the Jews because it was already sealed by the king's ring, a new royal order was now issued and also sealed with the ring. It allowed the Jews in each town to congregate and, in order to protect their lives, to destroy, kill, and annihilate their enemies, including women and children, and to engage in looting as well. The next day the Jews of the capital city of Susa killed five hundred persons, and the Jews of the provinces killed seventy-five thousand non-Jews. At Esther's request the king allowed for one more day of retaliation in Susa. By the next day all of Haman's ten children had been hanged, and three hundred more people had been killed. No looting, however, was done on either day because the killings were carried out for the protection of life and not for plunder. In other words, this was a justified killing in self-defense on the part of people who adhere to proper moral standards. After the great deliverance Mordecai sent word to faraway Jewish communities about the month of Adar, during which sorrow turned into happiness and mourning into a holiday. He therefore urged all Jews to celebrate the new holiday of Purim.

Perhaps the most striking feature of this tale is the rigid following of symmetrical rules of justice. Rigid symmetry is a characteristic of primitive justice, and in the scroll of Esther corrective measures have been set up for each malaise in a glaringly symmetrical contrast. In response to an irreversible decree that was sealed by the king's ring, another decree was issued that was similarly sealed by the king's ring. The original formula in the first decree allowed the non-Jews to destroy, kill, and annihilate all the Jews, including women and children, and gave them permission to plunder. Similarly, the new formula of the new decree allowed the Jews to destroy, kill, and annihilate all non-Jews who sought to harm them, including women and children and including also permission to plunder. Haman provided the details for a royal parade, believing that it would be in his own honor, yet he ended up personally conducting an identical parade in Mordecai's honor. Haman prepared a gallows tree on which to hang Mordecai, but he himself was hanged instead on the very same tree. Last but not least, even though a mass killing had been plotted for the Jews, it was finally executed by the Jews against the non-Jews. There is no question that the rendering of justice in the book of Esther is saturated with gloating over the success in turning the tables on the enemy. That is one obvious source of the symmetry of this justice. But there is something else in this symmetry that seems both familiar and old. It goes back to Yahweh's rudimentary conception of justice—"a life for a life, an eye for an eye, a tooth for a tooth," that is, the law of retribution, or lex talionis. For a better understanding of the triumph of symmetrical retribution during Purim, we need to explore the psychological origins of this conception.

The biblical code of a life for a life is actually derived from an older Mesopotamian heritage that had already promoted highly symmetrical notions of justice. The ancient juridical sources of this code can be traced to the laws of retribution to be found in the law collection of the Babylonian king Hammurabi, whose reign lasted over forty years (1792–1750 B.C.). They can also be traced to the middle Assyrian laws from the time of Tiglath-pileser I in the twelfth century B.C., some of which might go back to the fifteenth century B.C. The Mesopotamian law collections and, subsequently, the biblical rulings (Exodus 21) introduced some flexibility into the laws so that sometimes it was possible to forgo the principle of a life for a life. But the original harshness of the law of retribution that was attributed to Yahweh never dropped out of sight. It exerted a major influence in Western civilization that frequently excluded mercy from legal judgments. A life for a life is a gut-level impulse that mobilizes anger for symmetrical retribution. During the tense month of February 2000, as Hizballah (Party of God) attacks from Lebanon on Israel escalated, the Israeli foreign minister, David Levy, warned on one occasion that the Israeli government would follow a policy of "blood for blood, a life for a life, a child for a child." It was as if the spirit of Yahweh had descended upon him.

The archaic psychological origins of the symmetrical and primitive sense of justice are imbedded in a very early state of infant development (Gonen 2000, 110–16). At that semiamorphous state, one's body is not yet distinctly separate from the rest of the world, and the dividing line between feelings and actions is still blurred. What is more, when there is not yet a clear-cut distinction between wish and wish fulfillment, a thought is indistinguishable from a deed, and an impulse can be equated with an accomplished action. Similarly, the mere fear of harm seems like actual damage in the making.

This psychological state of affairs dooms aggressive impulses to a lex talionis fate of symmetrical retribution. In the absence of a clear-cut distinction between self and others, an aggressive impulse aimed at the ill-defined outside seems also to be an aggression that comes from the outside. Therefore the aggressive impulse becomes intertwined with the fear of retaliation. At the very same time both the felt urge to strike and the felt fear of being stricken are equated with an accomplished action and an actual damage. As if by poetic justice, it is therefore the very same projected stuff that was originally externalized by the self that now returns to haunt that very same self. And it is in this reencounter with the formerly projected aggression that one's own original drive—the crime—now returns as fear of the very same thing in a new form—the punishment. This is the original intrapsychic source of the rigid symmetry that characterizes a primitive sense of justice. Crime and punishment must be similar, since they once were practically identical during the early and oral developmental stage, when any new punishment was but a reincarnated return of the old crime.

We are in a better position now to understand the far-reaching ramifications of the triumph of symmetrical retribution in Purim. Although God is not mentioned in the book of Esther, his rigid law reigns supreme, and his symmetrical law is rooted in the primitive conditions of infancy. It would have been the law of a baby, had the preverbal baby been able to legislate. "Baby-God" was able to. The outcome was Yahweh's lex talionis. Therefore in a roundabout way we get a glimpse of Yahweh's origins as an omnipotent and yet a troubled baby. Although baby-God was given the name Yahweh, it became the ineffable name for Jews. Christians refer to him as Jehovah. They even gave him a baby who himself became a Messiah and a God of sorts. Perhaps God is a baby who needs a father, just as so many humans do. But, no less so or even more so, human beings need a mother too, and this creates troubles for patriarchal religions whose diminution of the feminine role can cause traumatic deprivation.

Symmetrical retribution stipulates a punishment that is basically identical with the crime. Its infantile psychological origin is the

metamorphosis of aggression directed outward (crime) into a retaliation that bounces back upon the self (punishment). If this hypothesis is
correct, then what follows is that during special times, during crisis and
volatility as many things are in a state of flux and as repressed material
breaks through, the two sides of the justice equation—namely, crime
and punishment—can change position in a way that exposes their
underlying similarity. What is more, this reverting of each action into its
flip side holds true not only for crime and punishment but also for identity at large. God can metamorphose into Satan, as happened during
the Holocaust. This will be discussed later. And Jews can metamorphose into goyim, as happens during Purim celebrations. This will be
discussed now.

The book of Esther described a court culture where wine was provided in abundance during feasts. This culture was adopted also by the
local Jews. It was therefore recommended in the book of Esther that the
Jews celebrate their victory with a "day of banquet and gladness." Eventually, the inducement to lavish drinking reached astounding propor-
tions with the notorious dictum of the Babylonian talmudist Rava that
"a man is obligated to intoxicate himself on Purim until he did not
know [*ad dela yada* in Aramaic] the difference between cursed Haman
and blessed Mordecai." The Purim carnival in Tel Aviv took its Hebrew
name from this dictum and came to be known as the Adloyada. It
would take a huge drinking binge to blot out in the mind of any good
Jew the difference between blessed Mordecai—descendant of the royal
house of King Saul, and cursed Haman—descendant of Amalek, who is
Israel's eternal enemy and against whom Israel must wage war for all
generations to come.

Who drinks like that anyway? The clear answer to that is "the goy."
The contrast between the sober Jew and the drunkard goy has been one
of the ingredients that has shaped Jewish self-image and perception of
Gentiles (Gonen 1975, 133–48). I vividly recall my late father teaching
me the words and music of songs that he picked up during his own
youth in Russia. He taught me a Russian song that vows to recapture
Port Arthur from the Japanese. That was the Russian in him. He also
taught me how to do a dance—hop and clap the hands—while singing
a Yiddish song that in an English translation runs as follows:

> Oy, oy, oy,
> A drunkard is a goy.
> Drunk he is,
> Drink he wants,
> A drunkard is a goy.

That was the Jew in my father, although he was not religious. And it goes to show that, even after secularization, internalized Jewish perceptions can persist. My mother disapproved of my father's jubilant act, fearing that it might teach us kids wrong and biased attitudes toward Gentiles. My elder brother and I thought that our father's performance was funny and that it disclosed a flair for acting, but we did not come to regard the more immediate "goyim" around us—the British and the Arabs—as a bunch of drunks.

So when is a Jew unable to distinguish between himself and a goy? When he himself behaves like the stereotypical goy and gets blasted. But there are even worse ways of behaving like goyim during Purim. Perpetrating pogroms is one of them. With this behavior we cross a crucial line that separates what is merely funny from what is utterly despicable.

In 1984, on Purim day, Jewish physician Baruch Goldstein burst into an Arab mosque in Hebron that is also the site of the Makhpelah Cave (the tomb of the Jewish Patriarchs) and sprayed Arab worshipers who were kneeling in prayer with bullets from an automatic weapon. Twenty-nine Palestinians were killed before the enraged crowd tore him to pieces. It was a shameful day in Jewish history, the memory of which should be injected into all future Purim celebrations as a sober reminder of the potential barbarism that is hidden within old myths of vengeance wrought by the Sons of Israel upon their enemies. Later on that day Hanan Porat, a right-wing leader and one of the founders of the pro-settlement movement Block of the Faithful, was heard to respond with "Happy Purim! Happy Purim!" when receiving word of the massacre. It might have been an allusion to the well-known song "I am Purim, I am Purim, happy and entertaining" that is sung mostly by children. Porat has been trying to play down this response ever since. He later attempted to explain his remark in the following manner: "Three years ago in Purim a beloved student of mine was murdered in the Old City. After we buried him in Mount Olives the guys crowded themselves around me like lost sheep, and I said, From here we go to a Purim feast. We believe that out of all the troubles redemption will grow. After the Hebron massacre I knew that people in Qiryat Arba are in a state of total confusion and in terrible duress. I came to them to say, Do not lose your senses. Lift up your eyes. One must be happy" (Kafra 1994, my translation). So presumably, his "Happy Purim" remark did not signify any gloating but rather was an encouragement to the befuddled. He certainly cared for his flock.

Eventually, a memorial plaque was set up on Goldstein's burial place that mentioned his family's roots in a Hasidic dynasty. It said that he "delivered his life for the people of Israel, its Torah, and its country" and described him as "clean of hands and pure of heart" (Psalms 24:4). If Baruch Goldstein was "clean of hands," then the book of Psalms must have been written by George Orwell. And in a further demonstration of Orwellian Newspeak, the memorial plaque affirmed that "he was murdered for the sanctification of the Name on the 14th of Adar, Purim 5754. May his soul be included in the bundle of life." In this manipulative phrasing the old Jewish ethos of martyrdom, the sanctification of the Name, was given new meaning—messianic, activist, and murderous.

With the active support of the municipal council of Qiryat Arba (the Jewish section of Hebron), the site of the grave became a place of pilgrimage. Fanatical Jews would come there to pray, to light memorial candles for Baruch Goldstein, and to buy trinkets and memorabilia offered at the spot. These activities by Yahweh's modern zealots became a national scandal. They clearly illustrated that the murderous act could not be explained as the act of one deranged individual. Among religious circles individuals such as Baruch Goldstein and Yigal Amir, who killed Prime Minister Yitzhak Rabin, are described as *asavim shotim* (foolish grass) or weeds. This metaphor is supposed to indicate a statistical rarity in the form of an individual aberration. Sometimes, however, weeds can take over the lawn, and, not infrequently, it is *hassidim shotim* (foolish devotees) who turn into asavim shotim. Had any European country tolerated a similar pilgrimage in honor of a murderer of praying Jews, the Israeli protests would have pierced the skies. But in Israel the army and the civilian authorities took their time in putting an end to the pilgrimages, even though they had the legal authority to do so. In response to criticism Gen. Shaul Mofaz, who subsequently became chief of staff of the Israeli army and later on defense minister, stated: "No one intended for a stele to be erected there that would turn into a site for pilgrimage. The Israeli army was told that it is a temporary grave and that it would be removed elsewhere in the future" ("The Disgrace of Qiryat Arba" 1997, my translation). General Mofaz was not the first or last either civilian or military leader who took the settlers at their worthless word while knowing full well that what they pretend is only temporary is meant to be permanent. Numerous tacit compliances like this one have resulted in the growth of the settlements to the point where the tail wags the dog and the manipulative settlers can bounce the whole State of Israel around. It is not likely that the Israeli government would appoint as the army's chief of staff a person who is truly that naive.

Purim celebrations in Israel in 2001 were once again blotted by ugly incidents. As Jewish hotheadedness increased in response to acts of

Arab violence that were committed during the second Palestinian uprising, known as the al-Aqsa intifada, harassments of Palestinians took place. During Purim it was a mitzvah, or good deed, to sock it to the modern Amalekites. At the Adloyada parade in Hebron, settlers harassed Arab onlookers and even bullied Israeli policemen who tried to separate the two sides. What especially provoked the Arabs and added to the Jewish disgrace was the fact that some of the settlers wore Baruch Goldstein masks. Several others drank wine from bottles labeled with a portrait of Baruch Goldstein. It was a saving grace that at least some of the participants tried to prevent others from waving photos of Baruch Goldstein. In Jerusalem dozens of Jews gathered in Sabath Square, pelted cars with stones, tried to set a minibus on fire, and threw various objects at residents of the Arab quarter. In Zion Gate Jews beat up Palestinians, calling them "dirty Arabs" and "terrorists." One drunken Jew who wounded an Arab in the eye subsequently attacked the police as he was arrested. There was no life lost in these incidents, but this cannot be said about the Baruch Goldstein precedence of violence that was deliberately injected into the Purim ritual. And if it has become a Purim commandment to drink and then attack Arabs, how should the Arabs react? Should they be singing "Ooh, ooh, ooh, a drunkard is a Jew"?

These unfortunate developments induced Yossi Sarid, leader of the secular and Left political party Meretz in Israel, to publish a condemnation of the holiday and its celebration practices. He also had a personal reason to be incensed. He had previously been called "the evil Haman" by Rabbi Ovadia Yoseph, spiritual leader of the Sephardic religious party Shas. In a speech at a synagogue in Jerusalem the rabbi asked God to obliterate Sarid's name and led the audience in a chant of "accursed is Haman, accursed is Sarid."

Had Rabbi Ovadia's remark been taken literally by his admiring followers, they might have tried to kill the contemporary Haman. Sarid divulged that he never liked the story of the revenge on the goyim with which the scroll of Esther ends. The Jews conducted a pogrom and then threw a banquet. Sarid particularly disliked the sight of Jewish children in Hebron masquerading as Baruch Goldstein, the murderous physician. Reflecting on the recent attacks on Arabs in three sectors of Jerusalem that were reported on television and in the newspapers, he concluded that he saw "an ugly and revolting picture: a thoroughly drunk Jewish Cossack bursts into an Arab house, smashes things to pieces, hits a father, hits a mother, while the children, even though Arab, gripped by dread and fear, cry profusely. Have we even in our nightmares seen drunken Jews, bottle in hand, perpetrating a pogrom?" (Sarid 2001, my translation).

Certain rituals were injected into the Purim celebration in order to strengthen a fused perception of time that draws a direct line from the remote past to the messianic future. The connection to the remote past is furnished by the fact that Haman the Agagite was a descendant of Amalek. This is why on the Sabbath day that precedes Purim a special Torah reading is mandated from Deuteronomy 25:17–19. It commands Jews to remember Amalek and to blot out his name from under the skies. On Purim morning there is a special reading of Exodus 17:8–16. It describes the difficult battle with Amalek in the Sinai desert and God's subsequent promise to blot out Amalek's name from under the skies and wage war on him for all generations. On Purim day itself, during the reading of the Esther scroll, whenever the name of Haman is mentioned children drown it out by making loud noises with rattles. The purpose is to blot out the memory of Amalek, as God promised to do (Exodus 17:14). It is also customary to recite the names of Haman's ten sons in one breath in order to show that they were all hanged simultaneously. According to Louis Jacobs, who authored the Purim listing on the *Encyclopedia Judaica* CD-ROM, this hurried reading was interpreted by some as an attempt to refrain from gloating over the downfall of enemies. There were probably quite a few Jews who were indeed bothered by the obvious gloating ambience of the Purim celebration, but reciting all ten names of Haman's sons in one breath is too reminiscent of extinguishing all of a birthday cake's candles in one breath. It is a victory of sorts. In a satirical Israeli song it is merrily stated that "Haman they hung on a tall tree — Vaizatha [the youngest son] on a plant." Thus there seems to be no lack of gloating in Purim.

The Purim celebration includes a series of ritualistic reminders of Jewish fate. The story of the costly war with Amalek that took place after the Exodus from Egypt is invoked. It is well understood that it was exactly because Amalek proved to be such a difficult enemy that an eternal war has been declared upon him. The recitation of the Purim story is the telling of yet another round of war with Amalek, this time during the days of Haman. And once again it was a close call, even though at the end it turned into a day of gladness for the Jews. For a while Jews were in great danger and very fearful, as their destruction seemed imminent. The blotting out of Haman's name by means of the noise of rattlers is another symbolic continuation, this time in the here and now, of God's order to blot out Amalek's name from under the skies. Blotting out someone's name stands for wiping out him and all his descendants. Finally, there is also the custom of reading more loudly four verses of the scroll of Esther that are interpreted as "redemption." The verses (Esther 2:5, 8:15-16, and 10:3) refer to Mordecai's royal origin and to the royal honor that was accorded him. These are considered to be messianic themes because the future Messiah is expected to be of royal descent and because following victory he would be recognized as king even by the goyim and be treated like royalty. Still, there is only a hint of redemption here, but by designating these verses as references to redemption and by their ceremonial reinforcement by means of reciting them in a louder-than-usual voice, the messianic future was incorporated into the eternal and fused Jewish mythical time.

Consequently, the duality of Jewish psychohistory has been reaffirmed once again. In a somewhat similar fashion to Passover, the traditional Jewish expectation from destiny has been instilled once more. What has already taken place in the remote past and what is always happening anyway will also recur in the faraway future. And, in accordance with Yahweh's rules of history, on each occasion there is plenty of trouble that precedes the joy. An added reminder of this double-edged fate comes on the eve of Purim in the form of Esther's fast. The fast brings back to life Esther's sense of trepidation concerning her life and the life of her people before the great deliverance took place. Thus the Purim joy is preceded by dread. Yahweh always brings suffering before he brings joy, so even though he is not mentioned in the scroll of Esther Yahweh is nevertheless alive and well.

Purim has traditionally been a happy holiday. It includes "sending portions" of tasty food or sweets to relatives as well as to the poor. Favorite items include the three-cornered pies known as "Haman's ears," which are also eaten on Purim day in a festive meal during the late afternoon. Children gobble them up throughout the holiday and not just during the festive meal. The cannibalistic symbolism that is embedded in this practice is fairly transparent, yet I have to admit that in my youth my mind was not focused on the notion of eating Haman's ears. What I did focus on was the hope that they would be filled with poppy seeds. These were the tastiest Haman's ears.

In his article on Purim in the *Encyclopedia Judaica* Louis Jacobs mentioned the tradition of staging parodies that sometimes mocked Jewish sacred texts. It was seen by some as an attempt to find annual relief from the burden of loyalty to the Torah. This Eastern European custom is not prevalent nowadays, but the Adloyada parade, which was influenced by the tradition of the Italian carnival, remains very popular. People, especially children, wear masks and disguises on Purim, and not only during the Adloyada parade. It was even permissible for men to be dressed up as women and vice versa. It all follows the non-Jewish tradition of the yearly festival during which taboos can be broken so that discipline can be maintained for the rest of the year.

One of the greatest Jewish taboos is to become a goy. This metamorphosis is not always done consciously on Purim. Nevertheless, at face value, the ways of celebration seem more "goyish" than Jewish. Thus, in a collection of comments by Jewish teachers on Purim, Rabbi Menahem ha-Kohen included the following saying by the Polish Hasidic rabbi Simhah Bunem of Pshiskha: "What is the difference between Purim and Yom Kippurim (the Day of Atonement)?—During Purim Jews disguise themselves as goyim—gobble up, drink up, and get drunk. On the Day of Atonement 'goyim' (nonobservant Jews) disguise themselves as Jews, including those who throughout the year do not behave like Jews—they fast on this day and come to the synagogue" (1981, my translation). Rabbi Simhah was clearly right in treating it all as a once-a-year behavior. On Purim Jews behave like goyim, but on the Day of Atonement even nonpracticing Jews become "religious." A discussion of the Day of Atonement appears later in this chapter.

God's absence from the Purim story did not go well with everyone. The right-wing publicist Yisrael Eldad (1981), an ardent supporter of the Greater Israel movement, was dismayed by the difference between Purim and Passover. The Passover story amounted to "immense troubles and complete redemption," but the Purim story culminated in a Hollywood-style "happy ending," in which the Jews got gladness and relief while staying in exile. It was not only God who was missing from the Purim story but the Land of Israel too. This led Eldad to conclude that the Purim story expresses the ideology and mentality of exile that is reflected in the failure to leave the Diaspora in preference to a continued stay in the capital of Susa. The fact that Mordecai (Marduk) and Esther (Ishtar) did not use Jewish names and chose to hide their Jewish origin also irked Eldad. It obviously pointed to the growing danger of assimilationism. One can sum up Eldad's major argument as follows: By favoring the Exodus from Egypt and returning to Israel, Passover represents proto-Zionism. By favoring staying put in the Diaspora and celebrating there, Purim represents the traditional Jewish malaise of an exilic mentality.

Yet in some dialectical fashion Purim can be seen as representing at least one major ingredient of modern and largely secular Zionism—activist self-help. Somewhat paradoxically, it may be the absence of any mention of God in the story that shifted the focus from turning toward heaven to turning instead to political machinations in the earthly court of King Ahasu'erus. Moreover, the Jews offered armed resistance in response to an extermination threat rather than going down like sheep to the slaughter. Yet in trying to prevent a holocaust, they engaged in over-kill by turning an aggressive self-defense into a pogrom. So Purim is fraught with dialectics. Where is God? What is self-defense? When does a kill turn into overkill? What about the Diaspora, and what about the homeland? How much assimilation is possible without losing Jewish identity? Should earthly actions be initiated regardless of God? It is obvious that the Purim story reverberates with many echoes from Jewish history that expose some of the contradictions and conflicts that dwell deep within the qishqes, the innards, of Judaism.

An even more recent example of the spilling over of the Purim story into current events took place in 2001. These were the days of the al-Aqsa intifada, and leaders of Jewish organizations in the Diaspora canceled Jewish youth summer camps in Israel for fear of Arab attacks. In chiding the Jewish leaders for letting fear overcome their solidarity with Israel, Yair Sheleg (2001) reminded them of Mordecai's words to Esther, "words that have been engraved deep in the collective Jewish memory." When Esther was tempted to flee and save her own life but abandon her people to their fate, Mordecai sent her the following message: "If you decide to remain silent at this time, comfort and rescue will be provided to the Jews from another source, and you and your father's house will perish" (Esther 4:14). This was an example of how Purim was used by an Israeli journalist to remind Diaspora Jewish leaders of their duties to Israel. Since the article also appeared in the *Ha'aretz English Internet Edition*, chances are that Mordecai's redirected message reached its target and that it stung. All in all, Purim ruminations illustrate how events in the here and now get tied to that mythical time in which past and future are fused by means of the expected recurrence of a fateful duality.

The holiest day of the Jewish year, on which Jews fast and repent their sins, Yom Kippur, or the Day of Atonement, retains that fateful duality. It is the last of the ten days of repentance that start on the first day of the new Jewish year. These days are also called the ten days of awe because of the Jews' fear and dread of God's impending judgment. Consequently, the holiday is also known as Yom Hadin, or the Day of Judgment. Jews pray and hope that God will be merciful as he passes judgment on that day, but they realize with trepidation that his verdict could nevertheless go either way—thumbs up or thumbs down. Unlike Passover or Purim, when the focus is on the fate of the collectivity, Yom Kippur focuses more on the fate of the individual, although not exclusively so. Therefore traditional "history lessons" and "time fusions" that apply both to individuals and to the Jewish group at large have found their way into the ritual of this holiday as well.

A history lesson is provided in the evening prayer on the eve of the holiday. "He who answered our father Abraham on Mount Moriah, he shall answer us." Moses, David, Solomon, and others are thrown into repeated variations on this basic formula. Purim is included too: "He who answered Mordecai and Esther in Susa the capital, he shall answer us." The form God's "answer" should take is made clear in a wish that is expressed during the evening service at the end of the Day of Atonement: "And God will remove from you all disease and all the evil sicknesses of Egypt that you know, [he] will not put them in you but give them to those who hate you." This is a reiteration of the familiar formula that is so dominant during the Passover celebration. It gives voice to the hope that the two sides of God will neatly diverge along the Jewish-Gentile split and that the Passover miracle of passing over the Jews will continue to recur. During the afternoon service for the eve of the Day of Atonement worshipers call upon God: "Sound the great shofar for our freedom, lift up the banner to gather our exiles, and gather us together from the four wings [corners] of the earth. Blessed are you, God, gatherer of the outcasts of his people Israel." Yet this act of love toward Israel cannot be accomplished without reckoning with Israel's enemies. This entreaty is therefore followed by another plea: "And let all your enemies be speedily cut off. And the kingdom of wickedness you will speedily uproot and smash and defeat and subjugate, speedily in our days. Blessed are you, God, smasher of enemies and subjugator of the wicked." At the end of the evening service on the Day of Atonement a last wish is made: "He who makes peace in his high places, he will make peace for us and for all Israel; and say Amen." The shofar is then sounded. Tradition has it that the End of Days will be heralded by the sound of the shofar summoning the exiles to ingather and awakening the dead for the Resurrection. With this reference to messianic glory at the time of the end, the fusion of all time dimensions in one mythical time has been completed.

We have already seen that in the Jewish tradition this most sacred holiday has two names that evoke different images. These images impinged upon the Israeli national psyche during the Yom Kippur War of 1973 (Gonen 1980). The better-known image is Yom Kippur. The original Hebrew verb from which the name of the holiday is derived has a few meanings: to atone and seek forgiveness, to pardon or grant forgiveness, to appease, and to expiate. When the verb is used in conjunction with other words, it takes on the meaning of paying ransom or paying blood money. These connotations allude to the ancient origins of the expiation rites. They go back to ritual sacrifices or to the banishment of animals that served as scapegoats and as ransoms or substitutes for the banishment or sacrifice of humans.

Indeed, on the day before the Day of Atonement, the rite of kapparot is conducted. A cock or a hen is swung three times around and over the head of a man who recites: "This is my substitute, my vicarious offering, my atonement, this cock [or hen] shall meet death, but I shall find a long and pleasant life of peace." The fowl is later given to the poor, minus the qishqes, which are thrown out to the birds or, for that matter, the cats, which consider them a great delicacy. The practice of kapparot is reminiscent of the older practice of sending a scapegoat to the Azazel wilderness to expiate the people's sins.

The range of meanings that are associated with the images of the Day of Atonement and the Day of Judgment includes both helpless and masterful roles. Nevertheless, the dominant stance has customarily been that of supplicants who meekly seek expiation and who humbly plead for forgiveness. A person's whole frame of mind is focused on this holiest of days on his own imperfect self as he agonizes over his misdeeds and confesses during prayer, "I have sinned, I have transgressed, I have rebelled [against the Lord]." The special prayer book for this day contains a long list of transgressions, some of which merit death sentences. It is therefore in a mood of submission and even depression that Jews repent in fear and trembling of the impending act of the Lord. The awesome God is about to pass judgment. For the coming year the name of each person will be written for life or for death in the book of remembrance. The decrees are written by the Lord on New Year's Day and are sealed ten days later on the Day of the Fast of Atonement. Therefore, the prayer book for these ten fateful days is full of pleas to the Lord to write one's name in the book of life. It is an awesome Lord who in-scribes names in the book of life and, by implication, also in the book of death. This is why the first ten days of the Jewish year that culminate in the Day of Atonement are known as ten days of repentance as well as ten days of awe. During this period greeting cards that are sent to friends and relatives include the wish that the recipient's name will be written in the book of life.

The new Jewish year thus starts with a dreadful waiting period in anticipation of fateful decisions by the Lord. This is made clear with blatant, even brutal, language in the additional service for the first day of the year, which is repeated also on the second day of the year:

> On the first day of the year it is inscribed, and on the Day of Atone-ment the decree is sealed, how many shall pass away and how many shall be born, who shall live and who shall die, who at the measure of man's days and who before it; who shall perish by fire and who by water, who by the sword, who by wild beasts, who by hunger and who by thirst; who by earthquake and who by plagues, who by strangling and who by stoning; who shall have rest and who shall go wandering, who shall be tranquil and who shall be harassed, who shall be at ease and who shall be afflicted; who shall become poor and who shall wax rich; who shall be brought low and who shall be upraised.
> But Penitence, Prayer, and Charity
> Avert the severe decree.

It is clearly implied in this prayer that all these judgments are rendered justly, as penitence, prayer, and charity are given full consideration. But this implication was too much to take for some New York City Jews, as the first day of the Jewish New Year fell on 18 September 2001, barely a weak after the devastation that was inflicted by the terrorist destruction of the twin towers of the World Trade Center, which took thousands of both Gentile and Jewish lives. With the whole country agonizing daily over the television images of the smoldering rubble, Jewish prayers and sermons concerning divine justice by fire, water, and quake could sound ludicrous. It therefore no longer seemed appropriate to embark upon the traditional ten days of awe, waiting for God's life-and-death deci-sions with an unquestioning attitude. A few rabbis in the New York area, albeit non-Orthodox, decided therefore to revise their sermons so as to soften the stark prayer (Waldman 2001). These were difficult psychological times for American Jewish believers, as a judgment of sorts in the form of terrorist attacks seemed to have been executed a week prior to the start of the ten days of repentance. Not only did judgment precede repentance but it also did not seem to have anything to do with justice.

Since mixed moods are Yahweh's hallmark, the first ten days of the year too disclose a mixture of moods. Concurrent with the humble stance of ten days of repentance that culminate in atonement, there also exists a different frame of mind that is associated with ten awesome days that culminate in judgment. As mentioned before, since Yom Kippur is the day on which the terrifying God passes life-and-death judgments, it is also known as the Day of Judgment or, in Hebrew, Yom Hadin. We are dealing here with a different set of images that complement those associated with the Day of Atonement. The focus now shifts from those who repent to him who passes judgment. There is a switch here from a passive to an active role. There is also an identification with the all-powerful one who passes life-and-death verdicts. Something of his omnipotence and mastery rubs off on his dependent flock as they wholeheartedly not only regret their own sins but also identify with his active sacred role of judging them.

The name Day of Judgment comes from a poem that is included in the morning service on the first and second days of the year as well as on the tenth day, that is, the Yom Kippur holiday itself. In the poem the phrase "Day of Judgment" is repeated eleven times. The first and eleventh lines are quoted here:

> To God, who orders judgment:
>> To the examiner of hearts on a day of judgment;
> To the guardian of those who love him in judgment:
>> To the supporter of his innocent ones on a day of judgment.

The basic idea that is repeatedly reinforced throughout the entire poem is that a merciful God is passing judgment on a day of judgment. But passing judgment on a day of judgment is nevertheless a fear-evoking image that serves as the culmination of ten days of awe or ten terrible days. It is interesting to reflect upon the fact that God is addressed as "the orderer [fixer, sorter] of judgment," a term that in contemporary Hebrew has come to signify "a lawyer." The very same term that in the old Hebrew of sacred texts denoted "God" was retooled in modern Hebrew parlance to denote "lawyer." What could this particular evolution in the language possibly suggest? It is not likely to evoke the association that being a lawyer is like being God. But God acting like a lawyer is another matter. Yahweh, the stickler for details, knows full well how to read the fine print.

The prayer book for the Day of Atonement is saturated with elaborate and repetitious enumerations of all sorts of possible sins that any of the worshipers may have committed. Not only are there all sorts of different sins to begin with, but they also carry different mandatory sentences, and they can be committed deliberately or nondeliberately, openly or secretly, knowingly or unknowingly. Perhaps the most inclusive among the various categories of sins are sins that were prompted by the evil urge and sins that were carried out with stiff-neckedness. True to its bad habit, old yetzer continues to be evil, and, true to their character, the modern Sons of Israel continue to be stiff-necked. This just about insures that each individual is guilty by definition and should therefore relentlessly seek out and repent all his sins without fail. Since all sins are prompted by the notorious yetzer, which has such a proven capacity to raise the ire of Yahweh, the situation is most dangerous. It therefore becomes necessary to implore him to shift his gaze away from the irksome yetzer, which evokes his anger, and to direct it instead at the covenant. As we may recall, the covenant in the flesh, or circumcision, is a token of submission. It is therefore more likely to arouse Yahweh's pity, compassion, and forgiveness. Thus in one of the poetic prayers on the eve of Yom Kippur, God is asked eight times to fix his gaze on his covenant with the Sons of Israel (and be merciful) rather than on their yetzer (and be vengeful). The sixth stanza is quoted here in full:

> For like an embroidery in the hand of the embroiderer,
> When he wants he goes straight and when he wants he curves it.
> So are we in your hand, God of zealousness and avenger.
> Gaze at the covenant and turn your face away from the yetzer.

This is not the only reference to a zealous or an avenging God. The morning service of the holiday pronounces that "God of vengeance is Yahweh, God of vengeance has appeared." But by and large, references to el kana, or the God of vengeance, in the Yom Kippur prayer book are drowned out by the numerous references to el ra'hum ve'hanun. This tenth and most terrible of the ten terrible days is not the most opportune time to remind Yahweh that he is an angry God.

The function of the obsessive-compulsive ritual of very repetitious enumerations of a whole smorgasbord of sins is to serve as an anti-sins defense shield. Not even a single sin should escape repentance. If each sin is targeted and shot down through repentance, el ra'hum ve'hanun's task of sealing merciful verdicts for all the repentant Jews in the book of life becomes so much easier. What one senses here is an enormous anxiety concerning what might happen if even a single sin escapes repentance. Yahweh being Yahweh, who knows what he might do. Worrying is therefore the Jewish way of life. As a child I used to meet my fasting and weakened grandmother at the end of Yom Kippur outside the synagogue in order to escort her safely home. Little did I realize that having just undergone this elaborate ritual, she must have been afflicted not only by a physical fatigue but also by a mental one. Chances are, however, that for the true believer sheer exhaustion as such also contributes to the personal conviction that the act of repentance was indeed thorough and genuine. Having thus done one's duty of carrying on an indefatigable hunt of all possible sins, a person could now hope that the Lord would do his duty as well of purging all the repented sins.

The shock of the Yom Kippur War in October 1973 stirred up the competing images that are associated with this holiday. It was shocking for Israelis to realize that on the very day of Yom Kippur the Arabs, who were so soundly defeated during the Six-Day War of 1967, had crossed the Suez Canal, carried out major incursions into the Golan Heights, and succeeded in dealing "Israeli-style" quick military defeats to the Israelis themselves. The overconfident Israelis were caught by surprise, with their pants down, so to speak, because military positions at the Bar-Lev defense line in the Sinai and in the fortifications at the Golan Heights were scandalously undermanned. Consequently, the initial shock was quickly infused with an added sense of shame. But what instantly caused the war to reverberate with old echoes of Jewish history was the fact that it was launched on Yom Kippur—the holiest day of the Jewish year.

The adoption of the term "Yom Kippur War" by the Israelis was not as self-evident as it might seem (Gonen 1980). On 8 October 1973, the third day of the war, the Israeli chief of staff, David Elazar, held a news conference, during which he declared: "I envision now that we shall continue to attack and hit, and we shall break their bones. I do not yet want to commit myself as to how long it will take us." In response to a question as to what this war should be called, he suggested that it should be called the "Day of Judgment War." The newspaper *Maariv* followed this suggestion. The next day its report on the news conference appeared under the heading "In a News Conference in Tel Aviv— 54 Hours after the Start of 'the Day of Judgment War.'" As it turned out, the war lasted for seventeen days. It resulted in an overall mixed politico-military situation that did not seem to support the image of a

Day of Judgment War. If anything, this term would seem to be more fitting for the Six-Day War of June 1967, which was characterized by swift and resounding victories.

In a certain way, the furious Israeli chief of staff was trying to tilt the mythohistorical balance of what is traditionally the most terrible day of the Jewish year. Sensing on the third day of the war that military success was about to follow the initial setback, he attempted to mostly enshrine the war with an aura of "judgment" rather than "atonement." He thus placed the burden on the Lord to live up to the long-held Jewish hope that in dangerous times God would pour out his wrath on the goyim but spare the Jews. In short, Elazar called for vengeance.

When vengeful impulses surge, Jews tend to identify with the Lord of vengeance as an available conduit through which to channel their emotions. The majesty of the Lord as he wreaks vengeance on Israel's enemies is a familiar biblical image. It is alluded to in the morning prayer on the first day of the Jewish year, that is, the first of the ten terrible days. In the prayer the Lord of vengeance is described as "a king with red-stained garments" who "trod upon transgressors," an obvious reference to Isaiah's (63:11–16) poetic and powerful portrayal of the God of vengeance. Lacking Isaiah's poetic prowess, David Elazar resorted to prose about breaking bones and about giving the war its name. Putting the accent on judgment was akin to tilting the Day of Atonement more in the direction of Passover and shifting the accent from the image of meekness to the image of might. Still another tilt in the mythohistorical balance of this holiest of days was the shift of stress somewhat away from individual fate toward the collective fate. This was a natural reaction to the given circumstances; in a time of war, people feel more intensely that they share a collective fate. And by putting the accent on judgment, contemporary Israelis were encouraged to emulate down on earth the active role of the Lord up in heaven. In sum, there was a gut-level and not fully verbalized attempt to shift the significance of Yom Kippur along several axes: from prostrate atonement by Jews to harsh judgment upon Gentiles, from passivity to activity, from individual repentance to collective vengeance. Put differently, it was an attempt to imbue Yom Kippur with more of the spirit of Passover.

A historical follow-up to this attempt was carried out during the first Passover after the Yom Kippur War (Gonen 1980). The recent trauma was fresh in people's minds and created an understandable inclination toward militancy in an attempt to compensate for recent setbacks. Such collective emotional needs to achieve restitution can be exploited ritualistically and cynically by an unholy alliance between secular and religious militant nationalists. A Passover celebration by soldiers on the Golan Heights was attended by Defense Minister Moshe Dayan and the chief military rabbi, Mordecai Piron. The religious rabbi honored the secular defense minister by inviting him to recite aloud from the haggadah the "pour out your wrath upon the goyim" passage. It was a symbolic ritual in a military setting that expressed the yearning for the Day of Atonement War to have run a different course and be truly a Day of Judgment War. Yet the name Yom Kippur War has been adopted in popular use, and its wide acceptance by Israelis reflects their intuitive understanding as to what happened. True to his favorite sequence, Yahweh ushered in deliverance only after dealing a deadly blow first. In spite of Jewish entreaties, he did not save all of his harsh judgment for goyim alone.

Even though the image of the 1973 Yom Kippur War has remained largely that of atonement and the recanting of political, intelligence, and military failures, the image of the Yom Kippur holiday itself has been infused with a greater awareness of the shared collective fate. Ever since the great scare of 1973 Jews in Israel as well as abroad are instantly reminded of the Yom Kippur War on each new Yom Kippur day. The atonement may still be carried out on an individual basis, but the awaited judgment, be it lenient or harsh, is expected to apply not only to each person singly but also to the collectivity. With this increased emphasis on the people at large, there has been an increased awareness of the need to deflect God's harsh judgment away from the Jewish group. Although this did not result in formal liturgical changes, ever since 1973 there has been a little bit more of the spirit of Passover suffused in the Yom Kippur holiday. The final psychohistorical outcome of all this is greater maneuvering room for Yahweh. One of the prerogatives of omnipotence is the ability to keep all options open. Disasters need not necessarily happen only on the ninth day of the month of Av, when both the First Temple and the Second Temple were presumably destroyed. In a similar vein, miraculous deliverances are not confined to the month of Nissan and the days of Passover. Mighty Yahweh can dish out all things at all times, depending on his mood.

CHAPTER 4

Love and Fear

Yahweh's mixture of moods presented an enigma. How is one to react to a father in heaven who at times is merciful and compassionate but at other times is angry and vengeful? A fairly obvious answer would be that for being merciful you love him but for being vengeful you fear him. No wonder that love and fear became a dominant theme in Jewish worship and that over the years it received a rather obsessive treatment in Jewish studies.

It is worth noting that in the twentieth century the conceptual pairing of love and fear was proposed by Sigmund Freud, and this time it was based not on religion but on psychoanalytic suppositions. Groping with the issue of the rudimentary origins of what was to become a sense of guilt that could induce a bad conscience, Freud brought forth the notion of fear of loss of love. In the seventh chapter of *Civilization and Its Discontents* he maintained that this motive can be easily discovered in the helpless infant: "If he loses the love of another person upon whom he is dependent, he also ceases to be protected from a variety of dangers. Above all, he is exposed to the danger that this stronger person will show his superiority in the form of punishment. At the beginning therefore, what is bad is whatever causes one to be threatened with loss of love. For fear of that loss, one must avoid it" (Freud 1961a, 124). The implication of Freud's assertion is that love represents the life-sustaining activity of the significant adult, whom the infant loves in return. But withdrawal of love by that same adult is a punishment that threatens survival. It is therefore an expression of anger and rage that the infant fears. All this must involve an early splitting of the adult figure into good and bad internal images on the part of the infant. For our purpose all this suggests that the archaic origins of the pairing of love and fear go back to the total dependence of the infant on the mother. This should hold true also for Jewish lore, even though in Judaism the mother goddess or goddesses have been repressed and replaced by the cosmic father, God. At any rate, because of this total infantile dependence on the parental deity, the proper management of love and fear was perceived by the children of Israel as involving nothing less than survival itself. This was the bottom line of the frenetic response to Yahweh that for being merciful you love him (in a certain sense also "her") but for being vengeful you fear him (formerly "her").

But in Judaism this rudimentary response forms only the beginning of an answer. How do love and fear relate to each other? Would it be possible for the two to blend in harmony? Lastly, and most important of all, is there any possible way of influencing the internal balance of harshness and benevolence in God's character in a favorable way? Such ability to exert influence over the disposition of God's personality would require, of course, a special, even secret, knowledge of divine matters.

The secret knowledge was the prerogative of the Jewish mystics first in Kabbalah, which is the handed-down tradition of Jewish esoteric and mystical speculations, and later in Hasidism, meaning "piety" or "devoutness." It was through modern Hasidism that kabbalistic notions were popularized and filtered into a wider public. The long-range impact of this popularization has been the messianic influence of what can be called "populist Kabbalah" on the politics of present-day Israel. For this reason we shall discuss the Hasidic literature at a somewhat greater length. One Jewish mystic who dealt extensively with these issues was the kabbalist Elijah ben Moses de Vidas, who lived in the town of Safad in the Galilee during the sixteenth century and who studied with Moses ben Jacob Cordovero, one of the major theoretical innovators in Kabbalism. In de Vidas's book *The Beginning of Wisdom* (named after Psalms 110:11: "The beginning of wisdom is fear of Yahweh"), the first two gates (parts) are dedicated to fear and to love, respectively. Right off the bat de Vidas affirmed in the introduction that the aim of the study of wisdom is to make it a tool of fear, especially fear of sinning. Man was not created except for the purpose of fearing God. Even more specifically, the Torah was not given to Israel except for the purpose of fearing God.

This assertion is fully in line with mainstream Jewish tradition that attributes supreme significance to the Mount Sinai event during which the Torah was revealed to the Israelites, who were trembling with fear. A special feature of that event was Israel's a priori acceptance of revelation: "And he [Moses] took the book of the covenant and read it to the people's ears and they said, 'All that Yahweh has spoken we shall do and we shall hear'" (Exodus 24:7). The Jewish people's response of placing "we shall do" before "we shall hear" has received countless praises from Jewish sages throughout the generations as an example of faith. It was upheld as the epitome of the purest and noblest religious commitment. When de Vidas's assertion that fear takes priority over wisdom is applied to this ancient Israelite commitment in Sinai, the inner core of religion that places fear ahead of knowledge is revealed. Long before modern nationalism created the sentiment "my country right or wrong," which is fueled by a sometimes misguided love of one's own group, ancient religion created the sentiment that might be termed "my God no matter what," which is propelled by an overwhelming fear of one's own deity.

Yet there is fear and there is fear. As de Vidas explained in the fourteenth chapter of the gate of fear, there is an extraneous form of fear such as fear of death or fear of going to hell. This is a cruder form of fear that focuses on the prospect of punishment rather than on the significance of the act of sin. Some ignorant or naive persons fear punishment more than the commitment of transgression. But even such persons, when they repent due to the lower-grade fear of punishment, can subsequently reach the higher stage of fear for its own sake—the "good fear." What is more, the lower-grade "bad fear" has an important protective function. The Jewish mitzvot, or commandments, are subdivided into two major groups, namely, the dos and don'ts. By preventing the would-be sinner from violating all the don'ts, the bad fear prepares the ground for a motivational upgrade to the good fear, when violation of the same don'ts is avoided out of fear of the sin itself rather than its punishment.

Just as fear precedes wisdom it also precedes love, as can be learned from the opening to the gate of love section. De Vidas's proof for that is taken from Deuteronomy 10:12: "And now, Israel, what does Yahweh your God require of you but to fear Yahweh your God, to walk in all his ways and to love him and to serve Yahweh your God with all your heart and with all your soul." Completing his previous line of thinking in the gate of fear, de Vidas maintained that just as fear was necessary to avoid violating the don'ts commandments, love is also necessary as an inducement to perform the dos. He also emphasized in the first chapter of the gate of love that whoever performs good deeds out of love has his reward more than doubled. We actually get a hint here of the voluminous Jewish dialectics concerning fear and love and their intricate relationship to ways of repentance and types of reward and punishment.

This dialectics of reward versus punishment required the correction of seeming injustice on earth through final justice in heaven. On earth the evildoers seem to prosper and to be the recipients of more reward and less punishment. But in heaven the evildoers will get their comeuppance for all eternity, while permanent reward will be bestowed on the pious persons. The common denominator that seems to run throughout these discussions is the determination of whether something is being done for its own sake rather than for an ulterior motive. Repentance is insufficient if it is motivated solely by fear of punishment. A good deed does not earn additional brownie points in heaven if it is induced by a desire for reward. As for fear, it does have its rudimentary merit, but it acquires its refined and ultimate value when it evolves into "fear of the highness" of God. This notion was emphasized by the Hasidic rabbi Menahem Nahum of Chernobyl. All in all, the discussions of love and fear in Jewish religious and moral literature seem to place a higher philosophical value on love but to give fear a psychological priority. Although not all roads lead to love, it nevertheless seems that all roads begin with fear. This unavoidable reaction is presumably rooted in man being a creature of yetzer. As a result man is destined to sin and be punished and is therefore born into the psychological primacy of fear. Wholehearted love of the Lord continues to be the quality that is appreciated most. Yet fear, perhaps because it is an inescapable reaction, is given more than a rudimentary and low-grade merit so as to enable man to elevate himself. It was therefore allowed to acquire its more refined and ultimate value by evolving into fear of the highness of God as compared to mere fear of his ability to inflict punishment. Its greatest merit, though, remains its ability to serve as a springboard to love.

The dialectics of love versus fear has also been connected by de Vidas to the contrast between Jews and Gentiles. In chapter 1 of the gate of love he compared Jews to a servant who loves his king. Therefore when the king goes overseas, the loving servant uses the time to plant gardens and orchards for the king. Upon returning the king delights in the trees. The king symbolizes God, and the trees provide the realms of the above with the taste of high illuminations. This is so because in Jewish symbolism an orchard, or *pardes,* serves as an acronym that stands for four different levels of Torah, or religious studies, ranging from simple denotative meanings to secret meanings that are embedded in the texts. The moral of the story is that an awakening or an excitation on the part of those who reside in the divine realm up above can be prompted and caused by a prior awakening among those down below. This is a key mystical concept that gives earthly residents some leverage over fate. They now have an influence over the heavenly entourage that can be used to promote personal salvation and even salvation for the world at large. Potentially, therefore, the loving servant, who is the Jewish mystic, can do wonders. Not so the goy. He is like a fearful servant of the king. Lacking love, he does nothing during the king's absence. Although the goyim admit that there is no one like God, they do not fulfill the commandments even though they remain fearful. The clear implication is that goyim cannot even use fear as a springboard toward greater holiness, let alone love, which is utterly out of their reach. The holy work of saving individual souls as well as the world at large by an awakening below that causes an awakening above must be left to the Jews, who truly love God.

As already can be seen, the dialectics of love and fear touches upon many issues in Judaism. In order to complete this discussion, it is necessary to briefly mention the kabbalistic doctrine of the *sefirot* (numbers) concerning God's nature and the successive stages of emanations by means of which he reveals himself in the world. The doctrine originated in the Book of Creation somewhere between the third and sixth centuries but was given greater popularity in the Book of Splendor of the thirteenth century and has become the pillar of mystical Kabbalah. Philosophical speculations too proliferated in the thirteenth century. But within Judaism the psychologically fertile mystical speculations won the competition against formal philosophical speculations over the hearts and minds of most Jews. And nowadays in Israel popular Kabbalism is gaining the upper hand over the more conservative and less mystically inclined talmudic and posttalmudic, highly complex rabbinic legal tradition. The latter is less emphatic in its insistence on the immediacy of Messianism than is the former. And as popular Kabbalism has grown more and more political and nationalistic it has increasingly become more populist and chauvinistic. This recent development has been repeatedly and powerfully exposed in Seffi Rachlevsky's book *Messiah's Donkey.* The idea of the sefirot has exerted a strong influence on Jewish spiritual life over hundreds of years. The ten sefirot that form ten successive numbers, or stages, of emanation represent God's unfolding process of sustaining the creation. They were given a superb exposition in Gershom Scholem's classic work *Major Trends in Jewish Mysticism* (1954, 205–43).

The sefirot stretch across the universe along two axes. The vertical axis represents drawing nearer and nearer to a corporeality that culminates in sexuality as the ten realms, which originated in the unknown En-Sof (the infinite), unfold in stages of emanation in a downward direction. This process represents the intricate way by which the unknown God was somehow able to reveal himself. Scholem underscored the fact that Kabbalism abandoned the biblical conception of God appearing in person to select people and adopted instead the notion that God reveals himself only through the process of creation. He therefore concluded: "It will not surprise us to find that speculation has run the whole gamut—from attempts to re-transform the impersonal *En-Sof* into the personal God of the Bible to the downright heretical doctrine of genuine dualism between the hidden *En-Sof* and the personal demiurge of scripture" (Scholem 1954, 12).

Scholem's statement clearly indicates that tensions between polar opposites habitually reverberate in Judaism. Let no one dare to insinuate that Jewish dialectics is anemic! As for the horizontal axis, along which the sefirot have also unfolded in stages of emanation, it stretches from right to left. The right represents the side of Hesed, or benevolence, that is also the fourth *sefirah,* while the left represents the side of Din, or stern judgment, that is also the fifth sefirah. It is no coincidence that these terms evoke associations with Yahweh that we have already encountered before.

The ten sefirot unfold roughly in the shape of a human body. The shape of the cosmos itself is therefore that of Adam Kadmon, or the primordial man. The illustration below of the order of distribution of the sefirot follows largely Scholem's design (1954, 213–14).

	1st Kether (crown)	
3rd Binah (intelligence)		2nd Hokhmah (wisdom)
5th Din (judgment) or Gevurah (power)		4th Hesed (love or benevolence)
	6th Rahamim (compassion)	
8th Hod (majesty)		7th Netsah (eternality)
	9th Yesod (basis, foundation)	
	10th Malkhut (kingdom)	

The sefirot are the limbs of the cosmic body of creation. The first is the skull, the second and third are the cerebral hemispheres, the fourth and the fifth are the arms, the sixth is the torso, the seventh and eighth are the legs, the ninth is the penis, and the tenth is the glans penis (Rachlevsky 2000, 263). In this capacity the tenth sefirah represents not only part of the male body but also the point of contact with the female. But the tenth sefirah is frequently regarded as God's spouse, the Shekhinah. Therefore, the tenth sefirah is also suggestive of the receptive sexual organ of the female figure; through her the precious sustenance reaches earth.

As can be seen from the numerical order of the sefirot, the ideal flow of sustenance to the world should always proceed from top downward and from right to left. This direction of emanation is known as "straight light." If the emanation changes direction it is known as "reversed light." Straight light is of course the healthy and preferred condition, but this is not what always happens. Consequently, disrupting influences flash back and forth among the sefirot. This is especially noticeable in the relationship between the last two. Yesod, or foundation, is also Milah, which means circumcision. It is the penis, and when all is well it unites with Malkhut, or kingdom, which is traditionally identified as God's spouse, the Shekhinah, to continue the downward flow of emanation. Shekhinah is thus the receptacle of God's divine flow, which through her infuses the world with sustenance, without which it would remain a dead body. Yet disruptive influences due to emanations in wrong directions among the sefirot result either in the separation of Yesod from Shekhinah or, what is even worse, in a contaminated union that gives rise to impure souls. It all comes under the so-called secret of (sexual) union, and many a zaddik (Hasidic rabbi) has focused his thoughts and actions on this secret in an attempt to unify the Holy One, Blessed Be He, with his Shekhinah.

What is the meaning of this elaborate scheme of complex interactions among ten realms that came into existence through the unfolding emanation of divine light? Clearly, there is a cosmology here that deals with how the world was created, how it is governed, and therefore how it works. And there is tacit recognition here that the created world is flawed and does not work too well. This recognition led to further developments in the Lurianic Kabbalah, named after another of Cordovero's disciples, Isaac Luria, in which the origin of the defect was traced back to the act of creation itself. When God "contracted" himself in order to make room for creation, a so-called break (shevirah) occurred. What happened was that as God revealed himself through a process of emanation the successive vessels, the light-holding sefirot, could not contain so much divine light without breaking. With good reason the Israeli scholar S. Giora Shoham regarded this "contraction" and "break" as a clear case of birth symbolism. It all suggests, of course, that God has realized the ultimate male fantasy of giving birth, but the result was not a healthy "baby" but rather a flawed creation. Because of the break, divine sparks fell with the broken-off shards of the vessels only to be captured in the domain of evil matter. In consequence, the fallen holy sparks need to be rescued by being lifted up. The current situation therefore necessitates tremendous "reparation" *(tikkun)* efforts in order to undo the damage. It is possible to paraphrase this bold doctrine by stating that God's own original sin has been the fact that an inherent flaw in his own make-up caused him to miscalculate the proper ratio of the amount of projected light to the limited capacity of the containing vessels. As a result he bungled the process of creation. This leads us from cosmology to theology with a heavy emphasis on psychology.

The ten sefirot that were distributed along the cosmic body of primordial man represent the inner workings of Yahweh's personality. They are akin to a personality profile or a diagnostic chart that enables its reader to decipher some of the psychological mysteries of the enigmatic God. The entire right side of the chart is characterized by Hesed, or benevolence, which takes us right back to Yahweh being an el ra'hum ve'hanun. But the entire left side of the chart represents the forces of Din, or stern judgment, that is, el kana. Given the ongoing clashes between the two sides, a special task of mediating and taming is relegated to the centrally positioned sefirah of Rahamim, or compassion, which plays a crucial role in keeping the opposing forces in a correct balance. Because of this opposition between the right and left forces, the vertical direction ran along three lines: the right line of Hesed, the left line of Din, and the central line of Rahamim. The Hasidic rabbi Jacob Joseph ha-Kohen used to emphasize that a central feature of the secret of union is the conquering of the left line by the central line in order to subjugate it to the right line (1881, 137, 231). In sum, the right side is God's good side or "right" side. The center is where freedom of choice prevails, which can tip the scales one way or another. And the left side is the harsh side or the bad side or the "wrong" side. When perceived as the Other Side, or Sitra Ahra, it plainly becomes the evil side not only of man, who possesses the evil urge, but also of God. Therefore the divine chart of the sefirot provides a glimpse at the dynamic interactions that reverberate within Yahweh's conflicted personality.

One should not ignore the Greek influences that impacted this man-made diagnostic workup of God. Both mystical and nonmystical Jewish works incorporated into their discussions the four elements, the four humors, and the Platonic or Aristotelian tripartite divisions of the soul. Ha-Kohen underscored that man is called "a small world" in analogy to "the totality of the face of the universe," and it is incumbent upon him to "convert matter into form" (a Greek image) in order to create union (a Jewish image of the secret of union) (1881, 7–8). With proper *kavanah* (mystical intention) an awakening below is an awakening above. In other words, man's activity in his small world can affect the divine realm in the totality of the universe. The diagnostic essence of the Greek medical model centered on detecting imbalances among the four humors that disrupted an ideally balanced bodily state and that sometimes led to mood disorders. Until recently, the adherence to this model in Western civilization discouraged any interest in the Sumerian and Akkadian medical breakthroughs in ancient Mesopotamia and significantly held back European medical advances. But this is a separate story. What is relevant to our story is that the Kabbalah adopted the Greek medical model of imbalances in diagnosing the divine realms. The Jewish mystics set themselves up as the physicians who volunteered to treat the ailing God, and a central treatment procedure was to engage in mystical acts that were intended "to include the left in the right," which meant to subjugate the left side to the right side so that the emanations always flow from right to left. This was the way to insure that the divine sustenance *(shefa* or *hiyyut)*, which flows down along the vertical axis and which supports the world, remains pure. Any reversal of this process not only deprives the world of much-needed sustenance but also injects it with additional impurities that further delay redemption.

The left side, the side of harshness, was derived from the zealous and jealous side of the angry God, which sometimes came to be seen as the Other Side. It was also the feminine side, which was regarded as being in closer affinity to matter, to sin, and to impurity. No motherly love could be expected to originate from there. In the reflected and analogous realm of the small world of an individual Jewish man, the left side was also the side of the evil urge. Succumbing to the urge to sin created new impurities. Impurity was always a danger coming from the left—the side of the evil urge, women, and goyim. It always resulted in severe punishments. The left was the realm of extreme harshness, which evoked fear.

The right side was the side of benevolence, which was derived from the merciful aspect of the loving God. It was of course the masculine side with a closer affinity to spirit. Because it was closer to spirit, masculinity was relatively less vulnerable than femininity to impurity and contamination. That is why in both the macrocosm of God and the microcosm of man masculinity belonged on the right side, which is also the theologically correct side, where the good urge resided. The right side of the sefirot or of the deity strove to ensure a steady overall flow of benevolent sustenance downward and evoked the response of love by grateful man.

What we once again encounter in this right versus left dialectics is the old gender bias in Judaism. Both men and women are highly compromised beings but to a vastly different degree. Masculinity represents something like tainted goodness, which retains some potential for doing messianic good. In contrast, femininity embodies evil, which can perhaps be redeemed if totally subjugated to the "right" side, namely, man. The daring kabbalistic notion of entering the domain of evil in order to lift up "holy sparks" is symbolic of sexual penetration or the entry of the male into the domain of the female. The highly paradoxical notions of "the holiness of sin" that were so emphasized by Scholem (1937) represented an attempt to harness sinful sex in the service of holy tikkun, or messianic reparation. The methodical, compulsive, and severe regulation of the rules of when intercourse is kosher turned copulation into a highly symbolic act of great religious significance. Through the properly conducted act of procreation holy work could be performed within the innermost innards of the domain of lowly matter and impurity, and knowledgeable man could gradually repair the originally flawed act of creation. The business of creation is therefore man's business. It is mostly what he does that determines the outcome. All a woman has to do is watch for her cleanliness and remain docile. Judaism thrives on male fantasies and antifeminine biases.

The waxing and waning of purity versus impurity in the sefirot was the outcome of the combined effects of the two axes. The vertical axis of the sefirot represented a progressive descent toward the world of sexuality, with its close affinity to the world of matter. And when man in his small world, which reflects the cosmic realm of the divine, engages in sexuality his proximity to a woman opens the door wide open to contamination by impurities. Sexual unions need therefore to be conducted under stringent restrictions lest the exposure to menstrual blood spread contamination all around, especially to the ejected semen. As a matter of fact, any faulty emission of semen, either during intercourse or through masturbation, creates impure souls and delays redemption. The pious man, who is aware of the secret of union, must ensure that all the strict conditions that permit sexual intercourse are fulfilled, and then he should do it with an intense mystical kavanah, or intent, to include the left in the right. By so taking care of the proper alignment of the right to left axis while doing the vertical thing, his awakening below excites an awakening above, causing Yesod and Shekhinah/Malkhut to consummate a heavenly union that benefits the earth.

The Jewish hypervigilance with regard to impurity led to defensive preoccupations with the issue of contaminated women and fragile men. By their inherent nature women are the source of the rise of yetzer in men. In the *Book of Hasidim* of the earlier Hasidic movement in Germany during the first half of the thirteenth century it was postulated that three yetzers oppress man via woman to make him heat up like an oven. The first type of urge manifests itself by incessant thinking about the woman. Should this happen during prayer the remedy would be for the man to stand up on his toes without leaning on a wall for support. If the social situation precludes standing up, then he should forcefully stick his toes to the ground while seated. The second type of urge shows itself through the sexual desire that causes an erection at the sight of the woman. The remedy for this problem of "heated desire" that is evoked by actual seeing is to stay away from women as much as possible and to curtail as much as possible any conversations with them. The third form is "the urge of a burning heart that does not extinguish, as the heart thinks every hour about the woman and is crazy over her [wishing] to be with her, and this is the hardest of them all. It is sometimes done by sorcery, even if he has never seen her." The remedy for this greatest predicament is to leave town (*Book of Hasidim* 1957, 179–81). By the way, sorcery, demons, and amulets are retained to this day in the Israeli practice of popular Kabbalah.

What can one say about all this? Not only is it difficult to be a Jew among Gentiles but it is difficult also to be a man among women. It requires a hypervigilant attitude for self-protection from the urge. To this day this hypervigilance vis-à-vis women remains strong among Orthodox Jews. Every so often discussions flare up in the State of Israel over the prospect of a compulsory conscription of Orthodox young men into the army, as is already the case with secular men and women. This raises the frightening possibility of Orthodox men serving in army units that include both men and women. Scenes of young men in close proximity to young women in the mixed crew of a tank are brought up in objection to the whole idea. These objections are not usually spelled out in graphic detail. Nevertheless they are not hard to fathom. The underlying notions of this stance are the same as the ideas in the *Book of Hasidim* as well as in kabbalistic notions: young male soldiers will not be able to control their literal as well as figurative "rising" yetzer. They will abuse either the women or their own bodies and spill their seed in a faulty manner. The mere sight of a woman can heat up the heart like an oven. A woman's voice is *ervah* (genital exposure), and likewise a woman's hair is certainly ervah. The sight of the hair on a woman's head is reminiscent of the pubic hair, thus providing yetzer with an opening. It is the same old attitude of hypervigilance that characterized the *Book of Hasidim,* but the aim there was confined to watching against sin for the sake of personal salvation only. It did not extend to the more ambitious goal of seeking out sin in an attempt to free the sparks of holiness that are captured there so as to hasten a collective salvation. This more messianic stance was the innovation of Kabbalism and subsequently has also been promoted to various degrees by the modern Hasidic movements.

These wider concerns are evident in the doctrines of Dov Bear, the maggid of Mezhirech, one of modern Hasidism's most important leaders. Relying on earlier statements in the kabbalistic Book of Splendor, he reiterated that when a man is captivated by the image of a woman so much so that it leads to nocturnal emission, it is as if he copulated with the evil Lillith. At this point man forgets that all beauty comes from God, and he consequently separates himself from God as he fulfils his desire by clinging to the world of matter. "When he wastefully spills his seed because of the dream image, it is as if he actually connected to Lilith as stated above, and by this he causes the birth of spirits and demons, may the Lord have mercy" (Bear 1927, 99). It is important to bear in mind that the birth of spirits and demons spoils the world and delays the Messiah. The arena of events has thus transcended the limits of personal salvation.

The dark themes of depth psychology that may be bursting through in this re-emergence of Lilith, who is Adam's shadowy mate in old Jewish legends, can only be guessed at. The psychohistorian Howard Stein has deftly and succinctly summed it up: "Behind the loving *Shechinah* is the witch Lilith who attacks and kills children—the phallic mother. Lilith remains the last but indomitable vestige of the Levantine fertility goddess in Judaism, a goddess who will not relinquish her reign of terror in the Jewish unconscious." Boldly tying all this to the age-old Jewish identification with the role of the victim, Stein also opined: "After all, the process of identifying with the victim begins with the mother. As she suffers, she expects her offspring to suffer duty bound to her. Wishing to annihilate and abandon them, she overcompensates with overprotection and worried indulgence. The living *Shechinah* on the surface masks a Lilith who lurks beneath" (1978, 196). Stein's assertions ring true. It seems likely indeed that an inordinate fear of women was a root cause of the old monotheistic revolution. In its aftermath the fear-evoking mother was done away with and supplanted by the fear-evoking father, who exercised the male fantasy option of creation by a male. Although this "creative" revision of the act of creation did away with the earlier images of the mother goddess, it could not actually rid itself of the earlier maternal split that was now repressed through monotheism. Consequently, Yahweh, who was both loving but also angry due to the loss of his feminine counterpart, was now endowed with a split personality that reenacted the infantile split of the mother image and was forced to preside over a split world.

The archaic fear of women, including their sexuality, blood flow, and impurity, was reincarnated in profuse obsessions over holiness and sin in relation to sexuality. That sexual transgression, whether in thought or action, goes beyond the issue of personal salvation becomes clear from Bear's discussion of the creation of a "destroyer" (1927, 71). Originally, the destroyer was the angel who killed all the Egyptian firstborn sons, but here it means a destructive demon. From a sinful thought the soul of a destroyer is created, and from a sinful action the destroyer's body comes into being as well. Thus when a man thinks of a virgin during the day he creates the soul of the destroyer, and when later it causes "the impurity of nocturnal emission" the destroyer is provided with a body as well. All this comes awfully close to the omnipotence of thought—a regressed psychological state in which the act of merely thinking is expected to produce material results. There is a good deal of grandeur here too. It is exactly because one's thoughts are so powerful and so consequential that a person needs to so carefully watch his steps. But this need for constant watching results in a miserable condition. One needs to be constantly on the alert, and this brings us back to the Jewish obsessive preoccupation with the issue of "Is it safe?" that was discussed in the first chapter. It is difficult indeed to be a Jew. How can it ever be safe when so many things such as goyim, matter, and women are inherently dangerous and since, at the very same time, they all are so alluring that yetzer can have a field day with them all? The only protection that is offered is to willingly be imprisoned in compulsive rituals that regulate every activity of both day and night and obsessively watch for all the tricks by means of which the urge will try to assert itself. This is no formula for safety and certainly not for happiness.

Influencing the above from below represented an attempt to heal an ailing God, and the healing followed the Greek medical model of restoring balance to separate parts that slipped into imbalance. The Greek model, which was a dismal failure in medicine, was, oddly enough, well suited for a psychological diagnosis of the enigmatic God who always seemed to suffer from an imbalanced personality. The stratification of Yahweh's personality into a special distribution of attributes allowed for a dynamic interplay between the various attributes and for mystical interventions leading to realignments that correct the imbalance. The result of such a correction is more purity and less impurity everywhere, which is better for everyone's health. In essence, personal health, the health of the chosen people, the health of the world, and the health of the deity itself depended on manipulating both axes so that sustenance would flow down in an uninterrupted and an uncontaminated fashion at all levels while the left continued to stay under the domain of the right. A different way of putting it would be that the therapeutic intervention aimed to place el kana, that is, Yahweh's left side, under the control of el ra'hum ve'hanun, which forms Yahweh's right side.

Although it is nowhere explicitly stated that way, it is nevertheless even possible to consider the vertical axis as sexuality or life-giving force and the horizontal axis as morality. The activities along the vertical axis should obviously be regulated by the properly aligned horizontal axis. This is easier said than done. Morality is the ability to choose the good urge over the bad urge, given the freedom of choice of whether to subjugate the left to the right. Since talmudic times the yetzer has been split into two, the good urge and the bad urge. Yet whenever it was referred to simply as "the urge" it was still the evil one. We may recall Ibn Paquda's vivid description of how clever yetzer, or the "friendly" stalker, was. Centuries later and with an established tradition of two yetzers, Ha-Kohen underscored the evil urge's cunning ability to appear in the clothing of the good urge and to present himself as such (1881, 57, 270). All these complications make it even more difficult to secure a proper regulation of sexuality by morality. But we went through this issue of regulation before as we dealt with Yahweh's vociferous insistence on removing the foreskin of the penis as well as the foreskin of the heart.

These two removals of the foreskin, one actual and the other metaphorical, stand for the up-downward vertical axis (sexuality) and the right-to-left horizontal axis (morality). On the vertical axis it is the ninth sefirah of Yesod (foundation) or Milah (circumcision) that clearly stands for the removal of the foreskin of the penis. Similarly, the horizontal axis that should result in the taming of judgment by benevolence as a consequence of choosing the right side over the left side (the good urge over the evil urge) could be seen as representing the removal of the foreskin of the heart, which results in moral elevation.

Because of the conceptualization of the sefirot in the form of the human body, there is an implicit suggestion there that when the left arm of Din (stern judgment) comes under the control of the right arm of Hesed (benevolence) through the decisive impact of the middle torso of Rahamim (compassion), the foreskin of the torso's heart has been removed. It all follows from the inexorable logic of the principle that an awakening below equals an awakening above. This could not happen unless it is implicitly stipulated that the above is similar to the below, including urges and foreskins. What applies to the body of every Jewish man in his capacity as a small world also applies to the cosmic body of God in the larger world of the sefirot. So, after all is said and done, it turns out that, like man, God too is tainted and therefore must clean up his act by removing the foreskin of his own heart.

An exhilarating sense of omnipotence must have surged within the daring Jewish mystics who assumed the role of physicians to the ailing God. They were engaged in the tremendous task of repairing the entire world. The psychological process of trafficking with omnipotence, however, does not start with grandiosity. Instead it consists of a two-step development that begins with a prostrate frame of mind in which one is a humble nothing at God's feet (Gonen 1978, 268). But this first religious stance leads to a second stance of grandiosity. When God is "my God," which is most certainly the case with the chosen people, then, God willing, one's very own personal will too will be done. Grandiosity was actually a response to "the psychological price" of Jewish existence (Gonen 1975, 28–29). Although in his home the exiled Jew could proudly absorb himself in worlds of spirituality created by previous generations of Jews, when he ventured out of his home and into the streets of the Gentiles he felt second class, unwanted, and vulnerable. The coexistence of spiritual pride and political shame exerted its psychological price. It was getting to be more and more of a strain to hover back and forth over a split existence of internal power but external powerlessness.

The therapeutic engagement in a cosmic repair job could set everything aright and provide a badly needed sense of competence.

Rachlevsky provided a beautiful simile to illustrate the split between the prevailing impotence on the outside but an omnipotence hidden inside: "It seemed that the whole world was folded within the body of the Jew. Within the lining of his coat, the whole cosmic drama takes place. With the proper kavanah (mystical intention), within the secret domain over his little kingdom that is within his coat—inside the holy *kapote* (long coat) the kabbalist was able to change the entire world" (2000, 264, my translation). What this meant was that, armed with kabbalistic awareness, a Jew could always bundle up within his coat. There the sefirot, the limbs of the cosmic body of primordial man, were reflected within his own limbs in his capacity of being a small world that mirrors the larger world. Worn out by external impotence, the Jew could instantly flip into the internal omnipotence that resided within his coat. In other words, by manipulating the contents of his own coat, his own body, thoughts, and conduct, the mystically empowered Jew could have a magical impact on the cosmos.

There is no question that the whole mystical credo that an awakening or excitation below equals an awakening or excitation above is a principle of magic, albeit not black magic. Its aim is to exercise a miraculous influence not for the sake of malfeasance but for the sake of doing good. It is magic nevertheless. And when the principle that an awakening below produces an awakening above is combined with Rachlevsky's simile of manipulating the self within the realm of one's own coat, the results are somewhat reminiscent of voodoo magic but with the aim of doing good rather than harm. The practitioner of voodoo manipulates the body of a doll in order to create a similar impact on another person whom the doll represents. In a somewhat analogous fashion, the practitioner of Kabbalah manipulates his own body in order to create a similar impact on the person of God, whose limbs (sefirot) are represented by the limbs of the Jewish mystic. The logic here is the logic of analogy, but the power to impact one side of the analogy by impacting the other side first is provided by magic that is derived from faith. As is the case with most magic, successful practice requires secret knowledge.

In his book *Light to the Eyes* the Hassidic rabbi Menahem Nahum of Cherbobyl has repeatedly emphasized the importance of possessing a complete knowledge. It was based on the comprehensive principle that God's Torah or God's hiyyut (sustenance) is the scattered holiness that can be found everywhere and is what keeps the world alive. It therefore becomes necessary to detect the inner and holy vitality that permeates all material things. With such discernment, the holiness within oneself and within the world connects to the holiness above. "Fallen souls," which sometimes interject themselves during prayer in the form of "foreign thoughts," are lifted up to join their heavenly "roots," which results in counteracting the impact of evil. In turn, the impact in the holy realms above is that of uniting the Holy One, Blessed Be He, with his Shekhinah. Sometimes this unity was literally called "copulation" with reference to Adam's "knowing" Eve, when knowledge was literally sexual. Without getting lost in the various intricacies of Jewish mysticism, suffice it to say that Nahum believed that man must have knowledge of the true nature of the divine and cosmic constellation in order to understand the significance and the consequences of his own choices. It was the revolutionary stance of many Jewish mystics who regarded their secret knowledge as a set of rules of God's worship that exceeded the framework of the formal religious law. Ultimately, what was a good deed and what was a transgression depended not on the formal law but on the determination whether each activity lifted up fallen souls, neutralized foreign thoughts, and contributed to personal salvation or the tikkun. And it was within this broad mystical tradition that for Nahum knowledgeable choices between good and evil in all spheres of activity, ranging from Torah studies to eating, represented the great work of reparation. It formed a blend of individual and collective redemption, which complemented each other.

For Nahum this was an incessant and dialectical process. He therefore kept reiterating that it was a back-and-forth process. He did this in a fashion that requires at least a brief discussion of the nature of deduction in talmudic and mystical studies. He kept referring to Ezekiel's vision of the chariot, during which the following phrase appears: "And the creatures are forth and back [*ratzo vashov*] like the sight of lightning" (Ezekiel 1:14). In Hebrew the creatures, literally animals, are *hayyot*, but the Hebrew writing system was originally consonantal, with vowels being a later addition. In Jewish religious interpretations reworking vowels was considered fair game as long as the consonants were kept intact, although not always in their original order. Nahum felt free therefore to take "and the hayyot are forth and back" and give it a new rendering of "and the hiyyut is forth and back." It so happens that hiyyut is the life essence of all beings. In Jewish mysticism it is similar to shefa, which is the divine providence that sustains the world. And by this change of hayyot (animals) into hiyyut (life sustenance) God's providential support of the world is converted into an incessant back-and-forth process. With the ebb and flow of the divine sustenance ride numerous mystical activities such as descent (into evil) for the purpose of a subsequent ascent, or a transgression that becomes a commandment, or malicious acts *(zedonot)* that through repentance become merits *(zekhuyyot)*. The whole of life therefore becomes a highly dialectical and very dynamic activity by the mere change of vowels from hayyot to hiyyut.

Vowel changes are not the only convenient gimmick of Jewish religious commentary. Another flexible tool of interpretation is gematria, or numerology, applied to the letters of the Hebrew alphabet, making it possible to create different codes for secret writing systems. The Hebrew letters have numerical values beginning with aleph, which is 1, and ending with tav, which is 400. Therefore any Hebrew word has a numerical value that is the sum total of the numerical values of its separate letters. Any Hebrew word can have a mystical connection to any other word or even a combination of words that add up to the same numerical value. This opens up endless possibilities for seeing connections and hidden meanings. With vowel changes as well as numerical equations of Hebrew letters, he who searches can always find. A fake "studied" quality allows the seeker to arrive at his heart's desire without seeming frivolous. The results were presumed to logically follow from the starting point rather than to wishfully gravitate to the desired end point. The "studied" results were therefore not based on literal and precise analysis of texts but on the twisting of words in pursuit of wish fulfillment. For generations Jews were engrossed with this kind of distorted reasoning process and convoluted studies, which were regarded as "the living words of God"; the worshiping admirers of such "studies" were oblivious to their inherent unreality. These ways of deduction were a joke, and their pathetic adoption by Jews to this very day is a sad testimony to the extent of Jewish denial.

Mystical pursuits can easily get entangled with dialectical plays of paradoxes, and Nahum was no exception. We have already mentioned Ha-Kohen's use of the Aristotelian concepts of form and matter. In Aristotelian philosophy a change from one form to another requires an interim state of lack of any form. With the Hasidic leader the maggid of Mezhirech this absence of form was elevated to the level of an ultimate form called Ayyin, or nullity. Immersing himself in the Ayyin, the zaddik returns to his roots in the divinity. He therefore strips himself of the material and cleaves to holiness. Sometimes the mere shame at thinking a sinful thought helps a person to turn himself into Ayyin. Last but not least, it is at the nothingness level of Ayyin that love and fear unite. In the world of matter, love and fear form two separate branches. Therefore man does not fear what he loves and does not love that which he fears. But in the root of holiness the formless state of Ayyin unites everything. Thus the cancellation of materiality and the immersion in God's holiness result in a world beyond form where love and fear dissolve into the same thing (Bear 1927, 25–26, 34–35, 78–79, 85). This doctrine holds a great deal of psychological fascination. Such a blissful mystical state that is devoid of splits transcends the schisms of the father and probably stands for a wishful return to the state of an archaic unity with the mother. It is a state that involves a curious blend of calm and ecstasy whose radical implications are that the complete renunciation of the self presumably enables a person to finally surmount Yahweh's duality, which has been so difficult to bear.

But embracing the holiness of nothingness that lies beyond fear of el kana and love for el ra'hum ve'hanun is not likely to be a workable strategy for the common man. Nahum too emphasized this transition phase of Ayyin as a way of canceling the individual ego by attaching oneself to the godly nullity, as he literally put it, "that he may kill his quality of selfness, and this is Ayyin" (1952, 35, my translation). Yet this state of absolute nothingness is but a reflection of En-Sof, the infinite and unlimited God that resides above the sefirot. In this connection Nahum stated, "For it is known that the Holy One, Blessed Be He, created the world as being [Yesh] out of nothingness [Ayyin], for the Holy One, Blessed Be He, is called Ayyin, something that cannot be apprehended, and prior to the creation of the world only En-Sof was incomprehensible and was called Ayyin" (1952, 90, my translation). Looking at it from a theological perspective, what we may have here is an attempt to resolve the age-old dialectical tension that arose from the question, How could the unknown God reveal himself as the God of creation? Nahum's resolution uses the formless Ayyin as the common denominator of the unknown En-Sof, who is called Ayyin, and the known creator, the Holy One, Blessed Be He, who is also called Ayyin. Nahum's statement was followed by a complicated discussion of God, creation, Jews, and goyim that involved the symbolism of words and letters. Following the central thesis of the Lurianic Kabbalah, he stated that the infinite God contracted himself to leave room for the potential Yesh (being) to evolve from the Ayyin at a single point.

Passages like these, which are reminiscent of the concept of singularity in modern physics, have caused some people to marvel at the surprising insights to be found in Jewish mysticism. But this is theology not physics. Nahum's convoluted discussion led him to conclude that the essence of the godly single point is in Israel alone, for whom the world was created, and not in the goyim, who do not merit being called Adam. This is a reference to the recurrent mystical notion that the creation of Adam was carried out from two components. This interpretation was also based on the usual freedom to modify vowels. The letter *a*, or aleph, at the beginning of the name "Adam" stands for Aluf, the sovereign of the world. It is therefore the godly part of human life. The remaining *dam* (blood) part of Adam stands for animal life. Only Jewish souls include the precious "A" part of Adam. The goyim lack it. Sometimes the deep disdain for goyim led certain Jews to conclude that the soul of a goy ranks even lower than that of a kosher animal.

Nahum's emphasis upon the underlying communality of Ayyin and En-Sof had its psychological correlates, which produced inevitable dialectical twists. If a man lowers himself into an absolute nothing, his implied reward is maximal—a share in the infinite. In a certain mystical sense the lowly psychological state of nothingness served as a direct pipeline to the infinite En-Sof. Nothingness was therefore allowed to embrace omnipotence. But in this created world in which the divine sustenance keeps flashing back and forth like lightning, it is forbidden to seek a lower step for the subsequent reward of ascending to a higher step. One can only exploit such a situation when it happens. Likewise, any gloating for being at a high step results in an immediate fall from the cherished state of Ayyin to the mundane state of being called Yesh (Nahum 1952, 9). In short, swinging between Ayyin and Yesh is a never-ending process that flashes back and forth and requires special knowledge for navigating among irresolvable paradoxes.

What seems to be involved in these mystical struggles is an attempt at a voluntary annihilation of one's ego and worldly individuality in order to ascend to a heavenly infinity. But an inevitable tension was created by the demand to renounce the self in order to join the eternal being. Nahum postulated the turning into Ayyin as a preliminary to ascending to higher steps. But who was going to ascend after the initial renunciation of the individual self? Clearly, it was still the individual mystic himself. By giving up his personality, he earned an ascent. Yet by somehow retaining his personality he also made the act of reward possible. That mysterious "somehow" that bridged the gap between the self-cancellation of descent and the self-affirmation of ascent is probably the psychological experience of rebirth. The fate of a mystic like

Menahem Nahum may therefore be to psychologically "die" and then be "reborn" in a lifelong ratzo vashov, or forth and back fluctuation, between the two.

We have seen that, after all the twists and turns are done, the principle of reward and punishment still requires an individual personality that serves as the recipient. A Hasid's belief system promises a reward for self-renunciation that is not done for the sake of reward. But it becomes exceedingly difficult for him to carry out the renunciation in total obliviousness to the prospect of a reward. Doing that successfully would require the negation of individuality to the point of ruling out the entire Jewish principle of rewards and punishments rendered justly to each individual based on his personal conduct. Nahum was enmeshed in this dilemma, as he promised a reward for the voluntary transition into the nullity of Ayyin. No reward can be given to an individual who is not a conscious person. Consequently, all mystical trafficking with the cancellation of individual personality is incapable of retaining the principle of divine retribution without dialectical plays with paradoxical thinking.

Tricky as the back and forth process of latching onto the deity may be, it carries great rewards. Hasidism emphasized the enormous joy that accompanies the worship of the Lord and cleavage *(dvekut)* to him. Nahum compared it to a child sucking sustenance (hiyyut) from his mother (1952, 178). But unlike infants, who are eventually weaned from their real mothers, men are never weaned from the Torah, which is called mother and whose nipples sate them at all times. It all comes under the principle that in his great love for them the Holy One, Blessed Be He, teaches his children how to worship him, that is, by sucking knowledge. Sucking knowledge, which is also identical to sucking the life-sustaining hiyyut, may constitute the ultimate mystical symbol for the perception of God. At this point it is worth noting that God was also known by the name of *el shaddai*. It means "God of the mountains" if one follows the Old Akkadian origin of the Hebrew word *shaddai*. But the Hebrew word could also suggest "God of breasts," and although this meaning is not likely to be the true origin of the word (even though breasts are mountains of sorts), the lingual suggestion is nevertheless there, and it could have exerted conscious or unconscious influence. We are back to a recurrent underlying theme that seems to be embedded in Judaism. It is difficult to be deprived of feminine sustenance, be it a mother or a mate. Therefore the merciful God of breasts, Blessed Be He, creates a Torah with nipples that provide the option of eternal sucking. But the Torah itself is hiyyut, in which case it would not have breasts but rather be the milk that flows from breasts. It is only too bad, however, that the nourishment that sustains all life flashes back and forth and does not seem to be continuously available.

Our brief excursion into Jewish mysticism fleshed out a worldview in which a vigilant scanning of impurities must be incessantly conducted under the guidance of both fear and love. Caught between the yetzer's proficiency at multiplying impurities and mighty God's ability to inflict punishment, the boxed-in Jews fell back upon compulsive rituals and obsessive thinking that typified not only the elaborate talmudic formal law but also the wilder mystical explorations that sought liberation from the oppressiveness of that formal law. In some intuitive way, the maggid of Mezhirech put his finger on the heart of the matter by means of a metaphor (Bear 1927, 72). Foreign thoughts, that is, sinful and impure thoughts, buzz around a person like bees. The trick for handling this situation is therefore to chase away the foreign thoughts just like one would chase away bees. In order to fetch the honey from the beehive, the bees are being chased away by means of smoke that has two shades, one dark and one light, symbolizing fear and love. This means that foreign thoughts too can be chased away like bees once a person lets fear and love enter his heart. I can only say that life must be difficult indeed if it is like approaching a beehive where the honey of holiness can only be reached by means of the two-shaded smoke of fear and love. Protective clothing would not hurt either!

CHAPTER 5

Bereavement and Resurrection

It is not for naught that Jeremiah was the favorite prophet of David Ben Gurion, founding father of the State of Israel who was its first prime minister. Even more so than other prophets, Jeremiah has been the most diligent teacher of the fateful duality that permeates Jewish history. It is impossible to read through Jeremiah's work without becoming only too painfully aware of what a horrible toll of bereavement must be paid by the Jewish group as the inescapable price of national resurrection. Ben Gurion, who shouldered more responsibility than any other single leader for the rebirth of the State of Israel, could not afford to lose sight of the tragic price. To him Jeremiah represented living history, and this is how it was taught in schools, where it was emphasized anew that devastation and destruction precede national reconstruction. In contemporary Israel this issue is sometimes discussed in terms of *shkhol* (bereavement) and *tkumah* (national resurrection).

The word *tkumah* appears in the Bible only once (Leviticus 26:37), when God warns the Israelites, "Thou shall have no tkumah in the face of your enemies." As is typical for Yahweh, the warning was part of a lengthy and ferocious forecast of a prolonged devastation that would finally force the uncircumcised heart of the Israelites to submit. When that finally happens Yahweh, who never forgot his covenant with his people, would relent. The postbiblical tract Shmot Rabah also warns in the name of the Lord: "If I let go of Israel and abandon them, they shall never have a tkumah."

When it comes to shkhol, there is no lack of biblical references to bereavement befalling Zion. Of particular importance to us is Isaiah's prophecy of consolation to Zion (Isaiah 49:14-21). There he promised the bereaved and lonely Zion that the so-called sons of her bereavement would return to her. It is in effect a promise of national resurrection, even though the word *tkumah* is not used here, while two derivatives of the word *shkhol* are. The underlying biblical notion is that bereavement and resurrection are closely intermingled. Each proclamation of Yahweh exists not only in and by itself but also in close context to all the other proclamations. Sooner or later, therefore, every vow of Yahweh turns out to be a mingling of a threat and a promise. This inevitable mingling is a result of his being the way he is. What is more, he is not the only one who takes care to make this message perfectly clear. His people do the same, as can be seen in the following case of a particular transformation in the Hebrew language.

Isaiah's consoling prediction to Zion that "your devastators and destroyers will go out of you" (i.e., leave you) has come to mean in contemporary Hebrew parlance that the destroyers will originate from or come out of Zion itself from within the ranks of the Jews (Isaiah 49:17). It has therefore become a catch phrase for sounding the alarm about self-produced dangers. For instance, in early 2002 a group of Israeli Reserve officers issued an open letter announcing their refusal to serve in the occupied territories. In response the Israeli army's chief education officer, Elazar Stern, issued a letter in which he applied Isaiah's phrase to the refusing officers, thus implying that they were destroying Israel. In a commentary on this episode with the title "Blows and Quotations" the Israeli journalist Meir Shalev (2002) set the record straight about the change of meaning from biblical Hebrew to modern Hebrew. Consequently, he emphasized that "the devastators and destroyers" in Isaiah were not traitors but, to the contrary, foreign occupiers. This is a crucial distinction indeed. If in the original biblical meaning the devastators represented the external enemy who is about to depart, in the current Hebrew usage the devastators are the internal enemy who is about to emerge from within the ranks of a flawed collectivity. It makes a huge difference whether the devastators and destroyers are about to depart and go back where they came from or are about to originate and emerge from within.

The change of meaning of the very same phrase from its biblical Hebrew sense to its contemporary Hebrew use amounts to a switch from being hunted by invaders to being haunted by inner demons.

Thus the shame of being overcome by enemies is replaced by guilt over being the originators of the self-inflicted devastation. The overarching theme that ties together all these different strands of meaning is sinning by the Jews and punishment by Yahweh. This is the ultimate explanation that is supposed to resolve all contradictions. It is nevertheless difficult to ignore the fact that if the original biblical phrase were to be reinterpreted in line with this new meaning in the modern Hebrew usage, then Isaiah's prophecy of consolation would be turned into a prophecy of self-destruction. Rather than finally departing, the destroyers would be emerging. So closely are the threat and the promise linked in Jewish consciousness that abrupt switches from one to the other can take place without any jarring effects being produced by awareness of any inherent contradiction. We know from psychology that the blessed domain in which contradictions coexist without friction is the realm of the unconscious. Yahweh's legacy runs deep.

Whether shkhol is the result of action by Israel's enemies or of the sinful activities of the Jews themselves, one thing remains clear. The crucial lesson to be drawn from many biblical prophecies is that in Jewish history bereavement precedes resurrection. The archaic perception of duality in the way Jewish history works left an indelible mark on Jewish psyches and finally left an impact on life in modern Israel. With the establishment of an independent state, a set of new rituals were established that are sometimes referred to as "the new secular civil religion." They were designed to instill a unified national ethos within a mixed society of new and old immigrants largely from European, North African, and Middle Eastern countries (Azaryahu 1995, 1–2). Although a lot of this has been artificially imposed from above by an administrative fiat, it nevertheless touched upon basic issues that have been floating in Judaism and that were shared to various degrees by most Israelis. How to properly commemorate both shkhol and tkumah became a focus for discussion and soul-searching among Israelis as they struggled with the age-old duality in the Jewish heritage. In exploring this issue, we shall see that a shared group fantasy of dual fate that once threatened ancient Israelites nowadays threatens contemporary Israelis. It is as if time is canceled so that psychologically Israelis become Israelites who are seemingly condemned to everlasting torments at the hand of a fateful duality of threat and promise. The old but crucial biblical as well as postbiblical lesson concerning this duality was clear: in Jewish history bereavement precedes resurrection.

The new Israeli state was established in 1948, three years after the end of the Second World War and the Nazi Holocaust. This close sequence of the Holocaust followed by Israel Reborn seemed to validate the old yet timeless expectations of a fateful duality that is inherent in the way Jewish history unfolds. Writing about "the Israeli sense of fate and destiny" in relation to the Holocaust, Eliezer Livneh (1971) maintained that modern history reaffirmed the old Jewish heritage of time expectations. Livneh referred to the poet Nathan Alterman's observation about the Holocaust, that Jewish fate comes in pairs so that both a new dawn and an annihilator come together. Livneh then reiterated that Jewish destiny does indeed come in pairs. He therefore upheld that the Holocaust confirmed in a most horrible fashion the old messianic notions. These were the well-known notions that the ingathering of the exiles and the return to Zion will be tied to horrendous messianic cataclysms that are unprecedented even in the Jewish past, which is so filled with scary events. And Livneh emphasized that this premonition of the future, which is part and parcel of the Jewish perception of time that fuses past, present, and future, proved to be akin to positive knowledge, that is, knowledge that is solidly anchored in facts. He intuitively sensed something important. However, the deeply religious Livneh was only able to go up to the point from which psychoanalytic insights depart. He was unable to see that the quality of timelessness of Jewish history is typical of the workings of the unconscious.

The unconscious is indeed characterized by a fused time or, to be more precise, by an everlasting present that consists of numerous emotional investments that are retained by an immortal memory. These invested desires have only a positive valence and cannot be canceled. They are therefore never negated, forgotten, or lost. It is important to stress the fact that there is no negation in the unconscious. This dispenses with the issue of logical contradictions and leaves only positive desire as the determining factor. In the absence of negation contradictory wishes coexist forever, while the self remains immortal. It is possible to be at many places at once till the end of time, since different spaces or times do not cancel each other out. In the unconscious "till the end of time" is actually the immediate and endless present, in which wishes are felt with great intensity. In the unconscious places cannot be negated — a Jew can always be in the homeland as well as in the Diaspora all at once. And since in the unconscious there is no negation of time either, it becomes impossible to divide time into mutually exclusive segments such as past, present, and future. Time then becomes an eternal and an all-encompassing present, as is the case with Jewish messianic time. And it is within this "eternal" domain of the unconscious that the immortal self resides to pursue the objects of its desire with omnipotence.

Another psychological conclusion that can be drawn from all this is that the traditional Jewish notions of premessianic cataclysms involved punishment not so much for acknowledged conscious sins as for repressed desires. The joys of disobeying the fatherly Lord are there even when they are unconscious. What consciously is a sin can still unconsciously remain a joy when it is repentance time. It is because of pre-Oedipal yearnings to merge with the mother as well as Oedipal urges to infringe on the territory of the harsh father that punishment for the "sinful" children of Israel is an ever-recurring phenomenon in Jewish history. So Livneh looked with wonderment at this recent recurrence of the old dreadful dualism, this time in the form of a Holocaust and a Zionist reestablishment of Israel, but was unable to draw a dynamic conclusion that could spring up in Jewish fantasy and that I once formulated as follows: "For infringing on father's territory one can be castrated or killed, and in return for Zionism one gets a Holocaust" (Gonen 1975, 22–23). Put differently, for the unconscious joy of ultimate sins one can expect the conscious suffering of ultimate punishments.

For generations now many Orthodox Jews used to fear that Zionism represents *de'hiqat haqetz,* or forcing the end. This term is frequently translated into "hastening the end," but it literally means pushing or shoving to bring about the messianic end. It even carries the connotations of crowding and elbowing, thus conjuring a notion of goading God almost physically to either speed things up or just step aside. As for the different but actual Hebrew verb "to hasten," it does indeed play a crucial role in the whole issue of the timing of redemption. This aspect will be dealt with in detail during the discussion of Rabbi Meir Kahane's ideas in the next chapter. Concerning the present notion of forcing the end, it was clearly regarded by the majority of Orthodox Jews as an arrogant behavior that consisted of dangerous pushing to update redemption regardless of God's will. They were therefore afraid that this brazen behavior was courting disaster. Then came the 1940s, during which the Nazi Holocaust provided further confirmation of the age-old dread. Yet this Nazi horror preceded the Zionist resurrection in 1948 of the Third Jewish Commonwealth (Third Temple). Once again, therefore, destruction preceded construction.

Since we are dealing with timeless messianic urges, it is worth noting that the notion of rebirth, which is so prevalent in Zionism, is dynamically tied to fantasies about a maternal entity. Such fantasies usually seek reparation for the earliest malevolent split in the life of infants—the split between good and bad maternal part objects, that is, internalized images of various features of the mother. At that early time, everlasting joy, on the one hand, and terrors of abandonment or of intrusive physical maltreatment (both a survival threat to the infant), on the other hand, lay in the balance. This archaic split was given its earliest formulation in the biblical duality of el kana and el ra'hum ve'hanun and has since received historical expressions or even collective re-creations in various forms. As previously discussed, these include the biblical prophecies of destruction and exile versus prophecies of consolation and return to Zion as well as the talmudic distinction between premessianic cataclysms and postmessianic redemption. They also include the contrast between *shevirah* (break) and tikkun (reparation) concerning creation as well as the opposition between the left and right side of the sefirot that are found in Jewish mysticism. The latest historical manifestations of the archaic split are reflected in the deeply felt awareness among contemporary Jews of the contiguity of the Holocaust and a Zionist rebirth or revival. This is reflected in the accentuation of the shkhol and tkumah duality in the current Israeli civil religion, which is discussed in this chapter.

Thus there are many opportunities and various ways of re-creating the dreadful early split that dominates Jewish thinking. In the cradle of Jewish psychohistory, the transition from a problematic mother who failed to deliver utopian goodness to an equally problematic father who presided over a disastrous reality was traumatic. The primordial good-yet-bad mother may have evoked the dual emotional reactions of love and fear. But with the onset of the monotheistic revolution, recorded Jewish history began with an internally split father in heaven without acknowledging that he inherited his frightening duality from the dethroned mother on earth. Consequently, he was set up as the originator of the ever-recurring bounce between disaster and utopia as a rule of history. It amounts to a major Jewish group fantasy that stipulates that you cannot have utopia without having disaster first (Gonen 1978). This is the way Jewish history seems to work. Why? Because group fantasies make history not only occur but recur. Psychohistorians Howard Stein (1975, 1977, 1978) and Avner Falk (1996) have provided some stimulating descriptions of the Jewish predilection to re-create the past in the future.

The latest manifestation of such a re-creation of the past in the present and future is the Israeli struggle with the issue of what would be the proper official commemoration of both shkhol and tkumah in the newly reborn state. Not surprisingly so, Independence Day has become the symbol of tkumah, or national resurrection. But what made independence possible were the soldiers who fought for it at the price of their lives and their families' bereavement. Setting up a Memorial Day in their honor was therefore a deeply felt duty. The only question was on what specific day to carry out the yearly national mourning. The decision was the outcome of a dynamic process that involved, among other things, conflicting interests between the needs of private mourning and of cultic national commemoration (Azaryahu 1995, 214–15). Bereaved parents did not wish to have a Memorial Day directly adjacent to an Independence Day that would eclipse it. But to the powers-that-be this very attachment seemed to be fraught with deep historical significance. The joining of the two days was therefore presented not as a solution to a technical problem of date setting but as an eternal connection that derives validity from tradition (Azaryahu 1995, 138–44, 214–15). The new custom took hold in the early 1950s and was enacted into law in 1963. Somehow it seemed natural to designate the official Memorial Day for Israel's fallen soldiers on the fourth day of the month of Iyyar—the day that precedes Independence Day. It was to be a reminder that national resurrection was acquired at the painful price of bereavement.

The wisdom of letting Memorial Day and Independence Day touch each other in an abrupt succession from one to the other came under increasing questioning in the aftermath of the Yom Kippur War in 1973. The war began on 6 October 1973, Yom Kippur Day, with successful surprise attacks by Egypt in the south and Syria in the north. It lasted for seventeen days and produced mixed results.

During the war Israelis experienced mounting concerns over the threatening possibility of an ascendancy of shkhol over tkumah, so to speak. There was great shock over the casualties suffered during the surprise attack. The bereavement over the new casualties was accompanied by a sense of tragedy. Not only was the price so high, but for a while it looked like it might not even be enough, as the survival of the Third Temple seemed questionable during the initial days of the war. There were rumors that Defense Minister Moshe Dayan lost his nerve and told Prime Minister Golda Meir that the Third Temple was falling. The rumors were incorrect but were widely believed and reflected the dominant national mood of that period. It was twenty-eight years before this myth about Moshe Dayan was debunked (O'Sullivan 2001).

At that time there was also a desperate sense of isolation from the rest of the world, as United Nations sessions served as an international forum for vicious attacks on Israel. Particularly revealing was the UN Security Council meeting of 9 October 1973 (Alden 1973). When the delegate of the Soviet Union, Yakov Malik, called the Israeli delegate "a representative of the murderers and international gangsters," the hall exploded with prolonged applause, although it is not traditional to do so in the council chamber. Comrade Malik also said, "Like savages, barbaric tribes in their mad destruction they have annihilated, destroyed and tried to remove from the surface of the earth; cities, villages, the cultural heritage of mankind. They have ravaged entire civilizations" (Alden 1973). It was impossible for Jews to greet with equanimity such a hostile diatribe even if others saw in it nothing but standard Russian propaganda. The Jewish-Gentile divide had once again widened into an abyss. When goyim accuse Jews of being the annihilators of cities and ravagers of civilizations, Jews dread that the only civilization that really ought to fear being ravaged is the Jewish one. Holocaustal fears were bound to arise when in the midst of a defensive war Israel was besmirched in the United Nations with such vituperative language.

It might very well be, however, that Israelis suffered the greatest psychological anguish as they fixed their gaze not on the Gentiles but on their own selves. It quickly became apparent that something deep and all-pervasive had happened to Israel as a result of the Yom Kippur War. The hawkish right-wing leader Ezer Weizman, who later moderated his views and became Israel's president, termed it "general devaluation." His phrase was picked up by the Israeli journalist Yoel Marcus, whose words on the subject in *Ha'aretz* of 25 January 1974 received notoriety and were quoted in both the *New York Times* of 30 January and *Time Magazine* of 4 March. What Marcus reiterated after Weizman was the following: "All in all, something happened to the country, something like a general devaluation, to use Ezer Weizman's definition. A devaluation in leadership ability, a devaluation in the army's ability. A devaluation in spirit, in values, in morale, in trust, and in self-confidence" (Marcus 1974, my translation). The rising self-doubts related to the most sensitive topic of all—the trust in one's ability to survive. This existential doubt was given expression by naming the recent tragic failure to be adequately prepared for war as the *mehdal,* a noun derived from the Hebrew verb *hadol* (to cease everything, even cease to exist). In my Alcalai English-Hebrew dictionary, Hamlet's famous question "to be or not to be" is translated as "to be or to cease." And I remember my teacher Baruch Kurzweil criticizing in class the poet Abraham Shlonsky for giving a precise literal translation to Hamlet's question. Kurzweil thought that the Hebrew verb *hadol* was uniquely suited to denote "not to be." The wide acceptance of the term *mehdal*, literally, "cessation," as a reference to the monumental self-failure that was responsible for the Yom Kippur catastrophe testified to a mingling of dread and guilt that plunged the Israeli national mood into depression as well as into a period of soul-searching that amounted to atonement for the sins of collective failure.

Israel's president at the time, Ephraim Katzir, sensed that the excessive preoccupation with renewed threats to Jewish survival could push Israelis into extreme psychologies of making a last stand till death. The notorious precedents in Jewish history for such stands are the individual example of Samson's uttering "Let my soul die with the Philistines" and bringing down Dagon's temple on himself and on his enemies as well as the collective example of the defenders of Masada, the last stronghold against the Romans. The "Great Jewish Revolt" against Rome ended in A.D. 73, when the zealots of Masada killed themselves with their own swords rather than be captured by the Romans. A modern Israeli fascination with suicidal psychologies that are based on the paradox of self-assertion through self-annihilation kept growing for a while (Gonen 1975, 213–36) and was tied to issues of Jewish self-image in relation to the Nazi Holocaust (Gonen 1978). The Israeli president chose the occasion of a memorial ceremony at Ben Gurion's grave in Sde Boker to address these well-known Jewish suicidal stands. The date was 31 March 1974, the thirtieth day since Ben Gurion's death. The occasion was very solemn. President Katzir quoted Ben Gurion's warning in 1946 that in these difficult days of struggle neither Masada nor wishing to die with the Philistines is a viable option. Tough days call for a tough stand but not for despair or suicide. The Israeli president was obviously giving credit to the late Ben Gurion's wisdom and foresight, but he was also referring to the present days of bitter struggle and reminding his people that Ben Gurion's prescription held equally well then. In other words, behaving as if a Holocaust was imminent was not the way to cope with a grave situation.

The deeply held conviction that a mehdal had happened reflected the mounting recognition that survival itself was unnecessarily jeopardized. In turn, the renewed consciousness of the danger to survival intensified feelings of identification with past eras of Jewish history. Realistic fears for Jewish survival have been one of the more consistent common denominators of different time periods in Jewish history. It is therefore revealing to watch how different historical times fuse into one time dimension under the immediate impact of a national crisis. In a symposium on the mehdal that was conducted in February 1974, the author S. Yizhar (pen name for Yizhar Smilansky) drew the following comparison between France and Israel: "Again, France was occupied by the Nazis, but the kind of basic questions that surfaced with us did not surface there. There was a bad war that eventually passed away from the world and merely left some bad imprints that were more or less overcome. But when it comes to the Jewish people, the entire world shakes from its very foundation, starting with its archaeology till today and till the end of time. And the threat—it's always to the point of final annihilation" ("To the Roots of the Matter" 1974, my translation). This perception of the timelessness of Jewish history is by no means confined to a man of letters. In the same panel discussion, the poet and journalist Chaim Guri quoted an equally revealing statement made to him by a soldier:

> Tell me where else in the world events that took place two thousand years ago influence people's contemporary life with such dreadful strength? In Europe history resides in libraries. It does not interfere with people's fate. Here it is as if the dimension of past time does not exist at all. Everything is present. Everything is open. It is as if everything repeats itself. The First Temple, the Second Temple, the Third Temple. Had we been defeated we could have had "the destruction of the Third Temple," not just a defeat in battle. You live in historical dimensions that Westerners do not share. ("To the Roots of the Matter" 1974, my translation)

"Everything is present" because Jewish time dimensions are compressed. And "it is as if everything repeats itself" because current historical plays are at the very same time psychohistorical replays of the past and prophecies of the future. This is the essence of the Jewish destiny of being chosen by Yahweh for a repetition compulsion of a horrendous dual fate. The unresolved question that still needed to be figured out was, Can secular Israelis escape Jewish fate? Struggling for an answer took an interesting form.

The renewed sensitivity toward the quality of timelessness in Jewish history prompted a debate about the advisability of letting Memorial Day and Independence Day remain adjacent to each other. In the gloomy days that followed the Yom Kippur War, many Israelis wondered whether the sudden switch from a day of mourning to a day of celebration was not a psychological mistake. This switch has always been hard to implement but never as difficult as in the depressed days of

April 1974. Articles and editorials in the press took note of this emotional difficulty but also revealed awareness of the symbolism involved in the contiguity of shkhol and tkumah, bereavement and national resurrection. The public was aware of the fact that this kind of duality appears time and again in Jewish history and serves as a common denominator of most of its time periods. Most everyone understood that a glaring symbolism was attached to the significant act of linking the two days by setting up Memorial Day on the eve of Independence Day. In America the two days fall in May and in July, and no one has a sense that there is anything wrong with this arrangement. But Israel was not supposed to share the ordinary fate of other nations. The uniqueness of Jewish history, the hidden hand of Yahweh, had to be proclaimed in a highly ritualistic fashion. For this reason Memorial Day was deliberately plugged in on the eve of Independence Day as a reminder that bereavement always precedes resurrection and is the inevitable price of the latter.

The most glaring example of this Yahweh-ordained linkage is of course the awful shkhol of the Nazi Holocaust, which was followed by the tkumah of the reestablishment of the State of Israel, which was perceived as the start of messianic redemption. The Holocaust was the kind of monstrous price that merited not merely the political remedy of creating a modern independent state but even more so the messianic remedy of ushering in redemption. These notions reverberated in Prime Minister Menahem Begin's mind when he stated the following during his acceptance speech for the Nobel Peace Prize on 10 December 1978: "I have come from the Land of Israel, the land of Zion and Jerusalem, and here I stand in humility and with pride as a son of the Jewish people, as one of the generation of the Holocaust and redemption" ("Text of Begin Speech Accepting Prize" 1978). It is clear that Begin's statement treats the creation of the modern Israeli state as a manifestation of redemption or at least as the start of the process of redemption. For this reason he identified himself as belonging to "the generation of Holocaust and redemption" or, one might say, the generation of premessianic cataclysms followed by messianic deliverance. Yahweh's decree of fateful duality being a basic law of history is never defunct.

This was made completely clear in a panel discussion at the Hebrew University in Jerusalem on 24 April 1973 that included among others the army's chief rabbi, Shlomo Goren, and the activist Labor leader Israel Galili, known for his lifelong ardent support for military security and for settlement activity. The subsequent report on the panel discussion appeared in the Independence Day edition of the newspaper *Maariv* on

6 May 1973. During the discussion Rabbi Goren stated the following: "Independence Day—it should not be devoid of any connection to grief and mourning and sorrow and the long Jewish history of being victims of bloodshed. To the contrary, it must be even more closely attached." This was a fair summary of the traditional Judaic outlook on Jewish history. Rabbi Goren went on from there to delve into the murky mingling of religion and politics: "This is Judaism, and we must know that all this gives expression to our vision, the vision of the third redemption of the people of Israel. We are therefore obligated to instill the values that the prophets of Israel attached to the national existence of the vision. It is not sufficient to be content with its physical implementation only but also [with the implementation of] the spiritual values. And there has never been a more propitious moment for engaging in this ordeal of instilling the values in the hearts of our youth than today" ("Panel Discussion on the Meaning of Independence Day" 1973, my translation). This was in effect a call to raise Jewish historical consciousness of a dual fate not just on the occasion of Memorial Day for the Victims of Israel's Wars that is attached to Israel's Independence Day. The instilling of the religious values of the prophets of Israel in the hearts of the youth should rather be carried out all year long with the active support of the state. The implications of all this are not hard to figure out even though they are not fully spelled out. There will be no separation of synagogue and state. Thus it would be difficult for such a state to be fully secular or democratic, but it would easily be very Jewish in its subscription to Yahweh's rules of history.

In talking about vision Rabbi Goren used a loaded term. It is the very first word in the book of Isaiah, which begins, "Vision of Isaiah son of Amotz," thus referring to the entire book. Vision has come to be considered as essential for collective health and survival. This is clearly implied in the well-known verse Proverbs 29:18: "Without vision the people unravel, but happy is he who keeps the law [Torah]." I remember how Ben Gurion loved this word "vision" and used it frequently to the point of being mocked about it. The general public took delight in the repetitions as well as in his funny accent. Ben Gurion's intent was to connect the new Zionist vision to the older prophetic vision. Rabbi Goren's intent was to harness the state's resources in the service of Torah vision lest the unraveling of the Jewish collectivity threatened even physical survival itself. Thus in the name of "vision" Rabbi Goren advocated not only the continued pairing of Memorial Day with Independence Day but also conduct by the state that amounted to a political support of religion.

One should not expect a different verdict as one moves from the religious nationalist Rabbi Goren to the secular nationalist Israel Galili: "I think about a deep historical sense and an educative national value of the highest importance and about a natural decision that could not be otherwise, that bound together and attached in an inseparable connection the Memorial Day for our dead with Independence Day. It seems that were they to separate the attached two, Independence Day would have been shortchanged. Something would have dwindled its contents. Its naturalness would have been spoiled. Something artificial would have been formed" ("Panel Discussion on the Meaning of Independence Day" 1973, my translation). With this endorsement of fateful duality in perpetuity, we witness the paradox and even tragedy that is inherent in Zionism. In a rebellion against the father in heaven during their youthful days, the secular old-guard Zionists strove to put Jewish fate back into Jewish hands. Explicitly, this meant the wresting of control away from the Gentiles. Implicitly, it meant taking it out of God's hands. Yet in their old age their behavior changed. They were old and weary after the waning of socialistic ideals and because of their mounting frustrations due to the incessant national clash with the Arabs that cast a pall over the justness of the Zionist cause. Having lost some of the secular gutsiness of their youth, they now retrenched in the timeless Jewish fate of threat-and-promise paired together like twins. They thus embraced the fate from which they earlier had tried to escape. Consequently, they ran back to the old religious conceptions of Jewish fate like scared children who run back to their mother.

Over the years Israelis have continued to struggle with the issue of whether the two days ought to be separated. Sometimes bereaved parents whose pain was very apparent joined the public debate. In a letter to the daily paper *Ha'aretz* one such parent, David Majar, objected to "the grotesque sight of the joy of resurrection emerging out of the agony of bereavement." He especially abhorred the heightened involvement of the media and the government with bereaved parents. He regarded it all as a cynical staging of "an instant national mourning." As a remedy, he recommended that more modest meetings and commemorations be held by bereaved parents on different occasions and on various days that are not far removed from Memorial Day and Independence Day. Moreover, he insisted that these be carried out without "the phony and bombastic pathos of apparatchiks" (Majar 1985, my translation). It is worth noting that the same issue of *Ha'aretz* reported an event that illustrates what David Majar was objecting to. During the official ceremony of lighting a memorial candle by the Western Wall with the participation of bereaved families, residents of Jerusalem, and tourists, Israeli president Chaim Herzog declared: "This time the casualties of Israel's battles fell not on the altar of destruction but of resurrection, survival, and life" (Memorial Service, 1985). This cryptic reminder, in front of tourists to boot, that there were other times different from this time is highly problematic. Its implied diagnosis of a historical advance from sacrifices to the altar of destruction to sacrifices to the altar of resurrection stems from an underlying perception of Jewish history as an obstacle course that leads from altar to altar, even though some altars are preferable to others.

In an interview that appeared on Memorial Day of 1986 another bereaved parent, the poet Yehoshua Tan-Pi, objected to the activities of bereaved parents organizations that amounted to a promotion of a form of bereavement worship. But he insisted that Independence Day was an integral continuation of Memorial Day and that separating the two would do damage to the significance and content that both days symbolize (Alon 1986). Another bereaved parent, Israeli professor Mordecai Rotenberg, injected a mystical notion into the pairing of the two days. Citing the Hasidic idea of "a descent for the sake of an ascent," he suggested that for the believer the transition from the dark night of the depression of bereavement to the bright morning of Independence Day is somewhat akin to the experience recommended by the Hasidic dictum (Rotenberg 1993). This amounts to a translation of the old fateful duality into the mystical language of a duality of descent and ascent that becomes akin to a personal mystical experience in a Hasidic style.

Over the years more and more voices could be heard questioning the wisdom of adjoining Memorial Day to Independence Day. But the official governmental line concerning this issue has remained unbending. Thus, at the lighting of the memorial candle ceremony at the Western Wall on 2 May 1995, which was broadcast on television, President Ezer Weizman made the following statement:

> The connection between the sorrow of Memorial Day and the joy of Independence Day is unique to us Israelis. To me this connection seems singularly right and proper. Twenty-four hours from now we shall lift our heads up with pride over our achievements. We do have that to be proud of. In less than fifty years we have created here a dynamic, progressive, and growing society. . . . For all this and even more we shall proudly lift our heads high during Independence Day. But this evening we shall bow our heads in view of the unbearable price. The shkhol has hit many households in Israel. The enemy's bullets never

distinguished whether their victim is secular or religious, leftist or rightist, which is why it is forbidden for any of us to enlist the shkhol for justifying his personal conviction. (my translation)

This was the official propping up of the national myth that aimed to counteract underlying cracks in the national unity that were hinted at in the speech.

The story became even more complicated when the civil religion of commemorating Jewish fate was extended to an entire week. This happened when Holocaust Day was fixed five days prior to Memorial Day. It was done not so much with the deliberate intention to create an entire week dominated by commemorations but for the purpose of emphasizing heroism. The twenty-seventh day of the month of Nissan was the day on which the Jewish revolt in the Warsaw Ghetto was finally brutally suppressed. Yet the choice of this day as Holocaust Memorial Day did not seem enough to ensure that the notion of the Holocaust would be sufficiently infused with the notion of heroism. It is as if a danger was sensed that in private some citizens could have perceived the day as "Holocaust and Cowardice Day" or, what is even worse, "Holocaust and Going like Sheep to the Slaughter Day." So the name of the day was changed from just Holocaust Memorial Day to Holocaust and Heroism Memorial Day in order to counteract and nip in the bud such scorching Jewish self-images. Many Israelis are aware of the manipulative distortion of history that is involved here. That is why Arieh Issar advocated that the Holocaust be portrayed as it truly was. It was a historical failure (mehdal) of the Jewish people in the Diaspora that caused them to ignore the threat to their survival. In this regard he issued a blatant statement indeed: "I want to say that the decision to call Holocaust Day also Heroism Day, thus giving equal weight to Holocaust and to heroism, means a distortion of the historical truth. In relation to the Holocaust, heroism was like the drops of water that the bird draws by means of its beak in order to overcome the rising tide" (Issar 1997, my translation). He was historically correct, but it would be only fair to note at this point that this case is typical of most other cases of the so-called identity politics either in Israel or in other countries in which considerations of the group's self-esteem are given priority over historical verity.

The Israeli rituals and activities that revolve around the Holocaust have become so numerous and elaborate that they led columnist Doron Rosenblum (1993) to talk about a Holocaust Day that lasts about a month and that stretches all the way from the celebration of Passover to

Independence Day. He was referring to a period characterized by Israeli scholar Maoz Azaryahu as charged with the symbolism that flows from the concentration of commemorations and holidays: "The order of commemorations and holidays in the national yearly calendar—Passover, Holocaust Day, Memorial Day, and Independence Day—has created an orderly construction that is significant in relation to the development of the national history saga from birth through destruction and sacrifice to rebirth" (Azaryahu 1995, 232). Now Rosenblum wondered whether recent developments in Israeli identity were responsible for Holocaust Day overshadowing Independence Day to the point that the latter now seems a mere twig of the former. He suggested that an erosion of Hebrew identity (mostly secular) and a growing identification with Jewish identity (more religious) were partly responsible for this outcome.

What Rosenblum was referring to was a growing process that Moshe Leshem has termed "the Jewing of Israel" (1989, 190–214). Leshem has given vivid descriptions of how daily life in Israel has been affected by the continued erosion of the political status quo between religious and secular Jews as the process of "the impregnation of the secular by rabbinical law" (205) continued. According to Leshem, the outcome of this process has been decisive. "It is the Orthodox camp that determines which matters can, for the time being, be left to the secular authorities and which ought to be defined in terms of *halakha* (the religious law). The Orthodox camp thus determines in essence what is Jewish and what is not" (204). Regrettably, all this is reminiscent of an old Jewish joke. Upon being asked, "Who makes the decisions in your home?" the man answers, "I make the big decisions and my wife makes the small decisions." The man is then asked again, "And who decides what is a big decision and what is a small one?" The man answers, "She does." Unfortunately, the relationship between secular and religious Jews in Israel has come to resemble the relationship between the husband and wife in the famous joke.

When Rosenblum detected the problem of a disharmonious identity, he posed the question, What defines Israelis more, the Holocaust or the national resurrection? He ventured the guess that any answer would have to include both (Rosenblum 1993). At any rate, when in the new Israeli civil religion the duality of Jewish fate escalates from bereavement and resurrection to Holocaust and resurrection, the cruelty of Yahweh's rules of history is given an ultimate emphasis. The Holocaust, after all, is the epitome of all bereavements. It seems that its cruelty and agony cannot be surpassed, although one should never underestimate man's capacity for evil. The Holocaust therefore makes the price of tku-mah unacceptable. At the very same time it foreshadows the similarly unacceptable price of premessianic cataclysms that Yahweh is bound to exact in the future for the delivery of messianic redemption.

In her 2001 article "Catastrophe Day or Victory Day?" Israeli journalist Lily Galili described a recent development that may provide some counterbalance to the overwhelming emphasis on the Holocaust commemoration. Israel nowadays includes around 1 million immigrants from Russia who brought with them a different outlook that has begun to penetrate the Israeli ethos. These newest immigrants have the strong tradition of proudly celebrating Victory Day on 9 May to commemorate the Russian victory over the Nazis that war veterans from their families helped to bring about during the Second World War. At this point it is important to underscore the fact that the tradition of celebrating Victory Day existed among the Russian immigrants on its own merit and was never set up as a means to infuse the Holocaust with heroism. It is therefore anchored in reality rather than fantasy. And in deference to the wishes of the Russian immigrants the Israeli Knesset (parliament) has begun to commemorate Victory Day in a special ceremony each year. In this connection Knesset chairman Abraham Burg stated that the cultural contribution of the Russian Jews could help his generation to resolve the inner tension between Holocaust and heroism. His state-ment amounted to a tacit admission that there was an inherent problem with the apparent unity of the "Holocaust and heroism" concept. There is no question that tilting the balance somewhat away from Catastrophe (Holocaust) Day and more toward Victory Day would be psychologi-cally helpful. Moreover, it is historically more accurate, since the tradi-tion of celebrating Victory Day is not an artifact of the need to infuse the Holocaust with heroism.

It is clear that criticism of the transparently manipulative rituals of the new Israeli civil and presumably secular state religion has increased over the years. In a 1990 article "Kitsch and Death in a Long Weekend" Israeli journalist Gideon Samet spoke of "the macabre collection of the days of bereavement and heroism." He also issued the warning that, in the crude hands of the politicians, the fallen and the dead in the chain of Holocaust-Memorial-Independence are turned into broadcast slo-gans for a policy that could bring about the next disaster. He was refer-ring to the stretch of five days that now includes all three commemora-tions. It stands to reason to assume that the root problem of the rituals of the civil and seemingly secular religion is the underlying messianic outlook they disclose. This was the opinion of Avner Ben Amos, head of the history department in the School of Education of Tel Aviv University. He maintained that the Holocaust Day and Memorial Day rituals form the current religion of secular Israelis. The rituals focus identity around bereavement, loss, grief, and destruction and then lead toward redemption, resurrection, and revival. To Ben Amos's mind, living between the stress of disaster and Holocaust and between resurrection and redemption constitutes a messianic outlook. It is a far too simple outlook that fails to accurately detect the much more complicated historical reality (Sa'ar 1998). On the whole, these criticisms by both Samet and Ben Amos seem warranted indeed.

Yet the fact that discerning critics were able to see through the manipulative programming of the newly created rituals for the Israeli civil religion does not mean that the public at large was able to escape the clutches of what adds up to a shared group fantasy. The historical background, cultural heritage, and psychological disposition to embrace the messianic outlook of a timeless and therefore ever recurrent fateful duality were all there. In consequence, the manipulations by the state's officialdom impacted receptive souls. By the year 2003 there were even references to the week of Holocaust and Heroism Memorial Day, Memorial Day for the Fallen of Israel's Wars, and finally Independence Day as "Days of Awe" similar to the ten days of awe that open up each new Jewish year. And so it came to be that, both consciously and unconsciously, the new state rituals were organized in a programmatic fashion. They were set up in a way that took extra care to anchor the new holidays of the evolving secular civil religion in the messianic spirit and ethos of the older religious holidays. By confirming the duality of Jewish fate the new holidays not only joined the ranks of the traditional fateful holidays of the past but also reaffirmed Yahweh's eternal rules of history. Such is secularism in Israel. It is like a rug that needs to be inspected so as to see what lies underneath.

CHAPTER 6

Messianism, Zionism, and Holocaust

The old messianic legacy included the all-important clause that final redemption can be ushered in only after premessianic cataclysms have run their full course. Moreover, Jewish history provided bitter past experiences with the tragic consequences of a sudden onset of messianic inflammation. Whether it was through the catastrophic revolt against the Romans led by Bar Kokhba in ancient times or the conversion to Islam of the disastrous "false Messiah" Shabbetai Tzevi in the seventeenth century, Yahweh's old historical lesson was given painful reinforcement. While premessianic cataclysms are delivered like cash on the barrelhead, redemption remains in the form of a promissory note. It does not pay off to crowd the Lord in an attempt to compel him to honor his old IOU of delivering a Messiah. Thus the people who deep in their hearts dreaded the end as such were certainly fearful of forcing that end needlessly. It seemed safer to let a sleeping God lie. Consequently, the notion of forcing the end gave most religious Jews the shudders and created ambivalent feelings. As we have already seen in the second chapter, the evoked fear gave rise to a conflicted, even contradictory, attitude of longing for the Messiah but dreading his coming. Theologically speaking, it was a duty to hope for him. Psychologically, however, it was safer to feel secure in the conviction that he would never actually arrive.

At the end of the nineteenth century Zionism injected itself into this uneasy emotional balance of forces as a new phenomenon of "secular Messianism" to be reckoned with. The sins of the Zionists were twofold. By organizing collective efforts to ingather the exiles and to resettle the Land of Zion without waiting for the Lord to do it in his own good time, they were forcing the end. It was like telling the Lord that they had given up on his seemingly worthless IOU of redeeming Zion. What was even worse was the fact that most of the early Zionists were secular. Therefore, their energetic actions on behalf of redemption were seen as a blatant declaration that a nonexistent God cannot keep promises. The message was not lost on Orthodox Jews. They could not swallow this new poison pill of secular Messianism that threatened to destroy their religious way of life. They knew that God is not dead. They trusted that Yahweh neither forgets nor forgives, and they were afraid that the new Zionist venture of forcing the end would provoke the zealous God to punish his errant children even more severely. A disaster was looming as a new breed of Zionist secular Jews, who in their dress and activities resembled goyim more than Orthodox Jews, ignored not only the Lord in heaven but also the rabbis on earth. This secular chutzpah was truly galling, and it scraped the qishqes, or guts, of religious Jews who remained in the fold.

But, as they say in America, nothing succeeds like success. The Zionists were getting somewhere with their efforts to resettle the ancestral land. The Jewish Yishuv (settlement) in Palestine was growing first under Turkish and then under British rule. Moreover, even the goyim recognized the seriousness of the Zionist undertaking. On 2 November 1917, with urging by Jewish leaders, the British government issued the Balfour Declaration, which stated that Britain viewed with favor the establishment of a national home for the Jewish people in Palestine.

This was a wake-up call for many in the Orthodox camp. The goyim, after all, are merely instruments in the hand of the Lord, even though they are unaware of it. God has used them in the past as unwitting tools of his will. This was the case when he imposed the destruction of the First Temple and the Babylonian exile through King Nebuchadnezzar or when he ushered in the subsequent return to Zion by means of the Declaration of King Cyrus of Persia. The Balfour Declaration seemed to confirm that God was following the latter and more favorable precedent. What is more, under the banner of "the-state-on-the-way" the growing Jewish settlement in Palestine, the Yishuv, organized itself successfully into voluntary bodies that regulated the political, educational, military, and most administrative and material aspects of daily life. It was therefore becoming increasingly clear that the secular rebels were well on their way to realizing statehood at some future point. Even though they lacked political independence, the Jews in Palestine were wielding actual power to an extent that was unheard of in the Diaspora. All this posed a challenge to Orthodox Jews of various strands and gave them some food for thought. Detailed descriptions of their various ways of struggling with this issue can be found in the work of Aviezer Ravitzky (1996). His explorations and analysis of the dialectics and nuances of the reactions of different Orthodox camps remain the best work on the subject to date.

For those Orthodox Jews who did not reject Zionism outright, new ways of relating to it needed to be found. They wished to endow the fruits of the labor of the Zionist secular Messianism with some legitimacy while avoiding the danger of forcing the end. At least two major avenues evolved in response to this challenge. The first was what Ravitzky called Messianism without a Messiah, meaning a redemptive process that takes place in the absence of a holy human redeemer (1996, 81). In this particular outlook, the beginning of redemption can be witnessed not through the appearance of a personal redeemer but through the collective activity of the people. In essence, this is an elaboration on the kabbalistic outlook of history. We have already mentioned Scholem's observation that, in the Kabbalah, God no longer appears as a person but reveals himself through creation. This represented a revolutionary departure of the Kabbalah from the original Jewish tradition. Now, and in a somewhat similar fashion, the Messiah could reveal himself not by a personal appearance but through the collective activity of the holy people. The kabbalistic work of reparation, or tikkun, has traditionally involved lifting up holy sparks that were scattered captives throughout the world of matter. The task of lifting them up and returning them to their heavenly roots has never been confined to a single person. The notion of a collective effort was imbedded there. The kabbalistic notion of reparation not only left room for a collective effort but also implied that such an effort represented helping the Lord rather than forcing his hand. Messianism without the Messiah could therefore proceed with God's blessing.

The second avenue was to treat the secular Jews like the goyim, that is, as unaware instruments of the Lord. In that case even rebellious secular Jews who have abandoned God still carry out God's divine plan even though they are oblivious to this fact. If their activities yield material results that bring closer the reestablishment of the Third Temple or the Third Jewish Commonwealth, then they too unknowingly work for the messianic goal of having the Torah law recognized throughout the earth. This is the major thrust of Seffi Rachlevsky's interpretation of the influential doctrines of Rabbi Abraham Isaac Kook in his book *Messiah's Donkey* (2000, 19-29). The Messiah is reputed to arrive while riding on a donkey. The Hebrew word for donkey is *hamor*. Apply the standard Jewish homiletic gimmick of playing fast and loose with a word's vowels and you get *homer*, or matter. Now identify this donkey turned into matter with the secular Zionists and you get the needed materials at the service of the Messiah. But he is on the rider's seat, that is, he represents the ultimate goals. By contrast, the secular materials with which he has to work—the secular donkey, so to speak—represent only the temporary means. Rabbi Abraham Isaac Kook's ideas displayed a revolutionary and even paradoxical way of thinking that sometimes has come to dominate messianic ideologies. What at first glance seemed to be a secular departure from the ways of the Lord was reinterpreted to mean that the divine course would proceed to its preplanned destination. And if the secular Zionists are indeed unwitting instruments of the Messiah— be they the donkey he rides on or the matter he works with—then cooperating with them and guiding them rather than fighting them is the holy order of the day.

Besides having its practical political implication, this doctrine offered also a messianic theological verdict that served to ease the traditional old fears. As goyim have traditionally been unaware instruments of God mostly for the purpose of destruction, so are the secular Zionists or Hebrew-speaking goyim unaware instruments of the Messiah for the purpose of redemptive construction. They are the unwitting pathbreakers of the road to God's renewed kingdom in Zion and on earth. And if this is indeed the case, there is no need to worry about the prospect of a horrible punishment due to de'hiqat haqets, or forcing the end. There is no shoving and pushing of the Lord here. On the contrary, everything is unfolding according to his plan, which is executed in part by persons who are unaware of it. So Yahweh is likely to be pleased and smile rather than be irked and frown.

The essence of Messianism is a myth that is accepted as bona fide history. A myth about the past acquires the force of historical determinism and is projected to the future and to the end of days as the inevitable course of history. From this derives the peculiar messianic time dimension. In one sense eternal time is frozen because past, present, and future are all the same, since they always abide by the same rules. In the Jewish tradition it is Yahweh's imposition of an apocalyptic fateful duality as a rule of history. Yet in another sense specific time periods may vary from each other depending on what phase they occupy in the evolution of the current unfolding of the old and repetitious messianic pattern. In other words, although specific time periods may differ, eternal messianic time does not, and in the final analysis things always end up the same. Therefore, the particular determination of how near or far away is the next repetition of the cataclysmic phase of eternal time from the transient present is of great importance in building up historical expectations. The dramatic succession of major events in the twentieth century provided fuel for rekindling both messianic hopes and fears. It also created sharp disagreements between secular and religious Jews concerning the true nature of each particular messianic phase.

The modern story begins with the rise of Zionism at the tail end of the nineteenth century. It was a continuation of earlier secularization trends of the Jewish "enlightenment" movement that were then augmented by the rise of nationalism in Europe. For Orthodox Jews secularization, even all by itself, was an unpardonable sin. Nevertheless, in combination with actual resettlement of the ancestral Land of Zion, secularization thrust itself into the heart of the messianic expectations from fate to create an enormous dread. The secular Zionists were not waiting for mighty Yahweh to send his Messiah. They ignored him and engaged in Messianism without a Messiah by ingathering the exiles on their own authority. Unfortunately, those secular fools did not seem to understand that by ignoring Yahweh and trying to force the end they were inviting punishing cataclysms. They were thus putting the collectivity of Israel in great peril. It was bad enough that as individuals they abandoned the faith. Why could not they at least refrain from collective dabbling in Messianism and just let sleeping el kana lie?

But even before and especially after the First World War, the ingathered secular exiles kept producing tangible results in the Holy Land. It no longer looked inconceivable that "the-state-on-the-way" would someday become an independent Jewish state. This prompted some, though by no means all, Orthodox Jews to reevaluate the Zionist endeavor in an attempt to discover in it positive developments that would be conducive to a smoother realization of God's divine plan. The most influential thinker along these new lines was Rabbi Abraham Isaac Kook.

The thrust of Rabbi Kook's vision of historical progress was the determination that history as a whole serves as a stage for messianic fulfillment. And the crux of the matter was that, at the material level itself, there was creative potential for reparation at the level of the spirit. This meant that the world of matter, including Zionist activities, is an indispensable stage for messianic evolution. In a penetrating analysis of this new trend Ravitzky underscored the importance of Rabbi Kook's notion that "destruction for the sake of construction is itself a kind of construction" (1996, 101–9). We can readily recognize that the ancient origins of Rabbi Kook's notions go back to Jeremiah. It was he who kept hammering the central theme of destruction that precedes construction and solidifying it as Yahweh's major rule of history. Very rightly so, Ravitzky singled out World War I and the doctrine of the Lurianic Kabbalah about the breaking of the vessels during creation as the catalysts that inspired Rabbi Kook's innovative outlook. The great devastation that was wrought by World War I raised the issue of whether there is any divine, albeit hidden, purpose to destruction. The old kabbalistic model could provide an answer to this question. Because during creation the vessels could not contain all the divine light and shattered, holy sparks scattered in the world of matter. But it was this initial destruction that created the opportunity for the messianic work of reparation by means of lifting up the fallen sparks. Ergo, from the very beginning an initial destruction served as a preliminary for construction.

It was Gershom Scholem who, in his 1937 article "A Good Deed [Mitzvah] That Comes through a Transgression," articulated the paradoxical and dialectical notions that were involved in the Kabbalah. The article became an influential milestone in the study of the theme of the holiness of sin in Jewish mysticism specifically and Jewish history in general. The following quote is a case in point:

> To put it differently, there was a touch of Zionism in the old Jewish mystics. They were not willing to let the Lord be. They opted for sharp reversal in the rules of fate. They were in a position similar to that which Zionists found themselves in relation to Orthodox Jewry. What the Orthodox Jews regarded as a transgression, the mystics and later the Zionists regarded as a mitzvah. In a way one could regard the State of Israel itself as "a mitzvah which comes through a transgression." The

Rabbis kept shouting "sin" but the Zionists went on with their transgressions until the results of a renascent Jewish state looked more like a
good deed ordained by God. (Gonen 1975, 287)

In the aftermath of the First World War, Rabbi Abraham Isaac Kook
looked with old kabbalistic eyes at "the-state-on-the-way" and did not
shout "sin." Rather, he saw in the Zionist buildup a messianic mitzvah
in the making.

As Ravitzky pointed out, Scholem claimed that the expulsion of the
Jews from Spain in 1492 served as the impetus for the later development
of the concept of the breaking of the vessels (1996, 106). It was therefore
actual historical events that were transfigured into cosmic events. But
not all scholars agree with this determination that the mundane symbolizes the cosmic, and Ravitzky himself concluded that Rabbi Kook
moved in the opposite direction: "The myth of the shattering and restoration of the sparks became, in his mind, a symbol of actual events in
the life of the nation and not the other way around" (1996, 106). This
was an activist stance. Holy doctrines of the past concerning cosmic origins were to be studied in order to understand what is actually going on
on earth now and in order to derive clues concerning what concrete
steps to take accordingly. What was going on was a seeming Zionist
destruction of faith but a construction of a forthcoming redemption.
Accordingly, what needed to be done was to cooperate with these new
secular Jews who were unwittingly serving God's divine design.

The horror of the Nazi Holocaust that was perpetrated during the
turbulent days of the Second World War catapulted the cataclysmic End
of Days time right into the present. The psychological roots of the collective German lust to annihilate lay in racial and "folkish" shared group
fantasies that incorporated anti-Semitism as an indispensable part of the
German identity and racist definition of self (Gonen 2000). For Jews,
however, the most rattling question was not what it was that was unique
to Germans but rather why the Jews were uniquely singled out for the
most thorough systematic and total destruction. As seen from Jewish
eyes, Hitler joined the ranks of Israel's other timeless enemies such as
Amalek and Haman. Did a cataclysmic disaster happen once more because the Jews had sinned once again? This would be the traditional
Jewish explanation of adverse fate. Some puzzled and increasingly
threatened Orthodox Jews remained stuck with this traditional albeit inadequate explanation. But there were also other ways of looking at how
it could have happened. It could also have happened because Jews

should have realized long ago that they had no business living among dangerous Gentiles and that they should have returned to Zion at least a century earlier. This would be the Zionist explanation.

The Holocaust was an event of such magnitude that it seemed to be a full-fledged fulfillment of the old threat of a messianic cataclysm that would precede redemption. Untold horrors of retail slayings and whole-sale exterminations to the sum of 6 million Jews made the scope of the murderous and barbarous destruction hard to even conceive. Just as in the creation of the world according to the Lurianic Kabbalah the vessels broke and the world ended up in a wrong state that requires reparation, so with the Holocaust the world of justice shattered. Taking the traditional concept of "for it is for our sins that we have been exiled from our land" and converting it into "for it is for our sins that we were afflicted by the Holocaust" would seem ludicrous. How many babies' skulls can be smashed and how many Jews can be gassed to death as just retribution for alleged sins? There have never been any Jewish sins that could even begin to justify the Holocaust as a deserved punishment. Only sick-minded anti-Semites believe that the Jews brought it upon themselves. There was therefore no justice. There could not be any justice. There was only a monstrous crime with perpetrators and victims. The Jews were the innocent victims. The Nazis were the perpetrators. But they were not the only ones. Someone had promised a horrendous cataclysm all along, and he has been notorious for his use of Gentile kingdoms as an instrument for carrying out his will.

Could Yahweh wash his hands of what took place? There is a telling joke about this issue. Two men meet, and one of them asks the other, "Did you hear that it is not true that God is dead?" The second man replies, "No, I did not." The first man then says, "He is alive and is retired in Argentina." It so happens that Argentina was notorious for being hospitable to many fleeing Nazis, who found refuge there. In this piece of macabre humor, God behaves like the run-of-the-mill Nazi perpetrator who escapes justice by escaping to Argentina. Psychologically speaking, the allusion to God as a perpetrator of the Holocaust is not as far-fetched as it might at first seem. After all, God is all-powerful. And, as Lord Acton's saying goes, "Power tends to corrupt and absolute power corrupts absolutely." His famous saying lends itself to suggestive conclusions. "The feeling of great power corrupts man. As we turn from man to man's projection, to the Lord of the Universe who was created in man's own image, we encounter the much envied image of an omnipotent being who has absolute power. If Lord Acton's dictum is correct then the Lord too should be most corrupt. He is indeed very power-ful and absolutely corrupt, but in such instances is known under such aliases as Satan, Devil etc." (Gonen 1978, 267–68).

The painful reality that there is no justice is sometimes expressed in the question, Where was God during the Holocaust? Believers were never able to come up with convincing answers. One notion to be floated around was that God was in Auschwitz suffering with his people. This sort of puts God on a par with the crying Messiah in heaven who was not allowed to appear and bring redemption and who could therefore only suffer like his people did. But what good is an all-powerful God who cannot prevent a Holocaust and who can therefore only join the helpless victims? Would they have been any worse off with a dead God rather than with a live God who is either impotent or evil?

For many persons, however, faith is indispensable, and the image of a living God must be preserved. An example of such a person was the German Jewish scholar of the gnosis, Hans Jonas. In an essay that was originally published in German in 1984, he dealt head-on with the problem of the concept of God after Auschwitz (Jonas 1994). Tradi-tionally, God was conceptualized as all-powerful, all-good, and com-prehensible to human beings. But after the evil of the Holocaust, a vi-able image of God could no longer sustain all three conceptualizations without exception. The fact that the Holocaust was allowed to happen indicated perforce that God either could not help it or actually willed it with an evil intent. Otherwise God becomes unintelligible to humans. Jonas suggested that the notions that God is not all-good or not com-prehensible thoroughly contradict the Jewish tradition. In contrast, the notion that God is not all-powerful is actually part of the Jewish mysti-cal tradition. The kabbalistic concept of "contraction," where God liter-ally shrunk himself to make room for creation (chapter 4), implies that by this withdrawal God gave up some of his powers. This conclusion led Jonas to speak about a suffering God who for his very own redemp-tion depends on the action of man.

Jonas maintained that his interpretation merely radicalized the no-tion of *tsimtsum* (contraction) of the Lurianic Kabbalah. His fascinating theological speculations were not directed at nonbelievers, for whom the harsh fact of the Holocaust does not contradict the notion of the nonexistence of God. The elaborate speculations were rather directed at those persons who adhered to the Jewish faith but needed to reconcile it with the horror of the Holocaust. For this purpose, however, his lines of reasoning were too intellectual, too reminiscent of formal logic, and much too philosophical to be able to satisfy the psychological needs of devout religious believers. What the latter need above all else are powerful but simple notions that provide absolute certainty that can be maintained, even if it violates the rules of formal logic and even when it flies in the face of reality. In the history of Judaism it has already been demonstrated that the more rationalistic Jewish philosophy has completely lost the competition for the hearts and minds of Jews to Jewish mysticism, be it Kabbalism or Hasidism.

In another attempt to protect the faith, the Jewish theologian Emil Fackenheim proposed adding a "614th commandment" to the existing 613 mitzvot stipulating that the Jews must survive, that they must remember the martyrs of the Holocaust, and that it is forbidden for Jews to deny or to despair of God. Failure to follow this commandment gives Hitler a posthumous victory (Fackenheim 1978, 19–24). Fackenheim may have reacted to an earlier remark by Isaac Deutscher, who stated: "It is a tragic and macabre truth that the greatest 'redefiner' of the Jewish identity has been Hitler; and this is one of his minor posthumous triumphs" (1968, 50). Clearly, Fackenheim was determined to deny Hitler a posthumous victory by not letting the Holocaust be the cause of Jews abandoning the Jewish faith. While seeing some sense in Fackenheim's new commandment to remember the victims, Peter Novick averred that "it would be an even greater posthumous victory for Hitler were we tacitly to endorse his definition of ourselves as despised pariahs by making the Holocaust the emblematic Jewish experience" (1999, 199, 281).

Moreover, for quite a while now there have been secular Jews, both before and after the Holocaust. Trying to deny them henceforward a secular option by emotionally blackmailing them to return to the fold seems suspect. It could be argued that such curbing of Jewish freedom of choice is actually self-defeating. It would actually be better not to drag Hitler's name at all into debates over Jewish identity or sectarian disputes.

For religious Jews, traditional modes of handling issues of justice were still available, although they were woefully inadequate. One could always escape into the good old blind submissive stance. The Lord understands the purpose of it all even as it eludes human understanding. Another traditional subterfuge was that a reward in heaven could always await those who suffered injustice on earth. From this vantage point the postdeath future could always rectify the scales of justice. Alternately, a present injustice may only seemingly be unjust because it represents current punishments not for present offenses but for past sins. This highly creative but past-oriented approach encompasses previous incarnations.

With reincarnation of souls coming into play, a seemingly unjust treatment in the present can still represent proper treatment for sins that were committed in previous incarnations.

This superstitious belief concerning justice is not new to Judaism, but its stunning application by Rabbi Ovadia Yosef to the Holocaust was nothing less than infuriating. In a live broadcast of his weekly sermon in Israel he made the following statement:

> The murdered people are reincarnated souls of sinners. All the horrors of the Holocaust, the unfortunate 6 million Jews, they all perished at the hands of the Nazis, may their name be eradicated, just like that for nothing? No. All this is the reincarnation of souls of previous people who sinned, who caused others to sin, and who committed all sorts of forbidden acts. [They] returned in a reincarnation in order to do reparation and thus received, the unfortunate ones, all those torments and troubles and deaths through which they were killed in the Holocaust. They are all reincarnated souls. It is not the first time in their lives that the souls appear. They came to atone for their sins. ("The Murdered Ones Are Reincarnated Souls of Sinners" 2000)

The ensuing public furor forced Rabbi Yosef to issue clarifications and retractions. But as is usually the case with such instances of damage control, the underlying true belief was reflected in the initial emotional outburst rather than in the subsequent response to criticism. The Judaic tradition contains legends and superstitions, including the reincarnation of souls. For some of those who literally believe in them, they come in handy in deflecting the ever-scorching question, Where was God during the Holocaust?

The Holocaust was a forceful reminder that sometimes there is no justice in the world. This grim realization put a greater pressure on religious rather than secular Jews. Religious persons, for whom there is a God, were stuck with the issue of where he was during the Holocaust. By contrast, secular Jews could see in the Holocaust an added and even greater justification for the self-initiated Zionist endeavor. In retrospect, the Zionist endeavor of taking fate into one's own hands seemed even more justified in the presence of a Holocaust but the absence of a helping God. But religious Jews who clung to their God were still left with the task of spelling out what possible sin against the Lord could have justified the infliction of a Holocaust. Some hard-pressed religious hardliners came up with an obscene answer. Zionism was the mortal sin. Its brazen embrace of forcing the end is what triggered the woeful punishment. This view was consistently held by the Satmar Hasidic rabbi

Moshe Teitelbaum. He and other like-minded religious hardliners have therefore been worried all along over what the zealous el kana would end up doing as his goyim-imitating children — the secular Zionists — persisted in forcing the end. They dreaded that evoking Yahweh's anger would end up badly. But even in their worst nightmares they probably did not imagine how bad it would really be. But once it happened, the religious hardliners were able to damn the pushy Zionists so as to give Yahweh a whitewash.

The destruction of the Holocaust was as big a cataclysm as they come or could be imagined. The Holocaust therefore seemed like the actual fulfillment of the old threat of a horrendous premessianic cataclysm that would precede redemption. It had an enormous impact on all Jews. For many religious Jews as well as for secular Jews who consciously or unconsciously subscribed to Yahweh's rules of history it created imminent expectations. Now that Yahweh had made good on his threat, it was time to hold him to his promise. He must not be allowed to renege on his IOU to deliver redemption in the aftermath of cataclysm. It was deemed unacceptable for the current generation to be shortchanged by Yahweh and to remain stuck as the generation of the Holocaust and nothing else. It was the prophetic duty of this tragic generation to evolve into "the generation of Holocaust and redemption," to use Menahem Begin's language.

Yahweh was able to come up with what amounted to a down payment on the promise of redemption. Aided by members of Jewish underground military organizations as well as by recent recruits from among newly arrived Holocaust survivors, Yahweh helped those who helped themselves. In the midst of war a Jewish state was reborn in 1948. David Ben Gurion, the founding father of the state, read the declaration of independence that proclaimed the establishment of the State of Israel. With this rebirth of the Third Jewish Commonwealth, the duality of Jewish psychohistory was reinforced anew. It now was the era of Holocaust and redemption, but in actuality it was only the beginning of redemption in the form of a mere down payment. The State of Israel was only a part of the larger inheritance of the forefathers — the Land of Israel. The Israeli national anthem, "The Hope," continues to express the hope "to be a free nation in our land." Although Israelis were already a free nation in the State of Israel, they were not yet a free nation in the larger Land of Israel. The messianic work of geographic expansion to the "borders of destiny" would still have to continue. As a schoolchild in the British Mandate of Palestine in the early 1940s, I was taught in geography class that there were actual current borders but that there were also borders of destiny that went back to biblical promises. The teacher left it unclear where exactly in Egypt and Jordan or Iraq these borders would run.

Yet this kind of forceful expansion in the face of Palestinian resistance, Arab objections, and international condemnations required the illusion of being a great power in order to be sustained. In 1967 the swift six-day Israeli victory over three Arab states triggered an unrealistic as well as arrogant intoxication with power. The result was the dazzling Israeli illusion of omnipotence following the Six-Day War (Gonen 1978). Tricky and largely unconscious psychological maneuvers enter into play here. A grab at omnipotence is usually implemented in a two-step procedure that ends up putting a lien on God's power. What begins in the first step of an utter humility of self before the might of God ends up in arrogating God's power for oneself. The utter humility of the self-prostrate person is not at all a helpless act. It reaffirms a special relationship to God and converts God into "my God," thus putting his powers at the disposal of the worshiper. Consequently, the hitherto most humble self becomes henceforward the mighty self that is capable of steering the Lord in certain directions. As psychoanalyst Sandor Rado put it: "My God is the One who will perform for my benefit, who will help me, and who will be, in other words, the executive agent of my omnipotence" (1969, 120). In some odd way this maneuver represents a variant of or a kosher form of de'hiqat haqets, that is, forcing the end. The Lord is being pushed and shoved in certain directions not by rebellious enemies who disdain him but by cajoling friends who love him. All this makes one wonder whether even an omnipotent being can get tired sometimes.

At the heart of what we call here "the kosher form of forcing the end" lies the conviction that it is permissible to compel God to act in certain ways by using the newly found might that is derived from God. Yahweh should not be allowed to wiggle out of a promise to deliver redemption in full. He who can deliver a premessianic cataclysm in full should not get away with delivering only a partial redemption. What is more, the delivery of a partial redemption in 1948 by means of a national resurrection, or tkumah, has exerted the additional price of bereavement, or shkhol, during the war of independence. This reinforced the underlying—albeit not fully verbalized—feeling that the balance sheet has not been evened. The father in Heaven still owed his children the delivery of redemption in full. Eventually, he was being aggressively held to his promise by some of his most ardent religious followers.

This happened after the Six-Day War of 1967. Now the Temple Mount itself was liberated. Rabbi Goren rushed there to blow the shofar, the sound of which is traditionally associated with the Messiah's imminent arrival. Great publicity was given to the fact that even secular Israeli soldiers cried at the Western Wall or were otherwise overcome by emotion. People could just about hear the footsteps of the Messiah.

Most important, Israel now controlled all the land west of the Jordan River. The State of Israel now seemed merely Small Israel. The possibility opened up for possessing more of the ancestral land and realizing a Greater Israel that stretches all the way from the Mediterranean to the Jordan River. A driving force in this messianic task was Rabbi Zvi Yehudah ha-Cohen Kook, son of Rabbi Abraham Isaac Kook. It was time to enlarge the State of Israel and establish the independent Land of Israel under Jewish control. Therefore, Rabbi Kook put a premium on the mitzvah of settling the land. The great victory of the Six-Day War, which came immediately after an anxious waiting period saturated by existential fears, was God-sent. A threat to survival was followed by a miraculous salvation as Yahweh continued his typical swinging act over the seesaw of fate. And his delivery was bountiful. The motherland of Zion west of the river Jordan was ready for possession. It could be claimed and cultivated and given new life by its messianically inflamed sons. And this time around, the husbanding of the motherland could be carried out with the massive support of state power. It could therefore be done in a fashion that would eclipse the piecemeal style of the previous Zionist efforts. The Arabs could be expected to put up a resistance, but a state government has many tools of power at its disposal in addition to an army, and the Six-Day War had just illustrated that the use of force was a very effective tool for handling Arabs.

Clearly, there was something expansionistic about the old messianic dream, which had not yet run its full course. The inherent logic of it is no mystery and was shared by both religious and secular militant nationalists. The immediate task at hand was to solidify Jewish control over the sovereign Western Land of Israel. The time for the Eastern Land of Israel, that is, the Transjordan, could come later. It was not forgotten that it too was the inheritance of the forefathers belonging to the tribes of Gad and Reuben as well as half of the Manasseh tribe. God could provide a propitious opportunity at a later date. After converting the entire west side of the Jordan into a Jewish state, a productive cataclysm, perhaps in the form of another war, could find the Israeli army as the new master of Jordan. This would be the time to recall the line taken from the anthem of the Beitar youth movement of the militant Revisionist wing of the Zionist movement: "The Jordan has two banks. This one is ours and this one also." This could therefore be the final opportunity to revive a Jewish kingdom in the complete Land of Israel on both banks of the Jordan.

But things did not work out that way. For good reasons, the Arabs did not cooperate at all, and, seemingly, neither did Yahweh. But there was a psychological readiness among those persons who were imbued by either religious or secular Messianism to hurl themselves at history and grab whatever opportunity comes their way.

Rabbi Zvi Yehudah Kook focused on the conquest and settlement of the land. His stance consisted of a political radicalism that stemmed from an underlying perception of a historical necessity (Ravitzky 1996, 131). In other words, it was destined to succeed because it was part and parcel of the inevitable messianic evolution as ordained by what we previously termed "my God." God's almighty power was therefore going to prop up the activities of the messianic settlers. As Rabbi Zvi Yehudah Kook put it:

> "The Glory of Israel does not deceive or change His mind" [1 Samuel 15:29]. We are stronger than America, stronger than Russia. With all the troubles and delays [we suffer], our position in the world, the world of history, the cosmic world, is stronger and more secure in its timelessness than theirs. There are nations that know this, and there are nations of uncircumcised heart that do not know it, but they shall gradually come to know it! Heaven protect us from weakness and timidity. . . . In our divine, world-encompassing undertaking, there is no room for retreat. (Ravitzky 1996, 132)

In short, God is by definition "my God" because he is "the Glory of Israel" rather than of other nations. And he sustains the Jewish position in a timelessness that is rooted in the true cosmic world that dictates historical inevitability.

Translating Rabbi Zvi Yehudah Kook's theories into a succinct operational definition, one could sum it up as "the Lord's Torah is complete, and so is the Land of Israel." The main implication of this assertion was that just as no part of the Torah could ever be given up, neither could any part of the Land of Israel. This was a messianic message that anticipated the imminent reign of God's law in the reclaimed and sovereign Land of Zion, Jerusalem. Naturally, it put a premium on the mitzvah of settling the land that is actually not listed among the traditional mitzvot. This new mitzvah, however, was the meeting ground for religious as well as secular militant nationalists. They all agreed that aggressive settlement activity must be diligently pursued. On the surface the joint venture may seem like a mere marriage of convenience. The secular nationalists agreed with their religious cohorts on settling the land for now but deferred the issue of the complete rule of life by Torah law for later, at which time they would register their noncompliance. Meanwhile, in the here and now the religious nationalists placed a Jewish kosher stamp upon their secular cohorts by considering that whoever keeps the one mitzvah of settling the land keeps all the mitzvot. The mutual affection that stemmed from the shared messianic aspiration contributed a certain quality of warmth to the marriage of convenience.

But the two-pronged realization of the messianic goals of complete Torah rule in a complete land carried with it the seeds of coercion. Complete Torah rule could lead to the coercion of Jews. They would have to give up the democratic option of remaining secular. And a complete Land of Israel could lead to the coercion of Arabs. They would have to give up their right to have their own country and possibly even the right to inhabit the land.

The vision of Torah law applying to the Jewish population of Israel was common to most religious factions. It was hoped that Jewish education of the secular part of the population would prepare their hearts for an eventual voluntary acceptance of keeping the commandments. The late Israeli minister of education, Zevulun Hammer, loved to refer to these educational efforts as "everything by soothing words, not by a beating stick." But the growing encroachment of religion on politics in Israel and the growing predilection in the religious sector to use the law so as to impose its ways made it clear that down the road lies the prospect of a massive coercion. It was sometimes referred to as being in danger of becoming a "Jewish Khomeinistan," a reference to fundamentalist Iran under the late Ayatollah Khomeini.

The Jewish messianic field of vision reclaiming the complete land for the revival of the old glory of Zion did not leave much room for Arabs. These aspirations gave rise to new militant interpretations of the old notion of transfer of populations. The transfer of Jews from Arab lands to Israel was regarded as mostly, though not entirely, completed. But most of the transfer of Arabs from Israel to other Arab lands still needed to be accomplished. The transfer idea is seemingly patterned after previous population exchange models such as the one that was concluded in a separate agreement that accompanied the 1923 Treaty of Lausanne. In the aftermath of a war between Turkey and Greece during

1922–23, this treaty provided for the compulsory exchange of nearly 1.5 million Greeks, 800,000 Turks, and 80,000 Bulgarians, all of whom were transferred to their respective countries but failed to adjust well to their changed circumstances. But the deeper roots of the idea are far more ancient. Israel is the biblical Promised Land of the Jews, not the Arabs. The Arabs had no right to make Israel their home, even though they had lived there for more than a thousand years and their third most holy religious site was in Jerusalem. A fulfillment of the old biblical promise would require clearing the land of Arabs by means of a transfer. How was this to be accomplished? Preferably by an approach similar to "everything by soothing words, not by a beating stick," but this phrase was reserved for Jews. Instead the promoters of transfer used to talk about how the Arabs on their own accord would come to realize that it is really better for them to leave. Somehow one gets the impression that in this mysterious process of an Arab change of heart the stick was going to play a very large role.

The idea of transfer has had many advocates during the years—some of them better known and some less so. Two of the most vociferous advocates—religious nationalistic hawk Rabbi Meir Kahane and tourism minister Rehavam Ze'evi—were murdered by Arabs. For Kahane, transfer was an integral part of the more general messianic call: "The call of the hour is to 'drive out all the land's inhabitants' (Num. 33:52). Woe to us for having dealt treacherously with the Land and its owner, G-d! Through our fear of the nations, we have refused to conquer the Land by banishing the enemies and revilers of Israel, the lowly Ishmaelites" (Kahane 1998, 995). As for Ze'evi, he was a secular nationalistic hawk who originally rose from the leftist ranks of Labor. In spite of being nicknamed "Gandhi" because of his appearance, he was anything but a Gandhian who espouses nonviolence. Throughout most of his political career he advocated a forceful expulsion of the Arabs as a preemptive measure to prevent them from doing the same to the Jews. These days Kahane's and Ze'evi's places have been taken by Benny Elon, one of the leaders of the Moledet (Homeland, literally, Birthland) party who succeeded Ze'evi as tourism minister. Elon's transfer hopes are pinned on closing Arab universities and making life so difficult for Arabs that they would want to leave. The advocates of transfer find added justification for their position in the demographic projections of a geographer from Haifa, Professor Arnon Sofer, who does not actually advocate transfer. Sofer's great concern is the demographic danger of Arabs becoming a majority in Israel. Consequently, he might advocate a modified position in which transfer serves as a backup plan in case a "separation" attempt of Jews from Arabs fails (Musco 2001). But many persons among the militant settlers continue to adhere to the notion of transfer as the primary plan rather than as the backup plan.

There is no lack of historical irony in all these developments. It was an aggressive and expansionistic militant stance that got Israelis after the Six-Day War to inject Jewish settlements into the midst of heavily populated Arab areas. This activity, which was designed to preempt a Palestinian state, has continued in full force even under Labor governments and even throughout the days of the Oslo peace process. As a result the map of the Arab part of the West Bank, which was sprinkled with Jewish settlements, has come to resemble a sieve. Add to this the numerous bypass roads, and the entire Arab area has been subdivided into so many enclaves that it cannot possibly function as an independent state. So far the Palestinians have responded to these aggressive incursions with two intifadas. The Jewish behavior is driven by a messianic urge that is either oblivious to or overrides compunction about the dispossession of another people, and it has fueled militant occupation policies.

Transfer was the most militant plan of them all. Merely biting bigger chunks out of the West Bank to be incorporated into Israel was somewhat less militant. When the Arab violent reaction to Israeli militancy made life too uncomfortable for Israelis, a clamor for a unilateral separation built up momentum. Yet for a long time nothing came out of the suggestion to impose a separation through a protective fence because of the political fears that it would be interpreted as a border and put a limit on expansionistic dreams. But in 2003, under the impact of increased Palestinian suicide bombings, the building of a wall began in earnest at the expense of more confiscation of Palestinian lands. Its planned major incursion into the West Bank in order to protect the Ariel settlement has become a bone of contention between the Israelis and the Americans.

Many Israelis feel that should separation fail to stop Arab bombardments of Jewish towns, then it would be time to go back to transfer as an ultimate solution. So what we have here is the dialectics of how to intrude upon the Arabs without paying the cost of being mingled with them. And in this dilemma of a search for a clean intrusion, transfer forms a preemptive defense that would prevent mingling to begin with. The Land of Zion would be emptied of its Arab intruders. Separation remains an ad hoc defense in case transfer is not carried out. But should separation fail, then transfer becomes a backup defense of last resort.

After Israelis were stressed to the extreme by the escalating violence of the al-Aqsa intifada, the idea of transfer gained in popularity during the last quarter of 2001 and the first quarter of 2002. More than one third of Israelis saw some merit in the basic notion. Ideas to be floated around included extreme plans such as transferring all the Palestinians west of the Jordan or transferring Israeli Arabs who live within the old pre-1967 green line to evacuated Jewish settlements across that line. Needless to say, there were plenty of Israelis such as Knesset member Avraham Burg and Holocaust researcher Yehuda Bauer who condemned these notions as morally utterly reprehensible. Among national religious Jews who had been mostly quiet on the subject up to then a new discourse arose concerning how to interpret the old transfer stories in the book of Joshua (Pfeffer 2002). Clearly, under the mounting pressure of the second Palestinian intifada, more Israelis were resorting to transfer as an answer.

It is true that the Israelis have to deal with very difficult neighbors. In the tragic Middle East the Palestinians have almost never missed an opportunity to miss an opportunity. But it is also true that the Israelis have missed a few opportunities on their own by rejecting King Hussein of Jordan's plan for federation with the West Bank or by dismissing President Sadat of Egypt's declarations before the Yom Kippur War that he would be willing to sign a peace treaty with Israel. Thus, on more than one occasion, a messianically inflamed territorial hunger overrode Israeli reason and prevented a possible political compromise.

"Transfer" is a euphemism for "expulsion." It aims to achieve ethnic cleansing by the less lethal method of expulsion rather than extermination. It is abhorrent that Jews could entertain such an idea and talk about it while at the very same time carry the memory of the historical trauma of the expulsion of the Jews from Spain. For many non-Jews the year 1492 stands for the discovery of America, which symbolizes expanding horizons. For Jews, however, it is the traumatic year of the expulsion from Spain that signals the imposition of geographic limits and the restriction of Jewish opportunities. But God forbid that this trauma ever be called "the transfer from Spain." It is true that Spanish Jews never threatened their host country as the Arabs have threatened Israel. But the Palestinians were not settled in a host country, with the Israelis engaged in a national clash with them as a result of the Zionist endeavor. Ultimately, the situation calls for a political settlement rather than for the impossible military solution of a clash. "Transfer" represents an envisioned solution by military means fueled in part by messianic yearnings turned lethal. What is more, Orwellian "Newspeak" does not make "transfer" of Arabs less painful than "expulsion" of Jews.

Throughout the second half of the twentieth century, the experience of sharing in state power had a radical impact on Orthodox Jews in Israel. As the actual power wielded by the religious sector steadily increased, so did their Messianism. Being able to apply the financial resources and the legal and military power tools of an actual state to Jewish education, on the one hand, and to reclamation of the "liberated" land, on the other hand, transformed the messianic experience and expectations. The messianic experience was now characterized by the application of Jewish force, including the use of the gun, mostly against Arabs but occasionally against Jews as well. This was the case with violent suppressions of Jewish peace demonstrators or with the murder of Israeli prime minister Yitzhak Rabin. And the messianic expectation was that the actual historical efforts to realize the messianic goals would bear fruit in historic time. In other words, it was something imminent rather than something that would happen in the End of Days. The old conviction that in reality the Messiah would never come (see chapter 2) now seemed largely a thing of the past; it was considered to be the product of powerless exiled Jews. One could therefore speak of a "new Messianism" as compared to the "old Messianism." Rachlevsky discussed how Messianism swept the majority of the Israeli religious society under its wing (2000, 141). He underscored the fact that this current society represents a religious reality that is radically different even from that of the recent past of the early years of the Israeli state, since it consists of a totally new theological and cultural creation in the history of Judaism. According to Rachlevsky, this "messianic fermentation" in Israel increased by leaps and bounds during the 1990s with the growing conviction that "we are the army, we are the state, and God is with us" (2000, 279).

The kabbalistic symbolism of the opposition between the left side and the right side played an important role in the Jewish messianic radicalization of the last decade of the twentieth century (Rachlevsky 2000, 227–29). It was Rabbi Abraham Isaac Kook who understood earlier in the twentieth century that the activities of secular Zionism represented the beginning of a reparation process that would lead to the inclusion of the impure left in the holy right. At the end of the century, the connection between the Israeli political "Left" and the cosmic left side was repeatedly drawn in the religious print and broadcast media. Rabbi Eliezer Schach went as far as to issue a religious edict that the "rule of persecutor" *(din rodef)* applies to the modern Jewish Left. The implication was that since the political Left represents the cosmic snake and the cosmic left side, whose influence prevents Jewish souls from going to heaven, its members might even be killed sometimes for being persecutors of Jews. All this illustrates how potent old myths can be symbolically applied to current political activities so as to infuse them with explosive dynamism. Speaking of old symbols, Rachlevsky underscored the old equation of Abraham the patriarch with "benevolence" and of his son Isaac with "judgment." Therefore, the biblical story of the "binding of Isaac" represented the subjugation of the left side (stern judgment) by the right side (benevolence). The same rationale applies equally well to the binding of the modern Isaac—Yitzhak Rabin, the assassinated prime minister of Israel who promoted the Oslo peace process. This seemingly heinous murder too enabled the "benevolent" right to dominate the "sinful" left.

There is a distinct totalitarian strand in the messianic ambition to impose an all-inclusive reign of holiness that has been purified of all contamination and impurities. Uriel Tal underscored this idea in his 1984 article on the foundations of political Messianism in Israel. The purification of holiness impacts both time and place. It converts current historical time into ultimate messianic time when the End of Days events are unfolding. It also takes the holiness that is symbolized by special places and attributes it to the places themselves. The result is the sanctification of Jewish sovereignty over occupied territories. Moreover, time and place, being totally existential categories, mandate the cleansing of foreigners from the land. Very poignantly so, Tal noticed the similarity of such ideas to certain doctrines that were promoted by twentieth-century totalitarian movements. He therefore condemned this kind of "mystical realism" based on a totalistic worldview that encompasses holiness and secularism, religion and politics, heaven and earth, and privileges and duties. It is a mystical unity based on an underlying duality—the attribution of holiness to the empirical political reality. And in this messianic outlook, "just as the purified land is redeemed from foreigners, so the purified personality is redeemed of foreignness" (Tal 1984). In a way it seems that there is nothing new under the sun. The preoccupation with impurity is as old as human history and reached monstrous heights in Nazi psychology (Gonen 2000, 99–136). Impurity implies a malevolent dualism of the pure and impure. It therefore gives rise to monistic yearnings for a thoroughly cleansed and consequently all-good holiness. As Tal put it: "It is thus possible to conclude that we face a political Messianism in which the individual, the people, and the land reach an organic unity under the wings of an absolute holiness." All this is very dangerous.

Jewish legend has it that in the sixteenth century the kabbalist Rabbi Judah Löw ben Bezalel of Prague created a golem, a humanoid made of clay who could be activated by placing God's divine name, YHWH, in his mouth. The golem used his superior powers to help the Jews. Unfortunately, one Friday the rabbi forgot to extricate the piece of paper on which the divine name was written from the golem's mouth. As the Sabbath drew near the golem grew agitated and threatened to destroy everything in his path. The rabbi was summoned from the synagogue and managed to extricate the divine name from the golem's mouth. The golem fell lifeless to the ground, and the rabbi never again revived that mass of clay. In the past Orthodox Jews looked at Zionism and its emphasis on secular nationalism as a new golem who posed a grave danger (Gonen 1975, 317-19). Now the tables have turned. With the stunning rise of a new Messianism in the State of Israel, it is the secular Israelis who now fear that they have inspired the creation of a new kind of golem—Orthodox Jews in the service of the Messiah.

There has always been something oppressive in Yahweh's harsh rules of messianic history with its apocalyptic cataclysm still to come in an undetermined time of the end. It produced discontent and the latching on to biblical phrases in search of escape clauses. A particular opportunity for creative interpretations presented itself in the wording of Isaiah 60:22:

> The small one will become a thousand,
>   and the young one a big nation;
> I am Yahweh;
>   in its time I will hasten it.

The first part of the verse is a promise of redemption. The second part promises that, when the time of redemption comes, God will not take his sweet time but will rather deliver it with all due speed. Thus Isaiah's statement refers to one redemption time and not to two or even multiple redemption times. But God's constraints are too oppressing, and Jews like to have more options available. Creative "readings" of the biblical texts may acquire the force of law and compel even the Lord himself to yield to the interpretative fine print that was added to the text. This happened during talmudic times, when Isaiah's wording was taken to imply two alternate redemption times, the first one delivery "in its time" and the second one an earlier "I will hasten it" delivery. Meir Kahane embraced with a passion these early reinterpretations of the Bible since they opened up the option of an earlier redemption devoid of the long-dreaded premessianic cataclysms.

Emphasizing that every day and every moment can be the appointed time for redemption, Kahane went back to talmudic sources:

> Such is the intent of *Sanhedrin* 98a:
> *R. Yehoshua ben Levi raised a contradiction. "It says, 'in Its time' and it says 'I will hasten It' [Isaiah 60:22 states, 'I the L-rd, will hasten it in its time,' and this is puzzling, for how can there be a fixed time for redemption, as is implied by 'in its time,' while at the same time G-d 'hastens it'? The Talmud answers:] If they are meritorious, G-d hastens it. Otherwise, it will be in its time."* (1998, 785)

So God's redemptive acts and their particular timings depend on what the Jews do. God's determination of whether the Jews have been "meritorious" indeed must depend on previous Jewish actions. This was the opening that Kahane needed. He was now free to elaborate a messianic doctrine of more numerous options that depended on Jewish action.

Correct Jewish actions could only come out of a renewed Jewish consciousness that was born of repentance. Repentance, a major tenet of the Jewish heritage, had already been emphasized in article 8 of *The Book of Beliefs and Opinions* of the tenth-century Babylonian rabbi Saadiah Gaon (1880, 157–58) on which Kahane relied. He did not bother to mention, however, that in the same discussion Saadiah Gaon went on to state that God's angel refused to explicate to Daniel what the meaning was of "in a time of times and a half" (see chapter 2), for sound reasons. Unlike wise persons, who seek their reward in the next world, credulous and naive persons are likely to misuse such knowledge and quickly desire earthly rule and honor. This was not a point that Kahane cared to emphasize, but he did underscore that repentance could result in corrective Jewish actions that would spare Jews the dreaded premessianic cataclysms. As Kahane put it: "If Israel merit it through the right acts of repentance, the war of Masshiach ben Yosef will end in speedy, glorious victory, without Messianic birthpangs" (1998, 924). Repentance must, however, "be complete with total submission to the Supreme Master, His sovereignty and mitzvoth." Then the Jewish lot will be pleasant—"the full redemption, in an instant, without Messianic birthpangs" (Kahane 1998, 780–81). In this formulation there is no such thing as a free lunch for anyone—not for each and every Jew, who need to resume keeping all the commandments in total submission to God so as to turn him into what we earlier called "my God," and not for the poor God himself, who may now be compelled not only to hasten the end but also to deliver it without its major punch line — the dreaded birth pangs of the Messiah, or *hevlai mashiah*.

In an implicit bargaining game with the Lord, Kahane evolved a theory of extending the deadlines of redemption:

> If Israel are unworthy of redemption "in haste," redemption devoid of terrible Messianic birthpangs, G-d, in His great mercy, will try to delay, so as to avoid bringing the world redemption "in its time." Like a merciful father, G-d extends His deadline again and again in hopes of His children repenting and returning to Him, so that He, in turn, can return to them instantaneously, in glory and majesty. (1998, 860–61)

Kahane thus influenced God's character, giving the edge to el ra'hum ve'hanun over el kana in his treatment of his children. In the process the anger and disappointment over the delayed arrival of the Messiah is assuaged by the knowledge that the extended deadlines are in effect the act of a merciful God. So merciful is he that he will pull off the extension gimmick as many times as necessary in order to insure that the punishing redemption "in its time" is avoided and that the pain-free "I will hasten it" redemption would inevitably come. His great benevolence thus amounts to a sabotage of Yahweh's own rules of history, which put a premium on premessianic cataclysms. What more could one ask for?

The anger over the constantly delayed redemption is therefore redirected at the errant children. As God delays his anger and grants one extension after the other, his children fail to realize that he postpones the terrible punishment in hopes of Israel repenting. The result is that the very fact that "the admonisher has blown the warning trumpet so often" and his warnings remain unfulfilled "makes Israel view G-d's warning with contempt" (Kahane 1998, 868–70). All that the people of Israel need to do in order to annul the postponements of redemption as well as to cancel its premessianic cataclysmic clause is follow a simple bargain. They need to observe all the commandments and follow the difficult Torah laws. As Kahane put it: "If we do not just study them mechanically but engage in difficult, discouraging toil, in faith and trust in G-d, which is what G-d yearns for, then He will bring redemption instantaneously" (1998, 862). There is the essence of the whole divine bargain. Give God total submission, which he yearns for, and in return have a share in his omnipotence.

Kahane's Messianism represents the most extreme manifestation of a fairly novel form that is sometimes called "Messianism with a gun." As Jews are finally able to be as well armed as goyim, the time arrives for them to apply force of arms in the service of the messianic cause. This belief of Kahane influenced his disciple Baruch Goldstein with very tragic results. In 1994 Goldstein ended up spraying bullets at Arabs who were kneeling in prayer in a Hebron mosque. In a typical mockery of justice the Israeli authorities imposed a curfew on the victimized Palestinian residents of Hebron rather than use this opportunity to evacuate the small and troublesome Jewish settlement there. The motivation of Baruch Goldstein received an excellent analysis by B. Z. Kedar (1994), who fleshed out the influential impact of Kahane's doctrines. Of central importance was Kahane's identification of the degradation of exile with "profanation of the name." By contrast, the return to Zion and the establishment of a state and an army represent "sanctification of the name." By transferring these two traditional Jewish concepts into the domain of power, Kahane ended up with the endorsement and even sanctification of revenge. By oppressing the Jews, the goyim are profaning the name. By taking vengeance on the goyim, the Jews sanctify the name. And if this Jewish action evoked an even harsher Gentile retaliation, then God would stop it by ushering in an "I will hasten it" redemption. A sanctification of the name by means of a vengeful act upon the goyim is therefore a way of forcing God's hand. It goads him to implement a speedy redemption by giving him the excuse to carry out that which he wants to do to begin with (Kahane 1998, 927–28). According to Kedar, this kind of rationale led Goldstein to sacrifice his life in a "sanctification of the name in a mosque." It was Purim time, that is, time for executing vengeance upon Gentiles. And it was the month of Ramadan, a perfect time for insuring that Arab reaction would reach the height of rage. Goldstein, the student, fulfilled his rabbi's dictum that "there will be no 'hasty' redemption . . . unless the Jewish people . . . are ready to sanctify His name through self-sacrifice" (Kahane 1998, 809).

Another notorious case of Messianism with a gun was the murder of Prime Minister Yitzhak Rabin by Yigal Amir in 1995. It was an attempt to kill not just one person but also an entire political process. The Oslo peace process was based on the principle of "territories for peace." But some fanatic Jews regarded this principle as a betrayal of the messianic process of redeeming the complete Land of Israel for the Jews. Some hotheaded rabbis were willing to affirm that *din rodef* as well as *din mosser* applied to Rabin. The first is the rule concerning a persecutor who is in hot pursuit of somebody in order to kill him. Killing a rodef is allowed because it saves the lives of his would-be victims. The second is the rule concerning someone who hands Jews over to their enemies or to the hostile authorities, thus putting their lives in jeopardy. It is permissible to kill him too in order to save lives. Neither of these rules is part of Israeli state law. In consequence, rabbis who are willing to pass such rules place themselves above the authority of the state. But for the messianically inflamed, Torah law and God's divine intentions stand above state law and state policy. And when it comes to Messianism with a gun, rabbinic rules can be executed through the execution of people. Yigal Amir did not divulge who were the rabbis who issued the specific rulings, and the desire by the Orthodox camp in Israel to find out was truly underwhelming.

Lots of water has flowed in the river Jordan since the end of the nineteenth century, when the secular Messianism of Zionism made its appearance largely on the European scene. Secular Messianism latched on to the old messianic yearnings while despairing of a weak and impotent Yahweh. It therefore injected the old dreams with a new vigor that stemmed from true political and material power. Being secular, it was free to emulate the ways of the goyim, whose strength lay not in their God or his Son but in their earthly ways of wielding power. By beginning to accumulate concrete earthly power and injecting themselves into the Gentile game of nations, the Jews have "returned to history."

The reaction to all this in Orthodox Jewish quarters ranged from utter rejection and condemnation to co-opting the Zionists and seeing the hidden hand of God looming behind Zionist activities. The Holocaust accentuated the chasm between those who regarded Zionism as the sin of forcing the end that brought about the Holocaust as punishment and those who regarded Zionism as the only solution to the precarious existence of the Jews. The creation of the State of Israel reinforced the tendency to view Zionist activities as the unfolding of God's divine plan. The Six-Day War of 1967, which put Greater Israel west of the Jordan within Jewish grasp, catapulted the messianic fever of both secular and Orthodox Jews to new heights. But many in the secular section of the Israeli population were growing tired of the high costs of trying to retain control over the entire land by lording it over the neighboring people who were settled there and who were only becoming more and more antagonistic and militant.

History was heading toward a moment of truth. Quite a few Israelis were willing to give up on total fulfillment of the messianic dream and settle for a "Small Israel" but a peaceful and a democratic one. This is where the militant activists of religious Messianism jumped into the fray to take the lead. Sensing the growing weakness of secular Messianism, they were determined to infuse it with Godly power in order to reinvigorate it. Then it could fulfill the messianic mission of possessing a Great Israel. The fruits of the Six-Day War could still be gathered in full, and God's hand would no longer have to remain hidden. With possession of the complete land would come the adherence by all to God's eternal Torah and divine law. Democracy would become a non sequitur. The Arabs will dissipate one way or another. God will find a way. And soon the age of miracles will dawn as all the nations on earth acknowledge Yahweh as the one and only God. It was time to push hard to force the end, and this included the use of arms. The age of Messianism with a gun has arrived. And the holy use of the gun was not merely the calling of individual fanatics but the task of the group.

The new Messianism that flowered in the 1990s is a dangerous golem, or a Jewish version of Frankenstein's monster. It could eradicate democracy. It could coerce all Israelis to lead a Jewish fundamentalist way of life, and it could also expel the Arabs. It is even conceivable that it could plunge the Middle East into an apocalyptic war that involves weapons of mass destruction. It therefore courts the ultimate disaster, thus giving Yahweh his chance to deliver the kind of terrible premessianic cataclysm that would make the messianic aftermath worthless. Although most Israelis and Jews are not Kahane types, the underlying logic of their belief systems and shared fantasies has the potential of escalating into a more fanatic form of Messianism. Even many persons who consider themselves as "secular" still subscribe to Yahweh's blueprint of history for the sake of a cohesive group identity. They therefore retain the potential of regressing to extreme behaviors whenever the group experiences national crises.

Perhaps the greatest historical irony of all is the certain resemblance between all this and some of the tenets of Nazi ideology. A messianically run Jewish state would not be democratic but totalitarian. It would homogenize its inhabitants through coercive fundamentalist practices. And as it expands settlement activities to the entire land it would engage in ethnic cleansing of the "foreign" Arabs. Unlike the Nazis of old, the Jewish clerical fascists of the future are likely to do this not by mass exterminations and gas ovens but through forced expulsion. The new Messianism with a gun would be capable of making the Arabs an offer they could not refuse. Expansion of the land, homogenization of the people, and purification from foreigners is a well-known ideological bundle that characterizes Nazi psychology (Gonen 2000, 99–136).

The Israeli Messianism with a gun is a new golem on the loose. Meant to add to Jewish power, it could end up destroying the Jews themselves. Where are the rabbis with the necessary foresight and courage to extricate the ineffable name from the golem's mouth?

CHAPTER 7

Alternatives

Once upon a time a vulnerable Yahweh acquired exclusive possession over the most precious of all peoples—the ancient Hebrews. They became his chosen people or, one might say, his transitional object, serving as a source of security for him without which he would have been at a loss. In turn he became the talisman of the chosen people. They therefore possessed a magical object that was to serve as a guarantee of ultimate success in facing the dangers of life.

But the mutual security bargain between Yahweh and the ancient Israelites turned out to be flawed. The Israelites had a predilection for turning to other gods, thus calling into question Yahweh's basic assumption that they were exclusively his precious object and likely perpetuating his sense of basic insecurity. Both sides were therefore more than a bit problematic. Only too frequently the Israelites were unfaithful, and Yahweh was a breached entity that could offer only inadequate protection against dangers that he engendered in the first place. Consequently, Yahweh, true to his inner duality, trapped his errant people into specific rules of Jewish history that locked them into ever-recurrent cataclysms of a messianic fate.

This was an enormous psychological burden for Jews. It is difficult to deal with a neurotic God of shifting moods who every so often explodes in an uncontrolled rage that suggests an underlying psychotic core. Eventually, the impossible task of incessantly trying to appease him took the form of an obsessive-compulsive adherence to a plethora of talmudic regulations that truly stultified the spontaneity of life. Very poignantly, psychohistorian Avner Falk characterized the Talmud as "a monument to obsessional thinking" that enabled Jews to avoid having "to grapple with the pain of Jewish life as a defeated, subdued and oppressed minority in their own land" (1996, 334). This was indeed the purpose of the much too complex law. But all the submission rituals of the world, no matter how compulsively enacted, could not placate Yahweh. For Jews, therefore, navigating through life resembled an attempt to walk in between drops of rain without getting wet. And there was more to it than the sheer impossibility of placating Yahweh. Because of his inherent duality, it was very difficult to figure out what kind of person he is or what it would take to placate him. Because of his contradictory nature, no amount of submission could guarantee that he would be appeased. It is no wonder that throughout the generations Jews have sought ways to escape this psychological oppression.

In the course of history several alternatives presented themselves. The oldest was probably reverting back to polytheism. Monotheism has been traditionally considered as a great conceptual improvement over polytheism. People used to think that the wind was created by a wind god, the sun by a sun god, and that trees and animals and hills were all created by gods that were specific to them. The realization that there is an underlying common regulation of the diverse phenomena of this world did represent a conceptual step forward. In time, however, science took over this task, while the monotheistic faiths, with their sets of eternal unchanging verities, have gotten more and more in the way of a free scientific enquiry into the underlying laws of nature.

On a social and political level the switch from polytheism to monotheism has had a detrimental effect that is frequently ignored. In the world of multiple gods a ruling group that temporarily becomes top dog militarily does not have to insist that subjugated peoples must abandon their local gods. There was therefore plenty of room for religious diversity. But with the triumph of monotheism there was less tolerance for diversity. Since there is only one God, and since each group's one God is the one and only true God, a holy duty emerges to eradicate other faiths and doctrines that must necessarily be false. The claim that one's truth is an ultimate dimension that should apply to all produces a license to tamper with the beliefs of others and to coerce other people's thinking. In other words, in the name of "absolutes" a fascistlike tendency toward mind control can easily put a curb on political and social tolerance. Unfortunately, every so often this totalitarian streak in monotheism has been historically acted upon with great cruelty, not least by Christianity.

One thing, however, is clear. In olden times, as the Israelites followed other gods, they temporarily escaped Yahweh's strict control of the rules of history. Yahweh was angered by their rebellious point of view and kept telling them what would happen to them at the end. But those who adopted other gods, sometimes even including Yahweh too in their pantheon of diverse gods, could see themselves as being safely out of his sole jurisdiction. At the time there was a double benefit attached to either the renewed or continued recourse to polytheism. For one thing, all of Yahweh's threats of horrendous ultimate punishments could be thrown out the window. For another, fertility cults could be savored once again, and ravishing contact with the missing fulfillments that come from the feminine side could be resumed.

It was difficult to deal with Yahweh because of his conflicted personality, which produced abrupt switches from one behavior to its opposite. This was confusing, and it was also hard to reconcile all this within the framework of a sole supreme being who is self-contradictory. Correlating the deity with its impacts on the world could be made simpler if there were two deities, one good and one bad, to begin with. Ongoing changes in both the good and the bad of this world could then be attributed to the shifting fate of the everlasting battle between the good God and the bad one. This is the doctrine of dualism or the two domains. It did not represent an evolution from polytheism into having just two gods but was instead the modification of monotheism from having a single God to having two Gods. The concept of two Gods may not make much sense from the standpoint of formal logic, but it is psychologically palatable. It answers the question of the origins of evil in this world and frees the worshiper from the need to address a single and conflicting God whose behavior is puzzling. With this conceptualization things may not be any better than they were before, but they seemingly make more sense. Understanding, even that which one cannot change, frees one from puzzlement, self-blame, or guilt and brings greater comfort.

Dualism exerted an influence on Judaism and was therefore subsequently fought by Jewish scholars. The thirteenth-century Jewish physician from France, Jacob Anatoli, wrote the homiletic work *A Goad to Scholars,* in which he objected to the belief in two domains because it cancels the principle of reward and punishment. He called this belief "foolishness." Moreover, he disputed the idea that the angel Samael enjoys independence vis-à-vis God, that he rules over demons, and that he became Lucifer (Anatoli 1866, 2, 173, 182). Nevertheless, Samael and his demons displayed great staying power and continued to be popular among Jews, especially members of Hasidic movements. Similarly, in the *Book of Principles* (pt. 2, chap. 13), the fifteenth-century Jewish scholar Joseph Albo objected to the influential ideas of Mani and his followers, who during the third century A.D. founded in Persia the new religion of Manichaeanism, which postulated a primal struggle between God's realm of spirituality and Satan's realm of matter. Albo rejected their two-domains hypothesis, which explained the presence of good and evil in this world by postulating two separate origins. In contrast, Albo underscored the notion that both the good urge and the bad urge came from God—the good urge to ensure the immortality of the individual soul and the bad urge to secure the continuation of the species (Albo 1893, 136–37). That was his answer to the issue of good and evil as he tried to battle with the traces of Manichaean influences on Judaism.

The allure of dualism was already noticeable in talmudic time during the second century A.D., as can be learned from Massechet (tractate) Chagigah of the Talmud. (In the following discussion quotes are taken from the English translation in the Soncino Talmud CD-ROM edition.) The general context is the severe restrictions placed on the teaching of mystical topics, especially "the work [account] of creation" and "the work of the chariot." These refer to the deepest secrets concerning the nature of the world and of the deity. Severe restrictions were therefore placed on whosoever speculates about "what is above, what is beneath, what before, what after" that clearly refer to knowledge of divine matters (Talmud, Chagigah 11b). Seeking such knowledge was considered very dangerous. In a famous parable in which four sages entered the grove—Ben Azzai died, Ben Zoma became demented, Aher mutilated the shoots, and Rabbi Akiva departed unhurt (Talmud, Chagigah 14b). The "grove" represents the garden of divine knowledge. The consonants in the Hebrew term for grove *(PaRDeS)* are traditionally interpreted as standing for *pshat, remez, derush,* and *sod,* which represent four levels of interpreting divine matters. In the "Kabbalah" listing in the *Encyclopedia Judaica* CD-ROM written by Gershom Scholem, these four levels are characterized as literal, allegorical, hermeneutical or homiletical, and mystical.

In this story of the dangerous excursion into the orchard of divine matters only Rabbi Akiva escaped unharmed, to the subsequent detriment of the Jewish collectivity at large. Unfortunately, the ability to exit the garden unscathed, still holding on to the correct theology, provided no immunity to Messianism, which was deeply imbedded in Jewish mysticism. With great messianic zeal, Rabbi Akiva joined the rebellion led by Bar Kokhba against the Romans that proved so disastrous to the Jews. It would have been better for the Jews had he died in the grove too. The rebellion broke out in A.D. 132 but was brutally suppressed by the Roman general Julius Severus, who embarked on a methodical isolation and destruction of Jewish villages and army units. By the time the rebellion was over in 135, more than half a million Jews were dead, many others were prisoners of war, and close to one thousand Jewish settlements across the country (except for a few in the Galilee) lay in ruins.

The most interesting character among the four persons who entered the grove was the one who was not mentioned by name but referred to as Aher, which means "another." His real name was Elisha Ben Avuyah, but he was referred to by the name Aher after he cut the shoots, that is, after he apostatized and deserted the Jewish religion. Shmuel Safrai, who authored the "Elisha Ben Avuyah" listing in the *Encyclopedia Judaica* CD-ROM, indicated that some traditions maintain that the latter's "belief in divine providence and in reward and punishment was undermined as a result of the persecutions following the Bar Kokhba revolt."

As we may recall from the second chapter, Harkabi (1982) referred to this revolt as a catastrophe second in magnitude only to the Nazi Holocaust. Using the language of the twentieth century, one could paraphrase Elisha Ben Avuyah's reaction as, Where was God during the Bar Kokhba revolt? His likely answer probably was that God was actually blocked by "another" *(aher)* God. According to Rachlevsky, Jewish historical memory did its best to paper over events, especially the connection between revolt and exile and the messianic origin of it all (2000, 253). Bar Kokhba (Son of a Star) was therefore referred to as Bar Kuziba (Son of a Lie), suggesting that he was the main culprit. In contrast, the name of the main fomenter of the rebellion, Rabbi Akiva, was removed from any connection to the disaster. However, modern secular Zionism reverted from Bar Kuziba to Bar Kokhba and turned him into a national, albeit not a religious, hero. Not to be left behind, religious Zionism named its youth movement Sons of Akiva. By thus choosing him as their admired hero, they tacitly reconnected him to the rebellion; Rachlevsky suggested that this act foretold the imminent rise of Messianism among religious Zionists.

It was not for naught that the talmudists renamed Elisha Ben Avuyah as Aher. The excuse for renaming him that way was a fairly flimsy one. A harlot asked him on the Sabbath, "Art thou not Elisha Ben Avuyah?" He then tore a radish and gave it to her. Because of this Sabbath violation she said, "It is another." The word "another," or aher, derives from the same root as Sitra Ahra, the Other Side. The real reason for renaming Elisha Ben Avuyah as Aher is that this term refers to dualism, while the real "Another" is "Another God." There are fascinating stories in tractate Chagigah 15a about the continued friendship and discourse between Aher as teacher and his student Rabbi Meir even after the former's apostasy. Aher tried to prevent Rabbi Meir from violating Sabbath rules even as he himself no longer kept them. Rabbi Meir continued to honor his teacher, but he did so carefully. "Rabbi Meir found a pomegranate; he ate [the fruit] within it, and the peel he threw away!" Great caution was necessary because Aher kept singing Greek songs and was reading many heretical books (Talmud, Chagigah 15b). It is very likely that at the heart of Aher's heresy lay dualism. This can be gleaned from his discussions with Rabbi Meir in which he emphasized the notion that for everything God created, he also created its counterpart (Talmud, Chagigah 15a). He seemed to imply that for each thing there is another and that this applies to God himself. The talmudists did not care to give full and manifest expression to Aher's heresy. They therefore left out specific details of his heretical beliefs and obfuscated the real reasons for the renaming. But chances are that he was renamed Another because he subscribed to some form of gnostic dualism and upheld the existence of another God.

The saga of Aher and his student Rabbi Meir held great fascination for Isaac Deutscher, the renowned Jewish scholar who wrote biographies of Trotsky and Stalin. He believed that Rabbi Meir continued to revere his mentor exactly because his teacher "appeared to be in Jewry and yet out of it." He "transcended Judaism." Deutscher was intrigued by the image of Aher not because he was charmed by dualism but because he was captivated by the general notion of Jews who transcend. He maintained the notion that "the Jewish heretic who transcends Jewry belongs to a Jewish tradition" (Deutscher 1968, 26). For him Aher was a prototype of revolutionaries of modern thought such as Spinoza and Freud who "found Jewry too narrow, too archaic, and too constricting" (26). These were Jews who dwelt on the borderlines of various cultures. Deutscher therefore applied to them the term "non-Jewish Jews" to signify that these were Jews who transcended their own culture.

It would be fair at this point to disclose to the reader that years ago I borrowed Deutscher's term to identify myself as a non-Jewish Jew.

As a secular Sabra who grew up in Israel, my choices were limited. I could be a national Jew or a universal man. Religion was not an option for me, since I had never embraced the Jewish faith, not even in childhood. When I came to the United States in my late twenties, I discovered that ethnicity was not an option for me either. Lox, bagels, and occasional broken Yiddish were not a solid base on which I could anchor my Jewish identity. Thus, only two "Jewish" options were available for me—being a national Jew or that kind of supersensitive universal man who is sometimes known as a "non-Jewish Jew." As I ultimately changed from Israeli to American citizenship, I have obviously become a "non-Jewish Jew." By now I know the meaning of the tension of two cultures, and I can no longer avoid it no matter where I live. (Gonen 1975, 341)

Nothing happened over the ensuing years to induce me to modify my views concerning my identity. Coming from Jewish origins, I have written this book as a secular psychologist.

We have seen that dualism provided an alternative to being subjected to the sole rule of Yahweh. Besides serving as an alternative it also continued to exert an influence on Judaism itself, inducing it to attribute greater duality to Yahweh by attributing an increasing role to the Other Side. It so happened that dualism was influential also with early Christianity. But what is of interest to us is the fact that Christianity itself, which was initially practiced by Jews, provided another alternative to the more traditional interpretation of Yahweh's rules. In effect, Christianity diluted somewhat Yahweh's exclusive powers. If one wants to use a corporation as a metaphor for the divine order of things, then it would be like having a chief executive officer kicked upstairs to become chairman of the board. With this dubious promotion of God, Jesus became the new CEO of the world. If one wishes to use a family as a metaphor, then God was given a son. From now on worshipers could turn toward Jesus as an intermediary between themselves and the Lord. The Lord can be harsh and the Lord can be merciful, but Jesus is always merciful. He thus softens the impact of the frightening father. All this touches upon the issue of father-son conflicts that are dealt with, albeit with different outcomes, in Judaism (the binding of Isaac on the altar) and in Christianity (nailing Jesus to the cross). Howard Stein gave it a focal expression: "Jews consciously identify with the 'good father,' while often acting according to the introjected dictates of the archaic 'bad father.' Christians are adept at noticing the latter and then identify the Jews exclusively as the 'bad father' rather than as both" (1977, 675–76).

Stein concluded that "we are all fathers and sons" and that it would be better for both groups to stop sustaining pseudo-identities that are based on projections with regard to the identities of others. Admittedly, this kind of healthy reintegration of religious identities could represent an improvement. But one wonders whether secularism could not provide a shorter path to health. At least secularism rids people of one of the two main causes of projected identifications—religion and nationalism.

In the process of giving the Lord a son, his children were also provided with a mother who could be worshiped with the kind of intensity that far outstrips the Jewish worship of the feminine and motherly She-khinah. It thus undid some of the Jewish repression of the feminine side, even though the Catholic Church as an institution continued to function with a decided antifeminine bias. Mother worship, albeit a virgin mother, gave Christianity a greater allure than Judaism.

The most important element in the Christian alternative was the claim that the Messiah has already arrived. This represented an abrupt clipping off of the continuity of messianic time. For Jews who converted to Christianity, the old fears concerning premessianic cataclysms could be set aside, since they were already living in a postmessianic time. Yahweh's old threat of ultimate disaster was seemingly nullified. At his death, the Christian Messiah granted forgiveness to all and caused the old rules to be defunct, thus providing a great opening for escaping Jewish fate that seemed attractive to some Jews, even though there were inherent problems with the Christian doctrine. The claim that the Messiah has already arrived implies that a utopian state should now prevail. And since this was obviously not the case, the official ideology was bound to clash with the existing reality. It was therefore just about preordained that Christianity would develop dreams of a Second Coming. Recently, the Vatican issued a paper signed by the pope's theologian, Cardinal Joseph Ratzinger, stating that "the Jewish wait for the Messiah is not in vain" (Henneberger 2002). Cardinal Ratzinger is the prefect of the Congregation for the Doctrine of the Faith—a venerable institution that in olden times was known as the Inquisition. Within the Church he is in charge of correct Christian doctrine, not unlike the way in which within the old Soviet Union Mikhail Suslov was in charge of correct Marxist ideology. At any rate, the recent Church document concluded that both Christians and Jews share the wait for the Messiah, though Jews are waiting for the First Coming and Christians for the Second. It thus seems that while Jews have to wait for a Messiah who will never come, Christians have to wait for a Messiah who makes more than a single appearance. At least by treating the Jewish wait for a Messiah as legitimate, the modified Catholic doctrine rids itself of the harmful tendency to condemn Jews for still denying the Son of God.

Polytheism, dualism, and Christianity represented alternatives to Yahweh's rules of history by means of switching religions. But another alternative was to change Judaism from within in radical ways by subtly shifting its accent away from religion and closer to philosophy. In the second half of the twelfth century the great Jewish scholar Moses Maimonides confronted closely interrelated personal and social issues. The personal issue was his conviction that the ultimate truths concerning the universe are anchored in philosophy (mostly Aristotelian) and not in religion. At best, religion represented second-rate approximations of the more refined and valid philosophical truths. The great value of religion lay in the important role it played in governance. Society was largely composed not of the minority of people who were philosophically inclined but of the large "multitude." Because these masses of people were largely driven by "imaginative power," their intellectual grasp was limited, while their potential for becoming unruly was great. Maimonides' personal issue was therefore that, as an individual, he had transcended religion and could have lived without it and with philosophy alone. But his social issue was the fact that society was composed largely of the multitude and not of philosophers. Doing away with religion was a sure formula for creating social chaos. He averred that even polytheistic religions of the past had had a useful value in preventing social breakdown. Faced with this sociopolitical reality as he saw it, Maimonides sorted out the various roles that the responsible philosopher ought to play in relation to the multitude as well as in relation to the few who seek philosophical knowledge.

Convinced that the philosopher ought not to delve only into philosophy without ever contributing to the social order that is sustained by religion, Maimonides wrote in Hebrew *The Second Torah,* a systematic summary of the talmudic law that aimed to facilitate its practice by the multitude, which included not only plain people but also rabbis and community leaders. This was his contribution to governance, which is the unshirkable duty of every philosopher. But there were also the intellectual few who sought philosophical knowledge. They were in danger of becoming perplexed and unsteady if they lost their footing in religion before becoming solidly anchored in philosophy. For them he wrote in Arabic *The Guide of the Perplexed.* He wrote it in a scrambling and disjointed style, making it difficult to pick up the continued discussion of each particular point. For good measure he kept dropping hints about greater secrets that are there for anyone who understands. All this did not represent feeble writing skills. The great systematizer of *The Second Torah* deliberately introduced choppiness and disorganization into the writing of *The Guide of the Perplexed* in order to insure that anyone with the mentality of the multitude will fail to get the point.

What was the point? In a nutshell the point was that Yahweh never existed except in the imagination of the multitude, that the world is eternal, and that if it has a God of sorts, it is the God of the philosophers, or the Aristotelian principle of the unmoved mover. There are enough hints in the guide to suggest that Maimonides' latent conviction was that the world was eternal. First, that was the opinion of Aristotle, and Maimonides habitually twisted the Bible to make it fit Aristotle rather than vice versa. Second, for Maimonides love of God consisted of an intellectual apprehension of the universe as a whole, as can be learned in part 3, chapter 28 of the guide (1969, 512-13). Moreover, Maimonides repeatedly signaled in part 1, chapters 69 and 76 and part 2, chapter 20 that the logic of any argument that entails an infinite regression of causes is fallacious (1969, 168, 230, 313). Taken together, these ideas call for a conclusion that Maimonides probably drew but never stated manifestly. If the world is viewed as a whole, the question of who created it is illogical and irrelevant. It could only open the door to a series of infinite causes. The assumption that the world was created by God raises the question as to who in turn created God and so on ad infinitum. The logical way to avoid this trap of an infinite regression is to stop with what is given to begin with—the world in its entirety. Within the world there are numerous chains of endless causes, but, taken as a whole, the world is eternal. The arbitrary step of assigning a creator to the world is based on religious faith and suits the needs of the multitude, but it is not based on knowledge of logic and philosophy.

Manifestly, however, Maimonides only stated that there was no way of ruling out either the possibility that the world was created or that it was eternal, even though there was greater weight to the arguments in favor of creation. But even this careful keeping of options open was enough to be seen by Jewish eyes as being heretical. The possibility that the world was never created and is eternal dispenses with God the creator, does away with miracles, and cancels the principle of personal reward and punishment from an external and transcendental source. These implications were not lost on traditionally devout Jews, who banned the book and burned it.

The guide consistently treats the Bible as a parable that illustrates philosophical truths; thus "angels" became the Aristotelian "separate intellects." Biblical and talmudic expressions were repeatedly allegorized, symbolized, and reinterpreted to denote Aristotelian notions but never vice versa. "The account of the creation" and "the account of the chariot" that were mentioned in the Talmud now alluded to "the natural sciences" and "the divine science," respectively, that is, physics and metaphysics. When I studied the guide under Shlomo Pines, he kept reiterating that these two terms, which in the talmudic source alluded to mystical secrets, were used by Maimonides to convey philosophical secrets. The two sources of truth, religious revelation and philosophic speculation, were not treated the same. The former was deprived of its original meaning in order to suit the latter. From Maimonides' formal point of view, no misinterpretation was involved, since both sources expressed the same truth, only in different languages. Therefore, demonstrating how the Bible and Talmud allude to the results of philosophic enquiries is but an explanation of what is already there. Yet Maimonides never twisted and turned Aristotelian expressions in order to make them conform to biblical or talmudic pronouncements. All this suggests that for Maimonides both religion and philosophy were needed—religion mostly for governance and philosophy for truth. Religion made life livable, but philosophy was the priceless jewel that contributed to the understanding of everything, including religion.

It thus seems likely that Maimonides knew that Yahweh was a fiction, but he also knew that the multitude could not live peacefully without some such fiction. There was no reason therefore why Jews should not continue to follow their tradition, no matter how fictitious it was. Consequently, Maimonides retained this fiction by references to the law, Torah, and prophets as if these were indeed ultimate sources of validity. They were so by definition for most Jews but not for him. Yet it remained his conscious burden to play along and practice all the mitzvot, as did most other members of the Jewish community. There was no philosophical society, a community of persons of a secular and scientific orientation, in which the intellectual few could live independently of the multitude. And even if there were such an option, he would not have taken it. His philosophy included a sense of duty for society at large. He therefore resigned himself to the fact that all that a philosopher can do is to persist in philosophical pursuits, on the one hand, and to educate the multitude, on the other hand. This education included the reinforcement of religion for the sake of effective governance, which insures a good social order. It also included the refinement of religion from conceptual crudities such as the corporeality of God. In other words, if you cannot lick religion, join it, but at least turn it into a pale reflection of philosophy. Maimonides, the philosopher and rationalist, had worked out a sociopolitical alternative to being a blind subject of Yahweh. It provided freedom of thought for the philosophical few while living among the multitude. As his God remained publicly the God of Israel but became privately the God of the philosophers, he personally freed himself from Jewish mythological rules of history. As Shlomo Pines put it in his introduction to the guide, for Maimonides "philosophy transcended religious or national distinctions. Qua philosopher he had the possibility to consider Judaism from the outside" (Maimonides 1969, cxxxiv).

By being able to consider Judaism from the outside, Maimonides was to some degree the spiritual forerunner of the great Dutch philosopher of the seventeenth century, Baruch Spinoza. He was of Portuguese Jewish descent of a family that fled to Holland in order to escape the Marrano fate of forced conversion in Portugal during the time of the Inquisition in Europe. Israeli professor of philosophy Yirmiyahu Yovel called him "the Marrano of Reason" and emphasized his double exposure to Judaism as well as to Christianity. Yovel underscored that "Spinoza 'transcended' Christianity and Judaism" (1992, xi). It thus seems that although in many respects Spinoza did not savor Maimonides' conclusions, he nevertheless followed in his footsteps in transcending Judaism. But he did it manifestly and did not mask the fact that he had become what we might once again call "another," or aher.

Unlike Maimonides, Spinoza did not give lip service to religion for the sake of social harmony. Validity rested with rational philosophical enquiries and not with religious fables of the past that do not stand up to scientific examination. The hallmark of his philosophical system was the identification of God with nature. Therefore some people see him as a pantheist, while others regard him as the first secular Jew. Shlomo Pines suggested that Maimonides' discussion of "divine," that is, natural, actions in part 3, chapter 32 of the guide forcefully calls to mind Spinoza. The idea that both men shared was, to quote Pines, that "the study of nature and of the order of nature is the only way open to man to know something of God" (Maimonides 1969, xcvi).

In *A Theologico-Political Treatise* Spinoza maintained that men mistake superstition for religion because they are driven by fear (1951, 4–5). The lack of set rules with which to govern all of life's circumstances evokes fear and makes men behave as if God has written his decrees not in the mind of man but in the entrails of beasts to be proclaimed by fools, madmen, and birds. Under the impact of fear and danger men abandon reason and "are wont with prayers and womanish tears to implore help from God." The derisive reference to "womanish tears" demonstrates that his antifeminine bias was as extreme as that of most Jewish sages, including Maimonides. He concluded another work, *A Political Treatise*, with a chapter on democracy in which he stated that because of their weakness women have been ruled by men and do not have by nature equal rights with men. Therefore "men and women cannot rule alike without great hurt to peace" (Spinoza 1951, 387). Having transcended Judaism, he had to base his conclusions not on Jewish law but on the basis of "if we consult experience itself." Thus, with a new grounding in reason, he displayed the persistence of the old Judaic antifeminine bias. In some odd ways even Jewish heretics remain very Jewish.

Spinoza's critique of Maimonides was analyzed in great detail by Leo Strauss. Suffice it to say here that Strauss detected two main differences between the two. The first was the distinction between intellect and between will in God by Maimonides versus the identification of the two in God by Spinoza (Strauss 1997, 153-54). Maimonides needed the distinction, at least in proper speech, in order to retain the role of God the creator; Spinoza did not. The second difference was the issue of human adequacy versus human inadequacy (Strauss 1997, 159). Maimonides maintained human inadequacy, thus justifying the need for revelation for the sake of social regulation. In contrast, Spinoza upheld human adequacy to sort things out by relying on reason to determine how the state should rule the masses. There is no question that when Maimonides is taken at face value only, thus ignoring all the hints and allusions to underlying different positions, the disparity between him and Spinoza is great indeed.

But there was also a difference in presentation styles. Spinoza did not care to obfuscate his writing in order to make it incomprehensible to the multitude: "Therefore the multitude, and those of like passions with the multitude, I ask not to read my book; nay, I would rather that they should utterly neglect it, than that they should misinterpret it after their wont" (1951, 11). He was an uncompromising intellectual who had nothing but scorn for Maimonides' "nonsense" of trying "to extort from Scripture confirmations of Aristotelian quibbles" (Spinoza 1951, 17). But Spinoza disdained Maimonides also for failing to do just that in the case of the doctrine of the eternity of the world: "For if he had been convinced by reason that the world is eternal, he would not have hesitated to twist and explain away the words of Scripture till he made them appear to teach this doctrine" (Spinoza 1951, 115). In some respect Spinoza was a cold-blooded intellectual who insisted on defining all terms used in philosophical discussions and who savored manifest statements sharpened by cutting-edge logic. He was therefore turned off by the multilayered and obfuscating style of Maimonides' guide, which was intended to send different messages to different audiences.

Spinoza, who unflinchingly advocated secular rationalism and paid for it with the price of being excommunicated by the Jewish community, was intolerant of Maimonides' sociopolitical compromise of reason with faith. For merely claiming that it is possible that the world is eternal, Maimonides' guide was banned and burned. Had Maimonides claimed that the Bible affirms the eternity of the world, thus doing away with the role of God the creator, Maimonides himself and not just his book would have been banned. Maimonides did not lack courage and did not fail to be "convinced by reason" of the eternity of the world, as he was accused by Spinoza. Instead he followed his own judgment concerning what roles a philosopher should play toward the multitude and toward the intellectual few with the sociopolitical aim of facilitating peaceful governance. The foggy quality of his writing was due not to philosophical doubts but to a deliberate policy. Spinoza, however, did not savor a writing style that says yet does not say what one means. This kind of style was "harmful, useless, and absurd" for treating the multitude, as it "does away with all the certainty which the masses acquire by candid reading" (Spinoza 1951, 116–18). Spinoza did not care to acknowledge that in many respects he made manifest that which was latent in Maimonides. He wanted everything fully manifest and expressed unambiguously in precise terms. In *The Ethics* he stated: "I shall consider human actions and desires in exactly the same manner, as though I were concerned with lines, planes, and solids" (Spinoza 1955, 129). Such a preference for scientific precision required him to get rid of the whole field of theology with its cluttered and ambiguous terms. It therefore meant first and foremost "the separation of philosophy from theology" period. "Theology is not bound to serve reason, nor reason theology." Philosophy's end is truth. Faith's goal is to instill obedience and piety. Philosophy's axioms must be sought in nature alone, while faith is based on history and language (Spinoza 1951, 42, 189, 195, 198).

These sharp distinctions also militate against a simple-minded interpretation of Spinoza's identification of God with nature as a pantheistic religion. Spinoza objected vehemently to the illusion of the masses that God and nature are two distinct powers, with God serving as a royal potentate and nature as force and energy (1951, 81). For Spinoza God and nature were the same. This was enough to preclude any old-fashioned worship of God as the Lord, or royal potentate, of the universe, but it also precluded casting nature in the role of a providence that regulates personal rewards and punishments. Guidance for proper conduct could be obtained by studying the rules of nature. All this certainly precluded any general notion of a God who selects chosen peoples. Such a notion may have been temporarily valid for the Jewish group only at the particular historical time of Jewish independence. Because it provided the heads of the Jewish kingdom with an authority to rule the multitude, it remained a within-state or local phenomenon. But the notion of being chosen lacked a universal validity that would apply to all human groups as a basis for the establishment of a ruling authority within each state. Yovel was strongly opposed to severing the link between God and nature in Spinoza's system on the ground that "nature" alone could not convey in full the sense of immanence that is inherent in the system (1992, 148–49). This surely is a plausible interpretation, but there may be more to it than that. After all, if one were to omit the term "God" from Spinoza's philosophical system, it would still stand on its feet. But take away the term "nature," and his system has no legs to stand on. Why then did he follow in the errant ways of Maimonides to introduce dual meanings in his writing through the seeming redundancy of nature and God?

It could be that, like Maimonides before him, Spinoza made concessions to people's habits of thinking. Maimonides emphasized that, by his wisdom and "gracious ruse," God, on the one hand, allowed the Israelites to persist in the habit of offering animal sacrifices but, on the other hand, transferred this practice from a polytheistic to a monotheistic worship (1969, 526). It is possible that likewise Spinoza engaged in a divine ruse of his own by letting people persist in the old habit of calling that which is ultimate, eternal, real, and true "God." With wily graciousness, he allowed people to continue with this old habit, but in the process he basically transferred the ultimate dimensions that were attached to the concept of "God" to the concept of "nature." These ultimate dimensions — that God's essence and his existence are the same — were already present in Maimonides, who in part 1, chapter 63 of the guide provided this interpretation of Exodus 3:14 ("I am that I am") to conclude that God is "the necessarily existent." In his fourteenth-century commentary on the guide, Rabbi Moshe ben Joshua of Narbonne extended the same interpretation to the ineffable name, that is, YHWH (Narboni 1946, 11). Spinoza adopted this concept of the necessarily existent and kept reiterating that it applies to God or nature (1955, 74, 117, 188, 243). It may therefore be the case that since people were already used to treating God as the necessarily existent, Spinoza, who wished to transfer this concept to nature, cunningly applied the concept not to "nature" alone but to "God or nature," thus providing a bridge on which to cross over from the old mode of thinking to the new one.

If it were not all a ruse, then the identification of nature with God was not meant to be redundant but to afford people a personal worship that leads to intellectual salvation through the knowledge and love of God. This certainly is a legitimate interpretation. But the way I read Spinoza, "knowledge" already includes "love," which is an inevitable outcome of any true knowledge of nature, that is, substance, or God. The redundancy was therefore Spinoza's way of bringing people aboard on the great philosophical train ride from transcendence (God) to immanence (nature). Either way, it all was a major shift in orientation, as was duly pointed out by Yovel (1992, 127, 136). Immanence was only latent in Maimonides, who on a manifest level preached transcendence. It was Spinoza who transformed the absolute into an immanent dimension of nature, including the mind of man. By sort of secularizing God but making nature divine, as emphasized by Yovel, Spinoza opened up the prospect of self-initiated action by man in a world where everything was now immanent. Transcendence leaves it to God to initiate action, but immanence calls upon man to act on his own. The worldview of this first secular Jew or, should one say, non-Jewish Jew can therefore also be seen as a precursor of Zionism.

There is a world of difference between the old-style messianic yearnings that were expressed by Maimonides (even though Messianism requires miracles, and he did not really believe in miracles) and the worldview of Spinoza, which shifted a good deal of the accent from God to nature and therefore also perforce from mythology to history or from miracles to science. The last chapter in Yovel's book offers a comprehensive and sensitive discussion of the ways in which to some extent Spinoza's ideas anticipated Zionism (1992, 172–204). By emphasizing nature and history Spinoza provided an inkling of the situation of the modern Jew that, according to Yovel, became secular, assimilationist, or national. Spinoza may have been a "closet Zionist." He expected that even after Jews secularized individually, they would still remain a distinct collectivity because of the sign of circumcision and because of anti-Semitism. A possible remedy for this problematic existence in the Diaspora could be for Jews to "raise up their empire afresh, and that God may a second time elect them" (Spinoza 1951, 56; Yovel 1992, 190). Yovel emphasized that this was not a reiteration of the old religious stance. It was a potential Zionism that represented a new development within secular history. Moreover, in anticipating a secular society that did not exist yet, Spinoza was ahead of his time. As Yovel put it: "None of these concepts—secular Judaism, Jewish nationalism, Zionism, even assimilation—has an a priori or supratemporal definition; their meaning emerges only in a historical context" (1992, 201).

Unlike Maimonides, Spinoza did much more than just subtly shift the emphasis from religion to philosophy. He was the harbinger of secularism who introduced it as an independent rationalistic orientation toward life. Spinoza's explosive potential can be understood best as releasing the secular genie out of the bottle. A secular mode of life was going to become an independent orientation toward life that would open up new alternatives. From now on Jews who did not stay in the religious fold could not only assimilate individually but could also become national Jews collectively. And since Jewish history is never devoid of dialectics, they could someday even commit collective assimilation. To some hard-line religious Jews, the whole Zionist endeavor of turning Jews into a nation like all other nations in a secular state of their own represents nothing more than collective assimilation in contrast to the individual assimilations of the past. From their point of view, the end product is of course the deplorable sight of Hebrew-speaking goyim. To where secularism would lead remains as yet an unanswered question concerning Israel's future historical course.

In the course of Jewish history Zionism represented a secular convulsion. It was a rebellion against what was perceived to be a deeply flawed Judaism whose diseased religion fostered a scattered and abnormal existence for the Jews. Under the banner of "the negation of the *galut* (Diaspora)," Zionism advocated the ingathering in Zion. In opposition to galut mentality it promoted self-reliance, productivity, self-defense, and national revival in the ancestral land. Following the previous secularization trend of the Jewish "enlightenment" movement in Europe, the ordeal of obsessively keeping the oppressing mitzvot was broken off to be replaced by secular freedom in daily life. The promise of a new freedom in a renascent national and democratic life would still allow the religious to remain religious and the secular to stay secular.

What is more, Israel would still be "a light to the nations" by providing a model example of socialistic justice inspired by the universalistic strand of the vision of the ancient prophets.

And there was the rub. Somehow Israel had to remain special while it served as a unique model of universalism and social justice. In other words, it had to practice universalism in a unique fashion. At a certain time the kibbutzim were heralded as a prime example of a unique model of how to implement general social justice. As if attached by a very strong rubber band to its Judaic origins, Zionism pulled as far away from Judaism as it could until the stretched rubber band forced the soaring secular rebels back to a more particularistic strand of Judaism and to the notion of being a chosen nation that can serve as a precious example for humanity only because of its undisputed uniqueness and separateness. Consequently, with all the secularism in the world at the end of the road, many Zionists had to remain "chosen," still serving as Yahweh's precious object. They did not have the heart and the staying power to wrench themselves so far from Yahweh's rules of Jewish history that the rubber band, so to speak, could snap, and they would finally exit Yahweh's orbit. Eventually, this loss of heart, which was imbedded in Zionism from the start, resulted in the subsequent Israeli failure to implement a separation of synagogue from state.

The Israeli psychology professor Benjamin Beit-Hallahmi pointed out that "the Zionist revolution was the attempt at cultural secularization" but that it resulted in "the defeat of secularism and the relative desecularization of Israeli daily life" (1992, 139–40). He attributed this to the decided disadvantage of secular Jews vis-à-vis religious Jews who are not on the defensive and need not explain in what ways they are still Jews. Put differently, secular Zionists suffered from what my high school teacher and literary critic Baruch Kurzweil used to call "the crisis of historical continuity." He issued warnings against the misleading secular "translation" of Judaic values into the narrow confines of petit bourgeois morality, class consciousness, or modern nationalism (Kurzweil 1969, 263–64). Because of this crisis of continuity, secular Zionists found themselves in a shaky position. They were caught in the contradiction of attempting to repair and safeguard the survival and continuity of the same sick Judaism that they were also out to annul and discard. Exactly because they advocated a sharp revision in the course of Jewish history and Jewish ways of life, the secular Jews were always pressured to demonstrate in what way they were still Jews. By contrast, religious Jews who remained loyal to a Judaism that needed a Messiah rather than a reform faced no crisis of continuity and were not put on the defensive regarding this issue.

In an attempt to soften somewhat his condemnation of the defeat of secularism in Israel, Beit-Hallahmi also took note of the fact that "the whole of humanity is still busy constructing a secular culture to replace religious traditions." This is certainly true. And it also brings to mind the difficulties that another non-Jewish Jew on Deutscher's list, Sigmund Freud, envisioned with regard to this process. In *The Future of an Illusion,* Freud characterized religion as "the universal obsessional neurosis of humanity" that brought with it both obsessional restrictions and wishful illusions (1961b, 43). Yet in spite of this unflattering opinion of religion, he remained somewhat ambivalent about the goal of casting it away. The reason for that was the danger that "the great mass of the uneducated and oppressed," that is, the multitude, could pose to civilization. Without fear of God, the mass would become socially destructive. Unlike "educated people" and "brainworkers," the mass could not handle the replacement of religious motives for civilized behavior with secular motives (Freud 1961b, 39). Jews who "transcend" seem to be fated to have their problems with the "multitude," which needs religion. It is evident, however, that Beit-Hallahmi had issued a timely reminder. The replacement of religious traditions by secular culture is a difficult process in many countries and not just Israel.

Yet after all is said and done, the fact remains that the Israeli failure to separate synagogue from state, thus providing religion and religious practices with state power, compromised democracy and freedom and encroached on daily life in many ways that evoked constant frictions in Israeli society. All this is well known, and it would suffice here to mention that the coercion even added insults to families injured by death. There have been attempts by the army to enforce religious funeral rites for fallen soldiers of secular families regardless of family wishes. And there have also been attempts by the religious burial authorities to prevent the burial of fallen soldiers whose Jewish origin was in question in plots inside Jewish graveyards. Once religion is not divorced from politics and there is no clear-cut separation of synagogue and state, freedom falls casualty to coercion. It is antidemocratic.

Identity issues such as "who is a Jew" as well as practical considerations such as Israel's right to demand of Jews to immigrate to Israel played into the reluctance to separate synagogue from state. Jewishness needed to remain a mysterious blend of national, religious, cultural, or ethnic identities to keep the Zionist calls for *aliyah* (immigration) by Jews abroad legitimate. If implored by their Israeli "fellow nationals" to settle in Israel, the majority of American Jews would reject the appeal because they are Americans not Israelis. But when the appeal is made in the name of a mysterious blend of identities, including a religious one, it may seem more valid. There was thus a decided advantage for Zionist appeals to all Jews to be based on the special circumstances of a hopeless entanglement of national, religious, and ethnic or cultural Jewish identity. This militated against a separation of synagogue and state. It also created a double standard on the separation issue with regard to the goyim versus the Jews. So what else is new? The following is a description of that double standard:

> The result is cognitive inconsistency concerning the relation between religion and state. One yardstick is applied to other countries while the opposite is applied to Israel. In every country except Israel, Jews ardently support the separation of state and church. Without such a separation, the adopted state religion is not likely to be a Jewish "church," which could place the Jewish religion in a disadvantageous position. That is why in the name of freedom and democracy Jews insist on keeping state and church apart, except in Israel. There is no separation of synagogue and state in Israel, but there are plenty of apologies concerning the reasons why. Presumably, the special nature of Jewish nationality is that it is so inextricably interwoven with Jewish religion that separation of the two is either impossible or at least very destructive. The implication is that what is fair to other countries is not fair for Israel. (Gonen 1975, 328)

This exemption of Israel from the democratic requirement of separation makes it a special case indeed.

The psychological bottom line of this specialness goes back to the conviction of being chosen by Yahweh. It makes Jews different. Being so chosen, they should become neither a nation like all other nations nor a democracy like all other democracies. Some religious Jews may believe that perhaps Israel should function for a while as a flawed democracy until such time as it can revert to theocracy, possibly with messianic help. Many so-called secular Israelis delude themselves when they believe that their temporary acquiescence to no separation of synagogue from state is motivated mostly by a desire to avoid a Kulturkampf. The culture war simmers continuously anyway, but the secularists wage it half-heartedly, except for a vocal minority that clamors for "change." Deep in their hearts, what frightens many members of the Israeli secular majority is the prospect that the separation of synagogue from state would result in loss of specialness. When push comes to shove, they are not willing to renounce the claim to a special destiny, to special powers, and to the "oy vay" fate. In short, they suffer from what can be termed "multitude mentality," which throws them back upon their specific religious heritage. Frightened by the wide-open space of secularism that surrounds them, they once again crave the certainties that come with their historical religion. These certainties made them special, even though they could be very painful. So even secular Israelis relish their chosen nation status, continue to cling to Yahweh, their talisman, and resign themselves to his rules of Jewish history. It is therefore not true that most secular Israelis are Hebrew-speaking goyim. They actually still are Yahweh's nonobservant Jews.

All in all, the clash between religion and state in Israel transcends mundane altercations between political parties and has its roots deep within Jewishness. This conviction led Gershon Weiler into a comprehensive investigation of the notion of "Jewish theocracy" in Judaism. As an admirer of Spinoza, he ended up with a razor-sharp analysis that advocated a separation of religion from state. Weiler maintained that after losing political independence, ancient Jews began to think in theocratic concepts because of their inability to forget the glorious past of political grandeur (Weiler 1976, 111). This assertion actually touches upon Falk's suggestion that the Jewish inability to mourn losses and then move on was the major factor that entrapped Jews in a kind of timeless fixation. This interesting hypothesis will be discussed shortly. As for Weiler, he drew the important conclusion that because of their inability to forget the glorious past, Jews had to adapt the memory of that past to the present reality of being only a religious community. The adaptation actually occurred during the Babylonian Exile, when the Hebrews were transformed from a nation into a holy community (Weiler 1976, 112).

The Halakah is the postbiblical oral law that has also been put down in writing. Weiler was correct in focusing on the Halakah's goal of transforming the exiled Hebrews from a nation into a holy community. Through the imposition of this radical shift in self-definition and group identity, the prolific Jewish law succeeded in preserving the existence of the Jews as a distinct religious community, but it was a limited success. In comparison to Christians or to Muslims, there are not many Jews left in the world. Over the course of two millennia countless Jews have been killed by Gentiles, but an even greater number of Jews have become Gentiles themselves through assimilation. What is more, the question of whether Jewish survival as a religious community at the price of a plethora of talmudic strictures was really worth it remains a disputed issue.

Weiler's assumption concerning Halakah law as specifically designed to safeguard Jewish existence only in the form of a religious community determines the conclusions that follow in the rest of his book. His careful analysis of the Jewish sources, especially the Halakah, revealed that the basic notions of Jewish theocracy, which aimed to regulate the life of a politically powerless religious community, could not possibly be suitable for the regulation of an independent state. What is more, the Halakah strove to convert the people's memory of independent Jewish kingdoms in biblical times into an ahistorical, utopian, and eschatological messianic doctrine. In short, the masters of the Halakah did their utmost to weaken the political elements of the earlier biblical heritage from which they derived legitimacy (Weiler 1976, 143-46). Noting this basic contradiction between the Halakah and the reality of a politically independent Jewish state, Weiler also concluded that there is nevertheless great reluctance to engage in open discussion of this issue rather than merely troubleshoot specific problems on an ad hoc basis that arise as a result of the pretense that no such contradiction exists. On his part, however, he clearly advocated the separation of religion from state in Israel so that the state would renounce any interest in forcing Halakah rules on its citizens (Weiler 1976, 178-79, 197).

This is not likely to happen soon. In a fairly traditional secular Zionist fashion, Weiler characterized the antipolitical and solely religious worldview of the Halakah as a distortion. Many ardent secular Jews have indeed looked upon Judaism as a diseased entity that Zionism was going to cure. The basic "distortion" that Weiler spoke of was the abandonment of the normal wish of any group to strive to be in charge of its own physical safety rather than be dependent on others. But the Halakah transposed such strivings away from collective action and self-help into the domain of God's mercy. In this connection Weiler suggested the provocative notion that the entire doctrine of being a "chosen nation" is actually the other side of the coin of this distortion. After all, the main thrust of being a chosen nation is the renunciation of earthly advantages in favor of total submission to the father in heaven (Weiler 1976, 307-9). This takes us full circle back to the meaning of Jewish specialness. As mentioned before, specialness affords the Jews an exemption from universal standards or ideals even though these standards should continue to apply to the goyim.

Unfortunately, Weiler's very enlightened discussion of the distorted worldview of the Halakah cuts more mustard with the intellectual few than with the multitude. The problem of the multitude that bedeviled both Maimonides and Spinoza continues to exist. Weiler made a convincing case to the effect that the Halakah has neither the tools nor the inclination to handle the political reality of modern statehood, but it remains a convincing case for the intellectual few. For the multitude "specialness" still comes in very handy. For the run-of-the-mill Jewish believer it does not seem far-fetched or problematic that a Jewish law could become the final authority in Israeli state law. A folkloristic notion such as "be'ezrat hashem hakol yistader" [with God's help everything will end up alright] can easily take care of most problems, and this includes the problem of reconciling state law, which is supposed to reflect the will of the people, with the Halakah, which is presumably based on the will of God. As long as either a conscious or an unconscious gravitation toward a self-concept of being special and an identity based on being chosen holds sway, separation of synagogue from state and a final plunge into freedom and democracy will be fudged and subverted. This is the way the ideology of "special circumstances" works. It puts religious brakes upon secular takeoffs, turning them into flights of fancy.

The Jewish inability to forget the glorious past as indicated by Weiler relates to the Jewish inability to mourn. Falk has emphatically stated that the inability to mourn is the most important issue in Jewish history, giving this long history its inner psychological coherence (1996, 17, 22). He further maintained that this inability to give up that which was lost was successively transmitted from one generation to the next. Consequently, for many generations the Jewish group lived in the past rather than in the present and in fantasy rather than in reality (Falk 1996, 17, 311). As mourning the terrible losses of their kingdom, independence, and motherland became too painful for Jews, they compensated for it with fantasies of restoration and rebirth (Falk 1996, 188). Thus instead of mourning their losses, Jews aspired to recover their losses. This was in effect a refusal to mourn that rested on massive denial of the reality and finality of the losses. With great psychoanalytic acumen, Falk traced this inability to mourn and to give up a loss to an earlier inability to give up fusion with the mother in order to separate and to individuate from her. In this connection Falk made the intriguing suggestion that the Jewish fantasies of restoration displayed a craving for rebirth and a return to the early Great Mother, who was symbolized by the Jewish nation and by the land of Judah (1996, 189–90). In earlier times the cult of the Great Mother was suppressed by the new Yahweh religion of Moses (Falk 1996, 98), but the Jews continued to miss her.

Falk raised the question, Why was their nation so important to the Jews that they craved a restoration that flew in the face of reality? His answer was that the nation and the land were symbolic of the early mother with whom they wished to fuse once again. Unable to mourn, they denied the loss and embarked on a course that typifies mysticism — they longed for the early fusion with the mother (Falk 1996, 444). To this one may add that a central feature of Jewish lore — the basic duality that is embedded in the concept of Yahweh — is what prompted as well as facilitated the process. This duality within the deity implies that a catastrophe is at one and the same time also a redemption promissory note that can be redeemed in the future. A divine IOU that is attached to each disaster turns it also into a gateway to salvation. Therefore mourning the loss and accepting it would be tantamount to an admission that Yahweh cannot restore and would require the abandonment of the impotent God. Eventually, secular Zionism implied just that during its brashest moments. But, frightened by its own boldness, it has largely retreated like a child who is being scared by its own shadow. It thus seems that when the Yahweh cult suppressed either the Great Mother cult or the cults of various mother goddesses, a specific immunity against any future countersuppression was injected into the system. This was accomplished by endowing the deity with an inner duality from which the special rules of Jewish history emanated. These rules made the mourning of disasters and then moving on very difficult because in the process one would have to abandon Yahweh.

Another way of putting it would be that, very ingeniously so, a program of anti-abandonment-of-Yahweh has been written into the software of the collective Jewish psyche. The program preemptively precluded the finality of past losses and kept them as unfinished business by inextricably tying them to future salvation. Since every disaster was perceived in an a priori fashion as unfinished business that would be finished only when redemption finally comes, it was practically impossible to mourn the loss and move on. Closure could not be arrived at because by definition each disaster remained unfinished business still awaiting the completion of the series of destructions to be followed by construction à la Jeremiah. It was a clever program indeed that was included in the old software of the Jewish psyche. It is even possible to metaphorically regard the two related concepts of a "chosen nation" and of a "covenant" as the click point on the computer monitor by means of which the duality of Yahweh versus Yahweh or of el ra'hum ve'hanun versus el kana has been downloaded into the Jewish psyche to become an unshakable part of it. And the poor Jews cannot shake Yahweh off, mourn the loss, and move on.

Unless Israelis and Jews succeed in discarding the uniqueness myth as a prescriptive formula for the future, moral and political crises will continue to build up. The moral crisis stems from the "original sin" of colonialism that in the name of the promise of the covenant perpetrated an injustice upon the Arabs. This sin received a sweeping indictment from Beit-Hallahmi, who overapplied it to all periods in the history of modern Zionism. It is true that the Zionist immigration waves and gradual settlement by buying lands from Arab landlords without military conquest did result in an injustice to Arab tenants, who were then legally evacuated. But this kind of injustice was not comparable to the colonialism that was organized in previous centuries by established European states. This changed after the Jewish victory during the Six-Day War of 1967, when Israel was in a position to use the organized power of an established state for the purpose of settling beyond its borders, as colonial powers typically do. This is not how it looked to messianically inflamed individuals, for whom the settlements represented a return to the ancestral land rather than an aggressive territorial expansion. But the Israeli political science professor Zeev Sternhell was correct in drawing historical distinctions (1997, 336). He indicated that the territories conquered in 1949 during the War of Independence stemmed from the circumstances of distress on which Israel was founded but that the attempt to retain the conquests of the Six-Day War had a strong flavor of imperial expansion.

The political crisis goes back to the failure of secularism. Secularism was most pronounced among the political parties of the Left, and yet, "in the Zionism of the Left, secularism was only a veneer." As a result, nationalism in Israel has come to rely less and less on rationalism, individualism, and genuine secularism and more and more on history, culture, religion, and mysticism. All this led Sternhell to a gloomy conclusion: "And indeed, peace is a mortal danger to the Zionism of blood and soil, a Zionism that cannot imagine willingly returning even an inch of the sacred territory of the Land of Israel" (1997, 341–43). Sternhell's reference to the German folkish slogan of "blood and soil" that was picked up by Nazism needs no further explication.

To fair-minded people liberal, democratic, and secular governance that separates religion from politics represents the optimal conditions for providing equality and freedom to Jews and Arabs everywhere. When peace prospects for the Middle East seemed bright during the first half of 1995, Falk expressed the following hope: "Modern Israel was a fantasy that became a reality. The price for living in that fantasy has been high. Perhaps now, if peace with the Arabs does become a reality, we Israelis will begin to live normally and let the rest of the world Jews take care of their own Judaism and be whatever kind of Jews they wish" (1996, 728). His hope has not materialized, as the extremists on both sides of the Jewish-Arab divide successfully reinforced each other in sabotaging political accommodation and peace. So what do the prospects for the realization of that hope look like at present?

For clues I resort to the outlook of the political scientist Alan Dowty (1998a, 1998b). He treats the universalist and the particularist orientations that are embedded in both Judaism and Zionism not as a matter of stark choices but as an invitation to a creative synthesis. In this he may be too optimistic, since such a synthesis would have to gradually take place in the mundane political world of Israel, which he himself described very realistically. It is a system of power sharing that relies on a bargaining process in which each community or sector has a voice and some influence. This is essentially what has been going on since Israel's foundation, what produced the uneasy status quo in religious affairs, and what is likely to continue. So far it has resulted in no separation of synagogue and state and no agreement on a constitution. Recent attempts at some gatherings of citizens to create a proposal for a "constitution by agreement" resulted in impossible mixes of the secular with the religious that were about as successful as an attempt to mix half coffee and half tea in a single cup. The practice of sectorial bargaining and power sharing can certainly perpetuate an uneasy accommodation. I doubt, however, that this ongoing reality would truly lead to a creative synthesis of opposing worldviews. In any power-sharing bargaining process, Yahweh is guaranteed to get his cut through his emissaries on earth. Consequently, there would be no abrogation of his special rules of Jewish history that preclude the possibility of Israel becoming a secular democracy. The true nature of the power-sharing process was illustrated by Rachlevsky through the metaphor of "the wall that moves" (2000, 243–44). The secular camp sets up a wall, the religious camp pushes against it, and the wall moves. In the process the weakness of the presumably reigning secular law becomes exposed, as it rests upon a shifting reality.

This shifting reality bodes ill for the future of Israelis and Jews alike. There is not much of a future in the twenty-first century for a religious orientation that in a cultlike fashion maintains that secular persons are criminals, that women are whores, and that the goyim are not human and are inferior to kosher animals (Rachlevsky 2000, 323–24). Neither is there much of a future for either Arabs or Jews in a messianic Israel that relies on blood-and-soil convictions and that contemplates going through cycles of expansions and separations in a futile colonial attempt to forcefully override the legitimate claims of the national antagonist to a part of the land. The future establishment of a Palestinian state is inevitable. And it is only just that Palestinians will have an independent territorial base as Israelis do. As for Israelis of all denominations, they can set their heart upon different religious and secular alternatives. Yet freedom and equality in Israel should belong to all its citizens, be they secular Jews, Reform Jews, Orthodox Jews, or even immigrants from Russia and Ethiopia whose Jewish origin is being questioned. Likewise, freedom and equality should belong to Christian Arabs, Muslim Arabs, members of the Druze community, and all other Israeli minorities. But the freedom for separate individuals to live in different ways without governmental interference can rest only on a truly democratic system that guarantees the freedom and equality of all without coercive impositions of any kind.

This, however, is unlikely to happen. The way things are set up at present in Israel—a flawed democracy that lacks a constitution and that is based on a tradition of sectorial bargaining and power sharing—Yahweh's special rules of Jewish psychohistory will continue to predominate. Clothed in transcendental attire as a compelling force beyond nature, he actually represents an internal psychological compulsion that has been historically maintained by shared group fantasies among Jews. The Lord of special dual fate for the Jews is written into the software of the Jewish psyche. Consequently, many Jews are no more able to let go of their mighty talisman than Yahweh is willing to relinquish his transitional object. Yahweh is very good at sticking to the Jews and sticking it to them.

Bibliography

Albo, Joseph. 1893. *Book of Principles* (in Hebrew). Warsaw: Feibel Rasin and Benjamin Kalinberg.

Alden, Robert. 1973. "U.N.'s Anti-Israel Tone." *New York Times,* 11 October.

Alon, Gideon. 1986. "The Pain Always Remains a Pain" (in Hebrew). *Ha'aretz,* 13 May.

Anatoli, Jacob ben Abba Mari ben Samson. 1866. *A Goad to Scholars* (in Hebrew). Lyck: Mekize Nirdamim.

Azaryahu, Maoz. 1995. *State Cults: Celebrating Independence and Commemorating the Fallen in Israel 1948–1956* (in Hebrew). Tel Aviv: Ben Gurion University of the Negev Press.

Bear, Dov. 1927. *Book of He Who Tells His Messages to Jacob and Collected Sayings* (in Hebrew). Lublin: N. Herszenhorn and Sz. Strazberger.

Becker, Menahem. 2001. "The Weekly Portion" (in Hebrew). *Yedioth Ahronoth,* 29 June.

Beit-Hallahmi, Benjamin. 1992. *Original Sins: Reflections on the History of Zionism and Israel.* Concord, Mass.: Pluto Press.

Ben Amotz, Dan. 1972. "A Palestinian Passover Haggadah" (in Hebrew). *Ha'olam Hazeh,* 28 March.

Book of Hasidim (in Hebrew). 1957. Jerusalem: Mosad Harav Kook.

Davidowitz, Moshe. 1978. "The Psychohistory of Jewish Rage and Redemption as Seen through Its Art." *Journal of Psychohistory* 6, no. 2: 273–84.

Dayan, Moshe. 1977. "The United States Will Not Decide Instead of Us" (in Hebrew). *Yedioth Ahronoth,* 28 January.

Deutscher, Isaac. 1968. *The Non-Jewish Jew and Other Essays.* London: Oxford University Press.

De Vidas, Elijah ben Moses. 1958. *The Beginning of Wisdom* (in Hebrew). Jerusalem: Ma'ayan Hachochma.

"The Disgrace of Qiryat Arba" (in Hebrew). 1997. *Ha'aretz,* 29 January.

Dobrowski, Elie. 1995. "Cherubim: God's Throne?" *Biblical Archeology Review* 21, no. 4: 36–41.

Dowty, Alan. 1998a. "Israel's First Fifty Years." *Current History* (January): 26–31.

———. 1998b. *The Jewish State: A Century Later.* Berkeley: University of California Press.

Ein Gil, Ehud. 1995. "In the Footprints of the Lost Cherubim" (in Hebrew). *Ha'aretz,* 14 April.

Eldad, Yisrael. 1981. "Of Purim's Intoxications" (in Hebrew). *Yedioth Ahronoth,* 20 March.

Fackenheim, Emil L. 1978. *The Jewish Return into History: Reflections in the Age of Auschwitz and a New Jerusalem.* New York: Schocken Books.

Falk, Avner. 1996. *A Psychoanalytic History of the Jews.* Cranbury, N.J.: Associated University Presses.

Freud, Sigmund. 1957a. "On the Universal Tendency to Debasement in the Sphere of Love (Contributions to the Psychology of Love II)." In *The Standard Edition of the Complete Psychological Works of Sigmund Freud,* ed. James Strachey, 11: 177–90. London: Hogarth Press.

———. 1957b. "A Special Type of Choice of Object Made by Men (Contributions to the Psychology of Love I)." In *The Standard Edition of the Complete Psychological Works of Sigmund Freud,* ed. James Strachey, 11: 163–75. London: Hogarth Press.

———. 1961a. *Civilization and Its Discontents.* In *The Standard Edition of the Complete Psychological Works of Sigmund Freud,* ed. James Strachey, 21: 59–151. London: Hogarth Press.

———. 1961b. *The Future of an Illusion.* In *The Standard Edition of the Complete Psychological Works of Sigmund Freud,* ed. James Strachey, 21: 5–56. London: Hogarth Press.

Galili, Lily. 2001. "Catastrophe Day or Victory Day?" (in Hebrew). *Ha'aretz,* 20 April.

Gaon, Rabbi Saadiah. 1880. *The Book of Beliefs and Opinions* (in Hebrew). Cracow: Fischer and Weindling.

Gonen, Jay Y. 1975. *A Psychohistory of Zionism.* New York: Mason/Charter.

———. 1978. "The Israeli Illusion of Omnipotence Following the Six Day War." *Journal of Psychohistory* 6, no. 2: 241–71.

———. 1980. "The Day of Atonement War." *Journal of Psychohistory* 8, no. 1: 53–65.

———. 2000. *The Roots of Nazi Psychology: Hitler's Utopian Barbarism.* Lexington: University Press of Kentucky.

Greenstone, Julius H. 1906. *The Messiah Idea in Jewish History.* Philadelphia: Jewish Publication Society of America.

Ha-Kohen, Jacob Joseph. 1881. *The History of Jacob Joseph* (in Hebrew). Warsaw: Rabbi Hirsch Bear Publishing House.

Ha-Kohen, Menahem. 1981. "To Beat up Haman" (in Hebrew). *Yedioth Ahronoth*, 20 March.

Halevi, Judah. 1964. *The Kuzari*. New York: Schocken.

Harel, Israel. 1992. "Better the Golan than Peace" (in Hebrew). *Ha'aretz*, 6 September.

Harkabi, Y. 1982. *Vision, No Fantasy: Realism in International Relations* (in Hebrew). Jerusalem: Domino Press.

Hazaz, Hayim. 1952. "The Sermon." In *Selected Stories* (in Hebrew), 184–202. Tel Aviv: Dvir.

Henneberger, Melinda. 2002. "Vatican Says Jews' Wait for Messiah Is Validated by the Old Testament." *New York Times*, 18 January.

Hestrin, Ruth. 1991. "Understanding Asherah: Exploring Semitic Iconography." *Biblical Archeology Review* 17, no. 5: 50–59.

Ibn Paquda, Bahya Ben Joseph. 1856. *The Duties of the Heart* (side-by-side Hebrew and German translations). Vienna: A. Klopf and Alexander Eurich.

Issar, Arieh. 1997. "Three Independence Days" (in Hebrew). *Ha'aretz*, 5 May.

Jonas, Hans. 1994. *Le concept de dieu après Auschwitz: Une voix juive*. Paris: Payot et Rivages.

Kafra, Michal. 1994. "What I Have Already Said" (in Hebrew). *Maariv*, 11 March.

Kahane, Rabbi Meir. 1998. *Or Hara'ayon: The Jewish Idea*. Vol. 2. Trans. Raphael Blumberg. Jerusalem: Institute for Publication of the Writings of Rabbi Meir Kahane.

Kedar, B. Z. 1994. "The Sanctification of the Name in a Mosque" (in Hebrew). *Ha'aretz*, 13 April.

Kurzweil, Baruch. 1969. *In the Battle over the Values of Judaism* (in Hebrew). Tel Aviv: Schocken Publishing House.

Lapid, Ya'ir. 1993. "A Passover Prayer, the New Version" (in Hebrew). *Maariv*, 2 April.

Leshem, Moshe. 1989. *Balaam's Curse: How Israel Lost Its Way and How It Can Find It Again*. New York: Simon and Schuster.

Livneh, Eliezer. 1971. "The Israeli Sense of Fate and Destiny" (in Hebrew). *Ha'aretz*, 9 April.

Maimonides, Moses. 1969. *The Guide of the Perplexed*. Trans. and introduction by Shlomo Pines. Introduction by Leo Strauss. Chicago: University of Chicago Press.

Majar, David. 1985. "Instant National Mourning" (in Hebrew). *Ha'aretz*, 24 April.

Marcus, Yoel. 1974. "A Fortress for New Illusions" (in Hebrew). *Ha'aretz*, 25 January.

Meidan, Anath. 2000. "When We Reached 'Pour out Thy Wrath on the Goyim,' Joe Asked to Tone down the Voice" (in Hebrew). *Yedioth Ahronoth*, 11 August.

"Memorial Service" (in Hebrew). 1985. *Ha'aretz,* 24 April.

"The Murdered Ones Are Reincarnated Souls of Sinners" (in Hebrew). 2000. *Ha'aretz,* 7 August.

Musco, Yigal. 2001. "What Can One Do, I Am Being Practical" (in Hebrew). *Yedioth Ahronoth,* 19 October.

Nahum, Menahem. 1952. *Light to the Eyes* (in Hebrew). New York: Twersky Brothers.

Narboni, Rabbi Moses. 1946. A Commentary to the Book "The Guide of the Perplexed" (in Hebrew). New York: Om Publishing Company.

"No, Mr. Sharon!" 2002. *New York Times,* 22 March.

Novick, Peter. 1999. *The Holocaust in American Life.* New York: Houghton Mifflin Company.

O'Sullivan, Arieh. 2001. "Debunking a Myth: Dayan Never Feared Israel's Destruction in 1973." *Jerusalem Post Internet Edition,* 28 September.

"Panel Discussion on the Meaning of Independence Day" (in Hebrew). 1973. *Maariv,* 6 May.

Patai, Raphael. 1979. *The Messiah Texts.* Detroit: Wayne State University Press.

Pfeffer, Anshel. 2002. "The Torah Called for Transfer, but Is It Still Valid?" *Ha'aretz English Internet Edition,* 25 March.

Rachlevsky, Seffi. 2000. *Messiah's Donkey* (in Hebrew). Tel Aviv: Yedioth Ahronoth.

Rado, Sandor. 1969. "The Primordial Self." In *Adaptational Psychodynamics: Motivation and Control,* ed. Jean Jameson and Henriette Klein, 117–22. New York: Science House.

Ravitzky, Aviezer. 1996. *Messianism, Zionism, and Jewish Religious Radicalism.* Trans. Michael Swirsky and Jonathan Chipman. Chicago: University of Chicago Press.

Rosenblum, Doron. 1993. "The Cruelest of Months" (in Hebrew). *Ha'aretz,* 30 April.

Rotenberg, Mordecai. 1993. "Remember and Keep" (in Hebrew). *Maariv,* 30 April.

Sa'ar, Re'eli. 1998. "The Rituals of the Secular Religion" (in Hebrew). *Ha'aretz,* 23 April.

Samet, Gideon. 1990. "Kitsch and Death in a Long Weekend" (in Hebrew). *Ha'aretz,* 27 April.

Sarid, Yossi. 2001. "A Holiday and a Pogrom" (in Hebrew). *Yedioth Ahronoth,* 16 March.

Scholem, Gershom. 1937. "A Good Deed That Comes through a Transgression" (in Hebrew). *Knesset,* 347–92. Published also in English as "The Holiness of Sin." *Commentary* 51, no. 2 (1971): 41–70.

———. 1954. *Major Trends in Jewish Mysticism.* New York: Schocken Books.

———. 1957. *Shabbetai Tzevi and the Shabbatean Movement during His Lifetime* (in Hebrew). 2 vols. Tel Aviv: Am Oved.

Shalev, Me'ir. 2002. "Blows and Quotations" (in Hebrew). *Yedioth Ahronoth,* 16 February.

Sheleg, Yair. 2001. "Failing the Leadership Test." *Ha'aretz English Internet Edition,* 13 June.

Smith, Terence. 1973. "Israeli Humor: It's Jewish, It's a Joke, but Not a Jewish Joke." *New York Times,* 1 August.

Spinoza, Benedict de. 1951. *A Theologico-Political Treatise* and *A Political Treatise.* Trans. and introduction by R. H. M. Elwes. New York: Dover Publications.

———. 1955. *On the Improvement of the Understanding; The Ethics; Correspondence.* Trans. and introduction by R. H. M. Elwes. New York: Dover Publications.

Stein, Howard F. 1975. "American Judaism, Israel, and the New Ethnicity." *Cross Currents* 25: 51–66.

———. 1977. "The Binding of the Son: Psychoanalytic Reflections on the Symbiosis of Anti-Semitism and Anti-Gentilism." *Psychoanalytic Quarterly* 46: 650–83.

———. 1978. "Judaism and the Group-Fantasy of Martyrdom: The Psychodynamic Paradox of Survival through Persecution." *Journal of Psychohistory* 6, no. 2: 151–210.

Sternhell, Zeev. 1997. *The Founding Myths of Israel: Nationalism, Socialism, and the Making of the Jewish State.* Trans. David Maisel. Princeton, N.J.: Princeton University Press.

Strauss, Leo. 1997. *Spinoza's Critique of Religion.* Trans. E. M. Sinclair. Chicago: University of Chicago Press.

Tal, Uriel. 1984. "The Foundations of Political Messianism in Israel" (in Hebrew). *Ha'aretz,* 26 September.

"Text of Begin Speech Accepting Prize." 1978. *New York Times,* 11 December.

"To the Roots of the Matter" (in Hebrew). 1974. *Dvar Hashavu'ah,* 5 April.

Waldman, Amy. 2001. "Rabbis Revise Sermons to Soften a Stark Prayer." *New York Times,* 18 September.

Weiler, Gershon. 1976. *Jewish Theocracy* (in Hebrew). Tel Aviv: Am Oved.

Weizmann, Chaim. 1966. *Trial and Error.* New York: Schocken.

Winnicott, D. W. 1986. "Transitional Objects and Transitional Phenomena." In *Essential Papers on Object Relations,* ed. Peter Buckley, 254–71. New York: New York University Press.

Yovel, Yirmiyahu. 1992. *Spinoza and Other Heretics: The Marrano of Reason.* Princeton, N.J.: Princeton University Press.

Index

296.3
Gon

Discard